T0274857

THE BETTER MAN

THE BETTER MAN

A GUIDE TO CONSENT, STRONGER RELATIONSHIPS, AND HOTTER SEX

ERIC FITZMEDRUD, PH.D

WONDERWELL

A portion of the proceeds for this book will be donated to
Love is Respect and The Rape, Abuse & Incest National Network.

Library of Congress Control Number: 2023908236

ISBN 978-1-63756-035-8 (hardcover)
ISBN 978-1-63756-036-5 (EPUB)

Editor: Jessica Easto
Cover design: Morgan Krehbiel
Interior design: Morgan Krehbiel
Author photograph: Martino Mingione

Published by Wonderwell in Los Angeles, CA
www.wonderwell.press

WONDERWELL

Distributed in the US by Publishers Group West and
in Canada by Publishers Group Canada.

Printed and bound in Canada

Written on unceded, Lisjan (Ohlone) and Esselene land.

For the next generation:
I learned these tools by making mistakes.
I am flawed. I have hurt people.
Any good communication tool can be abused.
Trust your heart, your community, and the principles.

CONTENTS

INTRODUCTION

YOU WANT TO BE A GOOD MAN. Since 2017, you've likely seen the stories from the #MeToo social media movement,[1] and you're horrified by the behaviors of the men in those stories. You may also be scared. Maybe you know that you haven't always lived up to your values regarding consent.[2] There may be some people in your past whom you hurt by having not skillfully navigated consent. Or maybe you haven't hurt anyone, but you also know the strength of your desire and you're nervous because you've never received much guidance about how to navigate consent. You know you're supposed to *get consent*, and you want to, but what does that mean? You might be afraid because you know that misunderstandings can happen even when you do have consent—and that can lead to emotionally and physically hurt partners.

The simple directive "Get consent" is a little like being told "Don't fall out of the boat" before going white-water rafting. Yeah, of course—but *how* do you do that? This book will teach you how to paddle, how to brace your legs, how to communicate with the other people in the boat, and what to expect while you're on the river so that no one gets hurt while you navigate the rushing waters of sexuality together.

You are not alone. Since 2011, I've been a psychologist in private practice focused on helping clients with relationship and sexual issues. I'm a member of the American Association of Sexuality Educators, Counselors, and Therapists (AASECT). As a psychologist, I have often helped individuals and couples with sexual issues.

Challenges navigating desire and consent are a consistent theme in my work with men. I've seen that many men want to be good but are aware that they've fallen short of their own values. Many men aspire to practice consent in sexual relationships but aren't sure how to go about it. In my practice, I have developed ways of helping men with these problems drawing on my education, training, and personal experiences as a bisexual, polyamorous,[3] and kinky man.[4] Straight or gay, dating or married, I've helped men be more effective in love and sex. This book brings those tools to you. Throughout these pages, I'll use the stories of fictional men (you'll see references to Jamal, Sanjay, and Luis later in the book) based on composites from my clinical practice to show you that many men share your experiences.

This book is for men like you, who are looking for a life of integrity with their sexual desires. You don't have to make an either/or choice between integrity and sexual expression. This book can help you manage and express your desire with integrity.

WHY DO MEN NEED THIS BOOK?

A patriarchy is a society in which the value of men (or some men) is higher than that of other people, and where gender roles are rigidly assigned in ways that eliminate room for naturally occurring human gender diversity and variation. We live in a patriarchy. We often hear that a patriarchy hurts women, but it hurts men, too. Author, professor, and feminist bell hooks wrote, "The first act of violence that patriarchy demands of males is not violence toward women. Instead patriarchy demands of all males that they engage in acts of psychic self-mutilation, that they kill off the emotional parts of themselves."[5] *The Better Man* teaches you how to reclaim the parts of yourself that you've cut off in order to survive in patriarchal society. Healing those wounds will give you the capacities to use consent in your sexual life. Using consent will help you love and be loved in the ways that you've hoped for, including making your sex life more satisfying.

In this book, we'll discuss five specific wounds of patriarchy:

1. **Entitlement:** As men, we are not taught how to take care of our feelings. Instead, we're taught to hide them—to be strong and toughen up—cutting us off from our emotions. We don't know what they are, and we don't know how to manage them. We're promised that, in exchange for being strong, others will respect us and take care of our other needs. This creates a sense of entitlement—a sense that others owe us respect, deference, and support because of what we've given up for them or had taken from us. In the bedroom, this becomes sexual entitlement. Sexual entitlement can make men blindly selfish lovers. We expect others to meet our needs, but we may not know what we want or how to ask for what we want. An entitled man believes that other people are supposed to fulfill his desires; he doesn't believe or feel a need to respect his partner's no. He becomes willing to use consent and boundary violations to get sex because he is starving for connection, companionship, and love. He has no other way to feed those needs because he has never been taught that he is responsible for those needs.

2. **Control:** Entitlement leads to controlling behaviors. If other people aren't fulfilling their ends of the bargain, then we use anger, rage, or dominance (the tools that a patriarchy gives us) to try to make them do what we want them to. This can be overt, with verbal threats, physical intimidation, or abuse. It can also take subtle forms, like

withdrawing; brooding; demanding; and making snide, insulting comments when we don't get our way.

3. **Performance demand:** Society puts a lot of pressure on men to be strong, resilient, and silent; to share feelings but only the right feelings; and to be ready for sex anytime— but only the right kinds of sex. This rigid set of expectations isn't masculinity. It is a caricature I refer to as *hyper-masculinity*. In the process of trying to live up to these impossible demands, men alienate themselves from their own lives. The truth is, we are too varied and unique to fit into the narrow definition of "good men." But we want to be "good men," so we hide our diversity, differences, and the real potency of our desire because so much of it is deemed "bad." Then we feel ashamed when our erections and our emotions fail to live up to the performance demand.

4. **Romantic myths:** The romantic myths of our culture seal the deal for us. We're told that real love comes naturally, is effortless, and lasts forever. We're told that real desire comes with nonstop erections and simultaneous orgasms. Yet, our real relationships don't match these experiences; they seem to require a lot of work. And that work requires good communication skills and the capacity to regulate our emotions, which is something most of us haven't been taught.

5. **Destructive masculinity:** Each of these wounds adds up. We're wounded by being given scripts telling us that we're entitled, but they make us dependent. We're given tools of violence and coercion to dominate and control others, but we can't control others. We're expected to do everything right, but of course, we can't. We're told that relationships should be easy if you're really in love, but they aren't. When other people see our human flaws, other people, often men,

will hurt us physically, emotionally, or socially. We become afraid that if we don't look powerful, we'll be belittled and victimized. So, we try to soothe our feelings of insecurity without letting anyone know what we're doing or why. We isolate ourselves from others by hiding our weaknesses, emotions, needs, and sexual desires. But hidden or not, we still need connection. So, we engage in secret sexual behavior, posturing, callousness, violence, and dominance battles with other people because we're trying to retain a sense of value despite our loneliness and helplessness. This damages our relationships with our community. We also destroy ourselves by demonizing our own sexuality and deciding that our desire was the problem all along. We conclude that the message we've heard from society all along is right: "Men are dogs. And I'm no different." This is the unending destructive cycle that turns our fear and vulnerability about not being "man enough" into the reasons we become violent and hurt others. This is what I call *destructive masculinity* (people also use the term *toxic masculinity*).

This book will help you heal the five wounds of the patriarchy by bringing your expectations in line with reality, focusing your attempts at control on yourself, helping you tolerate your emotions (including desire), teaching you how to accept your limitations, and giving you the tools to succeed in real relationships. Chapter 1 exposes the false promises behind patriarchal entitlement and shows how those false promises hurt you even while benefiting you in other areas. To begin healing these wounds, entitlement must be replaced with an affirmative consent process, which is addressed in chapter 2. This process will help you manage both your and your partner's expectations, place equal value on your and your partner's pleasure, and place equal value on your and your partner's safety.

Once you understand consent, it's time to consider what you want and what it's okay to ask for. To do so, you'll need a better understanding of both. Chapter 3 will guide you through myth-busting information about male desire and teach you how to eliminate the shame you might feel about your turn-ons. In chapter 4, you'll learn more about the difference between feelings of desire and your needs. This chapter will help you understand what's going on emotionally and mentally when you experience desire; and this information will help you express your desire skillfully, regulate your desire, and accept the elements of your desire that are out of your control.

To eliminate the processes of control and destructive masculinity from your life, you'll need to integrate not only your sexual desires but also the whole suite of human needs. Chapter 5 will show you how to gain the tools necessary to assess those needs and try to meet them so that you can live an abundant, fulfilled life. This chapter will help you shift your perspective about sex: you aren't a beggar, trying to get the sex you lack from others. Your sexuality can be a gift you share.

In chapter 6, you'll get the practical emotional education you've always needed but never got. The information here will increase your capacity to communicate with your partners so that instead of trying to live up to impossible performance demands and romantic ideals, you'll have the capacity to do the hard work required to have hot sex, whether as part of a quick hookup or decades into a relationship. This will also help you skillfully manage yourself during the painful parts of relationships. Whether you're managing rejection on a dating app or the inevitable pain that comes as part of a long-term relationship, navigating hurt is a part of loving.

Chapter 7 offers tools in four simple steps to improve your ability to share your feelings and listen to your partner's. This skill, which will help you communicate feelings like desire, is an essential element of practicing consent. Finally, in chapter 8, you'll put all of the background information and skills from the rest of the book together into a simple formula for practicing consent. You'll finish the chapter ready to begin the process of constantly learning, responding, and improving as a lover. I've made my fair share of mistakes while learning to express my sexuality, and I share those with you in the afterword.

IS THIS BOOK REALLY FOR ME?

This book is for anyone who identifies as a man. It often directly addresses cisgender (those whose gender matches the sex assigned to them at birth) heterosexual men to elevate consciousness about the pervasiveness of male-to-female sexual violence and to make this writing relevant to the #MeToo conversation. But it also uses explicitly inclusive language because the category "men" includes gay men, transgender men (whose gender is different from the sex assigned to them at birth), transmasculine people (those whose gender transition emphasizes a move toward masculine presentation), and gender-fluid people (those who have different gender experiences at different times) who sometimes identify as men.

Women and nonbinary people (whose gender identity does not conform to a man-woman binary) with intense sexual desire or with a history of difficulties navigating consent with their partners may also be interested in the lessons in this book. You are welcome in this discussion. Although this book often refers to men's consent violations against women, I also acknowledge male-to-male, male-to-nonbinary people, female-to-male, and female-to-female sexual violence and coercion. The pervasiveness of male-to-female sexual violence does not remove or invalidate the pain of sexual violence perpetrated by or against others.

In terms of sexual behavior, this book is for men who value and want consent from their partners. Many men fall short of this aspiration because we are not taught *how* to approach consent. If you are shocked and dismayed that you have fallen short of your own value of consent and you are motivated to prevent consent violations or miscommunications from happening again, then this book may help you.

Although much of this book focuses on regulating high desire, men with low desire may still benefit from reading this book if they experience their desire as intense when it does manifest. To be complete, our circle of men needs representation of many different forms of desire. Chapter 2 and chapter 4 may feel especially relevant for you.

This book is not for you if you regularly engage in, or if you desire, nonconsensual sexual contact. If you get pleasure from violating people's consent, this isn't a book that will help you. Even if you know that these practices can put you in jail and are looking for a way to stop before the #MeToo movement or the police catch up with you, this book still isn't the right resource for you. My best recommendation for you is to find a forensic psychologist who specializes in treating nonconsensual sexual behavior. I hope that you find a therapist to help you curb your impulses.

■

Our cultural conversation about consent has been fueled by trauma, fear, and shame. We're going to take a different approach: sex can be pleasurable! This book is about moving forward from our collective history of trauma with an ability to cultivate safety for yourself and your partner. This book will replace fear with tools that help you consciously navigate the risks of pleasure. This book will replace shame with acceptance of the nature of your sexuality and teach you how to express that sexuality in artful ways. This book will teach you skills so that the white-water rafting ride of sex is safe first, skillful second, and pleasurable from beginning to end.

Chapter 1

IS IT OKAY TO BE A MAN?

YOU MAY FEEL ATTACKED when you hear the term *toxic masculinity*. You may fear that the only things being associated with men are the behaviors of "a few bad men." You may even believe that our culture has stopped valuing or seeing the good qualities of men and wonder if it is it okay to be a man. Is it okay to be proud to be a man? Yes! But times are changing, people are being held accountable for causing harm, and many men have caused harm. Men are beginning to make men's violence a men's issue.

WHY SHOULD I CARE ABOUT THE #METOO MOVEMENT?

Founded in 2006 by sexual assault survivor and activist Tarana Burke, the "Me Too" movement helps survivors of sexual violence with empathy and empowerment.[1] In 2017, social media took the name "me too" and turned it into the viral hashtag #MeToo. In short order, many survivors of sexual violence shared their stories on social media and found support. Strength in numbers facilitated accountability for perpetrators of sexual violence. Early high-profile cases accused Harvey Weinstein, Jeffrey Epstein, Larry Nassar, Bill Cosby, Kevin Spacey, and Louis C. K.

Today, the "Me Too" movement and #MeToo hashtag continue to unite victims of sexual violence and demand accountability for perpetrators. Attitudes about sexual violence have changed in the years since 2017. Americans believe that, compared to before #MeToo, people who commit sexual harassment are now more likely to be held accountable, and victims are more likely to be believed.[2] Weinstein and R. Kelly were sentenced in 2022, and the landscape around sexual behavior in the United States has changed far beyond just boardrooms and Hollywood. For every extreme story of abuse of power and predation like these, there are many less-extreme stories.

In my office, I see the damage that men's lack of consent education can cause even when it isn't as predatory as those newsworthy examples. Even when it falls far short of rape or assault, men who pressure their partners for sex damage their relationships, limit or eliminate pleasure, and often create sexless relationships. The cultural changes caused by #MeToo embolden women to hold abusers accountable and support partners of all genders to say no to coercive or pressured sex in their everyday relationships.

One of these less-extreme examples did make the news. You may not have heard about "Grace" and her date with actor Aziz Ansari, which she described on Babe.net, accusing him of sexual assault. Babe.net and Grace both experienced a backlash for labeling the experience *assault*,[3] but many men felt uncomfortable, recognizing their own inadequate consent practices in the actions ascribed to Ansari.[4]

The #MeToo process changed the way couples show up in my office. Partners who had been accepting unsatisfying sex, pressure for sex, or emotional blackmail for sex have stopped accepting this in their relationships. Because of the movement, many partners are asking for the men they love to learn consent. A date gone awry is no longer just an "awkward sexual experience" after which a woman is unhappy or angry. A sexual problem in an otherwise happy marriage is no longer a woman's fault or a man's pain to tolerate in silence. She may secretly share her feelings with her best friends or publicly with the entire online community. Women who confront men about the harm our poor sexual-consent skills cause are being backed up by their community. People are holding their male partners accountable for regulating their sexual desire and insisting that sex be pleasurable for them as well. Men's private sexuality—including masturbation and pornography—may no longer be left in the privacy of a relationship. Partners are holding men accountable for relationship agreements (the things we agree to do and not do that form our relationship) about their sexual behavior, including masturbation, pornography, fidelity, and consent.

You should care about the #MeToo movement because it has increased the protections for you and your partners, it has changed the expectations about sexual consent, and it has increased the likelihood that if you are unskillful in navigating consent, you will be held accountable for your actions.

WHY FOCUS ON FEMINISM INSTEAD OF MEN'S MOVEMENTS?

I focus on feminism instead of men-led movements because the most visible communities defining sexuality for men are regressive groups that reject feminism—a movement that advocates for equal rights regardless of gender—and radicalize men. I'm referring to the four most prominent "manosphere" men's groups online:[5]

1. **Incels:** A portmanteau of *involuntary* and *celibates*, this group expresses entitlement to sex and advocates rape or violence to punish those who withhold sex. It has inspired several shootings.

2. **Men Going Their Own Way:** Often abbreviated MGToW, this group advocates that men drop out of society and avoid cohabitation and marriage. The arguments for this course of action are based on ideas about the superiority of men and demonization of women.

3. **Men's rights activists:** Nominally focused on equal rights for men, this movement in practice often rejects legal protections for women and children from male abusers under the guise of men's or father's rights.

4. **Pickup artists:** Under the guise of helping men have sex, these organizations or teachers objectify women and often advocate deception, pressure, coercion, and rape.

Movements like these are reactions against feminism. Most have responded to feminism by rejecting it and calling on men to return to a fictional past. They imagine a time when men got to be "men" and women liked it that way. They imagine a fictional history in which men weren't frequently sexually violent against women. Harnessing the polarizing power of the internet, these groups celebrate violence; speak to the pain men feel; and give isolated men a group identity and the cover of anonymity for their radical, isolationist, and violent views. Alone and reviled, men in these groups are vulnerable to the crossover potential of other radical political, racist, or terrorist organizations.[6] These online communities remove men from the context of culture and let them imagine that they can define themselves without dialoguing with women or other members of their community. These groups posture as being pro-men, but their rhetoric and recommended actions isolate men and don't solve men's problems.

At best, these movements will stoke your pain into an impotent anger that keeps you a member of the group but isolated from a larger community. At worst, they turn men into violent extremists. They will not improve their communities because they are not listening to the needs of the community. Men in these groups gather and talk about what it means to be a man without a large portion of their community (i.e., people who are not men) to inform them about what others need from them. They will never create a broader transformation in the culture of men because they forget what has always been true: not only fathers, but also mothers, raise men. Thank goodness. So, unless mothers and other caregivers also endorse a movement's ideas about manhood, the movement will never be perpetuated in the culture.

While empathizing with men's pain, these movements foment misogyny, hatred, and resentment toward women. It is true that some men are victims of domestic violence and sexual violence, and that men are victims of violence at about the same rate as women.[7] But stirring up more resentment encourages more violence. Lamenting the pain that only heterosexual men experience makes us tone deaf to the pain experienced by women, gay men, transgender people, and people of color—pain largely caused *by* men. Men make up 75 percent of the violent offenders, according to one Department of Justice report.[8] Trying to outcompete victims of men's violence by yelling louder sidesteps our responsibility as men to own up to the fact that people who share our male identity are the ones causing most of the pain to all of these communities, including our own.

The truth is, feminism is for men, too, and many men know it. The Good Men Project (goodmenproject.com), the ManKind Project (mankindproject.org), and r/bropill or r/MensLib on Reddit generally embrace feminism and are trying to envision "enlightened masculinity."[9] The core tenet of feminism is that people of all genders are equal. These groups, though small, know that under feminism, men's emotional needs are valid, our desires and sexual styles have value, and we can celebrate the diversity among men—we don't have to shoehorn ourselves or other men into a tiny, destructive masculinity box anymore. Feminism says that men have equal value with all genders. It also says that we need to not violate other people's rights when we try to get our needs met, that other people don't have to fulfill our desires, and that whatever our sexual styles, our partners have the right to say yes or no about joining us.

HOW DOES DESTRUCTIVE MASCULINITY HURT MEN?

Cultural images of masculinity have not changed much with feminism, and they are limiting. The image of the heroic masculine endures, whether the hero is in his thirties, like Chris Pine in the reboots of the *Star Trek* series; in his forties, like Dwayne "the Rock" Johnson in *Skyscraper*; in his fifties, like Tom Cruise in *Mission: Impossible—Fallout*; in his sixties, like Liam Neeson in *The Marksman*; or even older, as with Harrison Ford filming another Indiana Jones movie at the age of seventy-nine. The hypermasculine man never loses his appeal and keeps blowing things up, punching people, and having relationships with younger women his whole life.

In contrast, the image of women has changed and continues to change. From the Wonder Woman and Captain Marvel movies (finally!) to the heroic portrayal of Elastigirl in *Incredibles 2* to positive representation of older women's sexuality in *Queen Sugar* or *Something's Gotta Give*, women are demanding change and increasingly succeeding at transforming their broader representation in media. Time and women won't march backward for men. Feminism has empowered women to speak about their experiences and to insist that their needs for safety, respect, autonomy, and pleasure be respected.

In this cultural moment, the long historical arc of feminism has finally come home to roost for men. We can no longer sit back and watch women change and not make changes ourselves. Adult men—those raised within a world positively changed by feminism—are proposing masculinities that are in alignment with feminist values, the first of which is the equal treatment of people regardless of gender. One way in which this book exhibits the value of gender equality is by teaching men about emotions, an important life lesson left out of many men's childhood educations.

Another feminist value is intersectionality, the idea that people have more than one identity. Although the patriarchal system traumatizes men in general, it hurts Black men, Latin men, and Asian men in more and different ways. Men who are gay, bisexual, or transgender also experience more forms of oppression than heterosexual men. Men who like to be submissive sexually, cross-dress, or enjoy being anally penetrated are also hurt in more ways than men whose sexual desires are in line with the patriarchal image of sexual dominance. Although we are men, we may have identities that are discriminated against in different ways.

To illustrate intersectionality, imagine a married Black gay man, Jamal. Jamal's marriage is open—that is, he and his husband have agreed they can have sex outside the relationship. Jamal experiences racism on gay dating apps. He encounters profiles that say "Whites Only," and because he's Black, some prospective partners assume everything from the size of his penis to his preference in music. He also fears discrimination in his social circle for being gay or having an open relationship, something that is not an uncommon consensual agreement in gay relationships.[10] Jamal experiences an intersectional identity as a gay man and a Black man.[11]

This book is written with an inclusive definition of men, recognizing that all men have more than one identity. This means that I write assuming that some men reading this book partner with women, others with men, and others with gender-fluid or nonbinary people. Therefore, many of the book's examples refer to a man's "partner" unless it's illustrating something specific about male–female gender dynamics in the context of male-to-female sexual violence or about gay relationships. This book's inclusive perspective also means that it uses examples of men from several different racial backgrounds. Sometimes an example will attempt to illustrate a racial dynamic in a couple, and sometimes the aim will be to maintain representation of men from multiple racial backgrounds.

Although feminist principles benefit men, there's another essential reason to move forward with feminism. Although patriarchy harms men, it also benefits men in other ways. Some of the benefits we receive seriously harm women and transgender people. It is important to move forward with feminism because it isn't right to benefit from the oppression of others. Becoming men with integrity includes learning how to release some of the entitlement and benefits the patriarchal system gives us. This book identifies some ways of releasing those entitlements in the areas of sexuality and relationships.

The bottom line is, the old ways are not effective for men. In business, in our communities, and in our romantic relationships, we are increasingly isolated and rejected if we try to bring back those old, failed ways. If we double down on our misogyny, our isolation will radicalize us. If we want to stay in connection with our community, if we want sex, we need to take control of our own behavior. If we want love, we need to learn vulnerability, honesty, and self-soothing. This book teaches those processes.

WHAT'S WRONG WITH BEING A HERO?

When I talk about the performance-demand wound—that men should be strong, resilient, silent, and ready to have sex—a lot of men like the qualities I'm talking about. When I talk about the image of the heroic masculine, as I did when mentioning movies in the last section, a lot of men want to know, "What's wrong with being a hero?" The short answer is, there's nothing wrong with these qualities. There's nothing wrong with being heroic. But our culture's stories about heroic men have two problems, and these problems hurt men.

First, we only tell one part of the hero's story. The stories in our books, TV programs, movies, and video games focus on heroes fighting, killing, controlling, and manipulating. This reduces the complexity and diversity of life. It also encourages us to seek and create trauma to become worthy of being called a man. It makes older men who have more of their journey behind them feel like they aren't "real men" anymore.

Most men experience cluelessness, loneliness, and love. These parts of our lives are just as important as the times when we succeed on the soccer field, at school, or in the boardroom. Most men experience grief and inspiration. But we don't prioritize the value of men crying when a parent dies or of the art that they create. When society collapses the value of men from an entire life's journey into just the moments when a man is "heroic," it's easy to believe that the best times of our lives are when we are most physically strong, most easily aroused, and most successful. This is not real; it's impossible and unsustainable. Past a certain physical or intellectual point, we believe ourselves to be in decline.

If we can open ourselves to the dignity of age, then we can more easily embrace the fact that the role of ascendant hero is just a small portion of the journey. And there's a lot of joy to be had during the other portions of the heroic narrative. The impossible irrepressibility of young-adult male arousal is a lot of fun. When it passes, we get to turn our attention to connecting with our part-ners more emotionally and intimately, and learning how to let them into our hearts, not just our pants. Great lovers can please a partner without a hard erection and can find pleasure and orgasm without one as well. The way to these possibilities is not through the technical expertise of men's magazines, social media memes about what women want, or quick tips about giving or getting better head. These pleasures are found in the intimate and tran-scendent connections between people.

There's nothing wrong with being a hero. But if your image of what it means to be a man only includes being a hero, that'll be a problem: on the journey of your life, you'll experience many other roles.

Second, the hero narrative is entirely fiction. Stories are pow-erful and help us create meaning. The stories we tell about other people guide us in how to be. But they are stories, not actual descriptions of reality. Look at it this way: there are no heroic rivers. We could describe a river in heroic terms, but that's our story about the river, not the river. The river just does what it does. It gathers water from tributaries, joins other rivers, and eventually ends in a larger body of water.

A human life rises and falls like the rest of nature. Any narra-tive we construct around it is a story. Behind the story is the simple reality of our nature. To be kind, compassionate, and loving to others, we need to understand and accept our nature.

If we imagine ourselves to be heroes, we might forget to look at our actual nature. We can get caught in the trap of trying to make ourselves match the story instead of making a story that accurately describes our reality. When we do that, we can easily ignore feedback that doesn't fit with our story about ourselves. We might say, "What do you mean I made you scared? That doesn't make sense. I'm a hero not a villain."

Like a river, your sexual nature may be pleasant if you know how to navigate it. Like a rapid, your sexuality may be dangerous if you don't skillfully navigate the journey. Trying to be a hero may blind you to the potential for harm in the powerful forces of your sexuality.

HOW DOES DESTRUCTIVE MASCULINITY RUIN SEX?

The social and internal expectation to be a hero becomes a vicious cycle inside men's emotions and minds in the bedroom. He might feel inadequate because he compares himself to how skillful he thinks he's supposed to be. In his partner's mind, the myths about masculinity might prevent empathy for his experience. He wasn't allowed to talk about his feelings, so even if he wants to talk about how he feels, he doesn't know how. Finally, the fear of being shamed for inadequacies can make men defensive with respect to receiving corrective feedback. This leads men to damage their sexual relationships in several characteristic ways.

Damaging Relationships

A core script of destructive masculinity is that men have uncontrollable, rampant sexual desire and that other people must feed our sexual hunger or we'll go crazy. Combined with the scripts that men aren't emotional, don't talk about feelings, and aren't vulnerable, there's an inherent ticking bomb waiting to go off in our relationships.

If we do experience intense sexual desire, we feel justified in that desire. Feeling justified, we pressure or demand that our partners satisfy us. When our partner inevitably doesn't satisfy us because that kind of entitled sexual demand is both a turnoff and impossible to fulfill, we feel justified in hidden sexual behavior like secret porn viewing or affairs that break our relationship agreements. These kinds of broken relationship agreements hurt our partners, cause us shame, and damage our relationships.

This often brings men to therapy. Here's the kind of situation I see often in my practice: A man—let's call him Sanjay—feels that wanting to masturbate is "only natural." He justifies his behavior by telling himself, "This is just how men are." When he's caught, he apologizes and sincerely feels bad. He knows that he's "not supposed to" or "Good guys don't look at porn." He doesn't know how to be a good man while also desiring sexual pleasure in the ways that he does. The only script he has from his culture about his desire is contradictory—his desire is uncontrollable, but he's bad if he doesn't control it. So, he keeps making promises—and breaking them. He doesn't know what else to do.

Assuming Yes, Mistaking Silence for No

So many people in our culture have been harmed by men's violence that many sexual partners of men are afraid to say no. They fear violence, blame, judgment, rejection, and more. Even if you aren't a man who uses these methods, your sex with your partners may be affected by the culture of destructive masculinity because your partners may fear telling you no. If they accept sex, they don't want it to be painful, unsatisfying sex, and you may be blamed for not noticing that your partner wasn't that into it. This may ruin your sexual experience, your sexual relationship with that person, or even your whole relationship with that partner.

In addition, because our culture doesn't teach us how to seek, give, and receive consent, men and their sexual partners may not seek yes. Both men and their partners often believe that when there is consent, you should "just know." This sets up a dynamic in which both partners may expect men to be mind readers. This expectation can both cause us to misinterpret silence as no and silence as yes. This has the potential to create less sex, lower-quality sex, and trauma for both partners.

Lying about Your Sexuality

Destructive masculinity has two horrible contradictory messages about men's sexuality. The first is that "men are dogs," and the second is that "good men aren't like *that*." Both myths can cause men to lie about their sexuality. When talking with other men, the temptation to brag and tell stories to live up to the image of men as dogs is strong. A man trying to live up to this myth might lie about his sexual experience—or about being kinkier, hornier, or more desiring of sex than he actually is.

A man trying to live up to the myth that good men aren't like *that* may lie to paint himself as an exception to the rule. He might pretend to not be interested in sex when he is, deny masturbating or looking at porn, or hide his real sexual desires. Once his real desires or behaviors are discovered, he falls from favor in the eyes of his partner, who tells him, "I thought you weren't like other men." Or, if he is successful at hiding his real interests, he diminishes his connection to the vitality of his eroticism and decreases his and his partner's satisfaction about sex.

Lying about your sexuality—whether to overstate or downplay it—means that you won't match with partners who want your real sexuality. It also has a high probability of creating shame, disconnection, and fear.

Getting Stuck in Fantasy

In a world where porn is just a few clicks on a smartphone away but fact-based sexual education is difficult to find, confusing fantasy with reality is a problem for many men. This is a problem because destructive masculinity tells us that real men know how to have sex. Whether you imagine that most women get pleasure from men ejaculating on their faces or that anal sex requires no prep, no communication, and is never messy, fantasies can damage our real sex lives. We might blame our partner for not living up to fantasy with shaming scripts like "cold," "frigid," or "prude." We can easily hurt our partner physically or emotionally by not working with them to prepare for or talk about the fantasies we'd like to try to bring into reality.

Confusing fantasy for reality diminishes our real sex in our own minds and ruins opportunities for bringing fantasy into reality because we don't do the work to make that happen.

Behaving in Scary, Creepy, or Smarmy Ways

Destructive masculinity extends outside of the realm of sex. Romantic myths also damage relationships for men. For example, one romantic myth is that real men "don't take no for an answer" when courting partners, that persistence will be rewarded, and that ignoring the first no is what our potential partners want.

Destructive masculinity tells men we have to be persistent because our partners are obligated to say no at first. This causes us to ignore no when we hear it. We deceive ourselves that our feelings are reciprocated. We ignore objections from the other person. We then scare that person with our stalking, pressure, attention, or anger. These elements of destructive masculinity make us focus our attention on unwilling partners and can scare and hurt them. It also leaves us isolated because it is an ineffective courting strategy.

WITHOUT DESTRUCTIVE MASCULINITY, WHAT ARE MEN?

So far, we've learned that our patriarchal society produces destructive myths about men—we're always strong, heroic, and horny, and we know what our partners want. With so many myths flying around, what is true about men? Are men good for anything?

Men unfamiliar with feminism may believe that the message of feminism is that men are bad. But as we've already learned, the message of feminism is that people of all genders are equal and have value. In other words, there are—of course—good things about men. These truths can feel healing.

You Are Good

Men can be caring, supportive, helpful, honest, and loyal. Many
of us have some positive connotations to ideas of men as father,
teacher, mentor, coach, lover, or friend. Even though we all have
some pain in this life, there are men who do good in the world.
There are men who are kind, men who teach and protect. You can
be one of them. I think you already want to do good in these ways
or you probably wouldn't be reading this book.

You may be questioning whether you're capable of finding and
expressing your goodness. You know that you've hurt people, hurt
your partners, yelled at your kids, picked on the vulnerable kid in
school, or betrayed your values. I acknowledge your mental list of
the ways you've failed to reach your ideals. I'm not about to sugarcoat your offenses any more than I'm about to sugarcoat my own.
People have suffered because of your behaviors and mine.

I'll attend to the concept of accountability for old hurts in chapter 6, when I discuss guilt (see page 188). For now, I want to focus on
the present. No one is defined by their past. You have the capacity for
goodness, kindness, and love today. Despite the harm you have done
in the past, you can be a better person in the present and future.

Your wounds can be healed, and you can make amends for the
wounds you have caused. Many of us work in vain to wipe away
the negative image we have of ourselves as a victim, perpetrator,
or both. Only self-forgiveness and community forgiveness can do
that, and both of those concepts require you to make sense of your
wounds and your capacity for violence. This book offers processes
to reintegrate some of the parts of you that got covered by destructive masculinity and to support the better man inside you.

You Are Not Expendable

As men, we have a lot to unlearn about ourselves before we can be
the better men we want to be. If men victimized you, then you may
believe that this is what men do, and if men victimize, it can be easy
to devalue men. It may be hard to imagine something else because

there are a lot of other devaluing messages that our culture and our economy have about men.

One of these is that men are expendable, a message that pervades our social institutions, such as the military, police, and fire departments. Although women also have those jobs, men dominate these fields. A primary aspect of each of these types of work is that the person doing that work may die. The overarching cultural message is that the sacrifice of men's bodies is worth it. Whatever it is that we are protecting, whatever it is that we are asked to die for, that thing is worth our deaths, and by default we are expendable. The message is that property, wealth, and empire are worth more than men.

I'm not trying to diminish the call to those careers. Choosing to risk your life to protect others or save them from harm has dignity. I believe that, even in a just society, military, police, and fire services have a place. What I am calling out is a culture that tells boys that, when they put their lives on the line, they have more value than when they choose to be caregivers, teachers, or healers.

The expendable value of men pervades more than these service professions. According to a 2021 Bureau of Labor Statistics release, more than ten times more men than women were fatally injured on the job.[12] Cross-referencing that report with another from 2022, we find that the percentage of men employed in some of the most fatal professions include logging workers (93.5 percent), roofers (95 percent), structural iron and steel workers (98.9 percent), aircraft pilots and flight engineers (90.8 percent), drivers/sales workers and truck drivers (91.2 percent), and refuse and recyclable materials workers (89.4 percent).[13] We men seem disproportionately willing to accept work that puts our lives at risk.

To put this another way, people in our culture are offered money to sacrifice themselves, their bodies, and their relationships with their partners and their children. Men accept the offer disproportionately. Often, we do so because we don't believe that we have inherent value beyond the money we can earn. Often, we do so because our system puts us in poverty if we don't. Either way, only we can free ourselves from this kind of bondage. Men can protest pay for unsafe working conditions, trauma, and injury in male-dominated industries. To make those changes, we'd need to work with each other and strengthen workers' rights. But before we are likely to make that choice, we must identify that we have value as something other than as a martyr. If feminism says that men are equal, then we are not expendable, and we have a right to safe working conditions.

You Are Needed

While you are at work, you can't develop connection and intimacy in your relationship or family. In heterosexual relationships in particular, men often talk about the need to support the family, to create the financial freedom for anything from vacations to a home to more yoga. In my practice working with couples, this narrative has little to do with whether the woman works or how much money they already have. In fact, I've sat with men earning millions per year who honestly described to me a sense of captivity because they "need" to work to maintain the current lifestyle for their family. This is another example of people being asked to sacrifice themselves for increased financial gain, which men accept more often than women. Even on the high end of the income spectrum, I've worked with men who work sixty, eighty, or one hundred (and more) hours per week after they already have millions because they seem to believe the money is worth more than they are.

Our financial system offers money for sacrifices of self, family, and relationships. Women, as exemplified by the cultural tensions known as "the mommy wars," press to maintain time with family despite also feeling called to work. Men don't as often have confidence that their families are better off with them around. I ask my clients the direct question, "What do you think your family values more: your presence or the money you earn?" Many men will tear up at this question. A few say they think their family needs the money they earn more than their family needs them. Then I invite the man to turn to his spouse or partner and ask if that's true. I've never had a partner say they valued money more than the man.

Men are needed at home. They can provide parenting, another perspective, and all the unique love and gifts they have. Most men don't know that their presence is more important than the money they earn. Some men have never been told they have inherent value. Even the men who have been told rarely find the words of their partner enough to contradict a lifetime of performance-demand messages. Performance demand tells us that men's work and income are more valuable than work in the home, interacting with our kids, and providing love and connection to our partner. Performance demand tells us that if we don't know how to do something at home, we're incompetent, and that makes it difficult tolerate the necessary feedback to get better at it. The entitlement wound never taught us how to refresh and reset after stress, so many of us are emotionally overwhelmed when we get home. And so, we have a hard time believing that, aside from our work, we have value—as a person, as a presence, as a family member—without regard for what we can do for others.

When we sacrifice our energy, health, and mental health at the altar of work, our families get upset with us. We feel hurt, angry, and betrayed because we made those sacrifices for them in the first place. We end up hearing their calls for our time and attention as criticisms because we can't believe that we are valuable enough to be needed. Many of us never learn that our real value is inherent. Our presence and our attention are some of the most valuable things that we can give. Our families and our partners are looking for us, not our money. Learning to get better at taking care of our homes and families might bring us the love, meaning, purpose, respect, and connection we desire.

You Are Wounded

The evidence shows that men are more violent than women by every metric. According to the most recent FBI arrest statistics for 2019 on the topic, men accounted for 88 percent of murder and nonnegligent manslaughter arrests, 96.6 percent of rape arrests, 84.2 percent of robbery arrests, 76.5 percent of aggravated assaults arrests, 78.3 percent of violent criminal arson arrests, and 90.4 percent of weapons-related arrests.[14] By contrast, men only make up 57.4 percent of theft arrests. Considering these statistics, you might reasonably ask why I would maintain my assertion that men are not inherently violent.

Men's perpetration of intimate partner violence (as one example of violent behavior relevant to this discussion) is caused by a complex web of factors. Some of those include adverse childhood experiences (ACEs), such as physical trauma, sexual trauma, poverty, and witnessing violence);[15] poor economic experiences, such as being low income or unemployed;[16] posttraumatic stress disorder; depression; and experiences with substance abuse or addiction.[17] Men with fewer of these experiences are less likely to be violent. Men with more of these experiences are more likely to be violent. Maybe it isn't that men are inherently violent. Maybe men metabolize traumas that they have experienced by becoming violent more often than women do. Hurt men use violence to control, dominate, and abuse others. They do so to protect themselves from more pain. This protective, defensive impulse causes more trauma and threat to us.

Instead of looking at the data about male violence as an indicator that men are inherently violent, I think of male violence as evidence that men are *wounded*. We express our wounds in high rates of violence. We turn our wounds into wounding others.

Think about this cycle: We men fight others so that we are not victims. We fight against the economic tide with our work so that we are not victims of poverty. We fight wars, injustice, business competitors, fires, crime, drugs, or "them"—whoever they are—so that we can find value for ourselves in fighting something. We have been bullied, beaten, teased, stolen from, emasculated, not touched, not hugged, not comforted, and shamed. Often, we experience these wounds before we can even fight back or ask to be loved. Instead, we learn to fight back in an attempt prevent that pain from happening again. We continue to fight so that our loved ones don't have to. We try to be good warriors to protect ourselves and others from being wounded, but we ignore that being a warrior means wounding someone else.

ENDING DESTRUCTIVE MASCULINITY STARTS FROM WITHIN

Once we look at male violence as a result of wounds, it opens a space for hope. If we men heal ourselves, if we heal each other, we can end the cycle of violence. And that starts by going inside.

First, think about the kind of person you would be if you had not been wounded. What would you be like if you hadn't experienced the traumas of your life? If you hadn't been bullied in school, how much easier would it be to open up with your friends? If you hadn't been called a pussy when you cried after losing a baseball game, how would you treat other people differently at work now? If you didn't feel that working until exhaustion was necessary just to keep your family healthy and well, how much more emotionally engaged would you be when you aren't at work? If you had never been told to "man up" when you were hurt or scared, how would you react differently to conflicts with your kids? If you had never been told that men don't cry, how often would you cry? If you had been told that male sexuality is a beautiful and good thing, how much easier would it be to only offer your sex to the people who enthusiastically want it?

Underneath the experiences of your trauma, probably interrupted at a time before you even have memory, there's a man that you could have been if you hadn't been hurt and isolated. He knew how to be touched, how to love, how to be vulnerable, how to be a heart friend to other people, and he had the capacity to become a kind and generous lover. That man is still there inside of you, and this book is intended to help you move closer to being him.

If you really want to become that man, you must go back to the source. Of course, we can't go back in time; the wounds of our past traumas are in us today. If we don't want to pass those wounds on to our partners, children, families, friends, and communities, we need to heal our traumas and fill in the gaps in our education. We need to learn the skills the better man we want to be would know. We need to refocus our goal: instead of striving to become warriors or heroes, we can strive to become lovers, sages, and wise men.

To do so, we must focus our attention inward. We need to make our external behavior and communication effectively convey our inner intention. That means we must learn how we are heard when we speak. We must shift our focus from controlling others to being masters of ourselves. That includes taking responsibility for our sexual desires, emotions, and relationship needs. When we can speak and act with that kind of integrity, we are able to look closely at and learn from our mistakes. With integrity, we can accept the faults and flaws in ourselves without giving up the aspiration to be more kind, whole, and compassionate. Then we can pass our healing and our wisdom on to the next generation.

Chapter 2

WHAT IS CONSENT?

THE OTHER DAY I WAS OUT WITH MY SON, and he had just eaten some chocolate ice cream. We were about to take a picture with some friends, and he had the telltale lines of chocolate around his lips. I wanted to remove the chocolate before the picture was taken. So, I knelt and talked to him. "Hey, buddy, you've got some chocolate around your mouth, and we're about to take a picture." At this, he sent his tongue on a tour to seek the remaining chocolate flavor. I continued, "Can I lick my thumb and wipe the chocolate off, please?" He nodded and said, "Sure."

This was a consent encounter because I wanted to do something with his body, I asked, and he consented. It wasn't sexual, but it was a demonstration of my respect for his bodily integrity and autonomy. By treating him this way, I hope that I'm building a habit of consent that will then carry over into the bedroom. Furthermore, I hope that I'm instilling in my son the value that he should be treated this way, which will teach him that others should be treated this way, too. The foundation of sexual consent is this simple:

1. Other people have a right to their autonomy.

2. I don't know what someone else desires, needs, or feels.

3. I have desires, needs, and feelings, but no one else is obligated to fulfill my desires, meet my needs, or tend to my feelings.

4. So, before I engage someone else's body for my pleasure, or try to give someone else pleasure with my body, I must have permission for what I want to do.

When we begin with these truths about human experience, the need for a consent process becomes clear. If I want to meet your desires and you want to meet my desires, we need to talk about what they are and how to fulfill them. Not asking for consent risks violating the other person's autonomy—that is, sexual pressure, coercion, assault, or rape.[1]

Most men in my office are hurt or offended when I point out their sexually pressuring behavior. They say, "I'm not that kind of guy." They're rightly uncomfortable with the fact that pressure is on a continuum with rape. But that's just the point—in order to not be that kind of guy, you have to work with the other person. Their feelings determine whether their encounter with you feels like sexual violence or feels consensual. Consent is how you protect your partners from those negative experiences.

In this chapter, you'll learn the foundations for consent. First, I'll address some concerns many people have about consent and how it might change the process of connecting sexually. Then I'll give a brief introduction to the value of consent for you and what consent means.

WON'T CONSENT INTERRUPT MY FLOW?

Whether it's because they already have a way of "feeling" during sexual encounters or because they're comparing a consent process to a sexual or romantic myth, many people are concerned about how consent might interrupt the flow of a sexual encounter. At least at first with a new partner, a consent process may interrupt the flow. But there are different kinds of consent processes, and not all need be an interruption.

Long-term relationships benefit from trust and experience. Using consent from the beginning of the relationship builds trust. When you have consenting sex with the same person enough, you learn the body language and vocal tones that indicate their pleasure or discomfort. With even more experience, you can develop patterns to adjust what you're doing when it isn't working. Trust and experience help long-term couples maintain consent without interrupting flow.

This is called the Consent Castle, my favorite metaphor for consent.[2] The Consent Castle is a building of familiar sexual patterns created over time by a couple. Experience is the foundation. The walls are the understandings and agreements built on that experience. The walls are the structure that makes the building safe. Explicit consent—a clear verbal process of asking for and receiving verbal agreement for a sexual behavior—becomes less essential when the couple who built the Consent Castle follows their established sexual patterns.

But the castle does not need to be stagnant. A consenting couple can add new sexual behaviors to the castle, just like someone may remodel a building. When they add new behaviors, they use explicit consent practices, just like you'd wear a hardhat and safety gear when constructing a new floor on a building.

If you're having sex with someone for the first time, you don't have that trust and experience together. You don't have an established pattern of consent or behavior. So, you must be more explicit to get consent. You also must be more careful to monitor consent. Monitoring consent includes paying attention to ongoing verbal or nonverbal cues of continued positive engagement (see page 221 for more on this topic). If you aren't finding that idea very compelling, I understand that feeling.

Robotically asking consent questions can kill a hot mood, but there's no need to be robotic. If you become skillful at consent for hookups, you can keep it hot. For example, you might ask, "Can I hear you moan, so I know that you're loving it?" What you asked is, "Can you verbalize your pleasure, so I know you're still into it?" Your partner's response could be, "I'm gonna pull your hips toward me 'cause I can barely talk." The consent response is, "I'll use my hands to show my ongoing consent because sometimes I don't make noise." Veiling consent language in dirty talk like this can be very sexy. It increases anticipation and helps people maintain consent in novel situations like hookups and casual sex.

The challenge is that using consent language this way requires practice, and that means you might have to do it robotically at first as you are learning. This is where men often encounter the performance demand in their heads. We get afraid that if we're learning, we won't look manly or be desirable. Protecting your partner from trauma is important enough to fumble a little while learning.

"PARTNERS DON'T WANT ME TO TALK LIKE THIS"

Some men think their partners don't want them to use consent language in bed. They're both right and wrong. Some partners won't want to talk through consent like this, and many will. In fact, you might have more potential sexual partners if you can help them feel safe and respected.

If you have a partner who doesn't like explicit consent conversations, you have a choice to make. Would you rather that your partner gets turned off by you demonstrating respect this way, or would you rather risk that your partner feels violated by your lack of consent talk? Would you rather have a partner who is willing to risk violating you, or a partner who is willing to talk about how to fulfill your desires?

What kind of partner do you want to be? What kind of partner do you want to have? Is the person asking you to deemphasize consent for them also de-emphasizing *your* consent? Are they wanting you to be a stereotypically strong, silent type who withholds his feelings and is numb to the feelings of others? If so, how does that feel for you? Similarly, you could ask the person who gives you that feedback, "I recognize that you don't like that kind of consent process. How would you recommend that we navigate protecting consent and safety while trying to express sexual desire?"

Beware of responses that suggest that you should just be able to "read" or to "feel" their responses. Those kinds of experiences can and do happen. But "feeling" and "reading" are subjective experiences and can be inaccurate. For some rare couples, that works intuitively, and for others, inaccurate interpretations lead to unintentional consent violations and trauma. The challenge is that no two people are exactly alike, and when we get down to the intricacies of sexual expression, people are quite unique. Explicit consent is the conversational oil that coats the gears between our differences.

YOU GET TO CONSENT, OR NOT, TOO

If you think that negotiating consent with your partner is like getting the keys to unlock doors to get the things you want, then you are missing the point. Consent is for *you*. Clear consent processes help you make sure you avoid a friends-with-benefits relationship when you want a long-term loving relationship. Clear consent processes help you avoid a makeout session that ends without an orgasm when you know that would likely leave you feeling rejected or frustrated. A clear consent process can help you avoid unwanted pregnancy, a sexually transmitted infection (STI), misconduct, feeling violated or used, a bad reputation, and unfulfilling sex. Consent conversations aren't about you getting the other person's consent. Consent conversations are about finding what you both say yes to and then doing that.

Men are often surprised by these statements. Remember, masculinity myths are pervasive and tell us that men want all the sex we can have. If a man doesn't want sex, he often thinks something is wrong with him. He's less than a man. That's not true. Every man has some kinds of sex he isn't interested in. Men deserve to be protected from negative sexual experiences, too. You are allowed to protect yourself. You are valuable. You are sacred.

Use thorough consent conversations to protect yourself. Then you'll use them to protect your partners, too. Use consent processes to avoid the sex you *don't* want. That'll make it easier to make sure your partners aren't getting sex they don't want from you, too.

Beyond protection from harm, consent is for pleasure. In a robust consent process, you can be selective about your partners. You can choose partners who are willing to do the things that drive you wild. You can teach new partners how to drive you wild. You can ask partners what drives them wild. Partners can teach you new things that you didn't know would drive you wild.

Consent includes listening and learning so that you become a competent, capable, and generous lover. Consent includes the tools to adapt to each sexual partner in a unique way. This will make you a better lover for each partner, not just a good lover for some and an okay or bad lover for others. Consent can also help you adapt your sexual skills over time. This will make your sex life more satisfying as you age.

SOMETIMES YOU NEED TO SAY NO

Much of the focus on consent culture is about helping men listen to their partners. Men also need help knowing when to say no. The myth that men always want sex and our cocks are hard on a moment's notice is destructive to us, too.

You probably don't want to have sex with every person whom you could have sex with. For example, perhaps you already know some partners who are sexually irresponsible in ways that you find dangerous. If your hookup from the bar doesn't want to use a condom or talk about their STI status, that risks your health. If your partner from the party doesn't want to talk about what this sex means, that risks your emotional balance. In these cases, you have a right to say no. Here are some other examples:

- If you have a partner who keeps asking for more commitment than you want, it doesn't matter if the sex is good or if you're afraid of hurting their feelings. You have a right to say no.

- If a partner can't talk about the sex they want, what they desire, or what their boundaries are, then you won't trust them. You have a right to say no.

- If your partner or spouse keeps shaming you because you aren't getting an erection after they've criticized you for being a bad husband, father, partner, worker, student, or man, you have a right to say no. After all, your penis already is saying no, so listen to it!

- If you aren't sure why, don't have a reason, but it just doesn't feel right to you, you have a right to say no. You have a right to decide when, whether, how, and with whom you will share the gift of your sex. There is nothing about your gender or any other identity or circumstance that obligates you to perform sexually for someone else. You have a right to keep your sex to yourself, for yourself, for any reason or no reason.

Saying no in any of these cases protects both you and the other person from potentially bad sex. Great sex—really satisfying sex—is sex that is freely and mutually given, gratefully and mutually received, and it takes some effort to calibrate your sexual communication about those gifts enough to make that happen.

One beautiful thing about sexuality is that it belongs to you. In the private corners of your mind, in the quiet of a room alone, your sexuality belongs to you, no one else. Connecting to your sexuality can be a source of freedom from even the most powerful forms of oppression.

BEYOND YES: ENTHUSIASTIC AND AFFIRMATIVE CONSENT

We've discussed explicit consent—in which verbal agreement is given—but the word *yes* alone is never enough. Legal definitions of consent include that the person must be of an age and adequate cognitive capacity to give consent. The legal standard of affirmative consent is that the consent is knowing, voluntary, mutual, verbal, and explicit. That means you must know what you're consenting to. All people involved (including witnesses or bystanders) need to consent.

Consent needs to be given verbally with yes. And consent needs to be explicit: "Yes, I agree to have vaginal intercourse with a condom on with you." Imagine a situation where just one detail is changed: "Yes, I agree to have vaginal intercourse with you." No mention of a condom. The couple begins having sex with a condom on, but then the man removes the condom without her knowledge. This is still a consent violation.

Other definitions of affirmative consent identify that the consent must be ongoing. In other words, either partner can remove consent at any point and the activity must stop. Put another way, for sexual activity to continue, all people involved must continue consenting. There's a very simple, common, ongoing consent process that many couples use. After the penetrating partner begins penetration and before beginning any thrusting, the penetrating partner might simply ask, "Good?" and the partner being penetrated can confirm, "Yeah, good." This confirms that no pain or discomfort is taking place during the penetration.

Affirmative consent establishes only the minimum bar for consent, but enthusiastic consent provides a maximal standard. With enthusiastic consent, you are looking for excitement, eagerness, and interest. The standard of enthusiastic consent helps ensure that communication barriers—such as the ways in which destructive masculinity can make it difficult for our partners to give us a clear no—aren't impeding the consent conversation. Imagine how you'd feel if your partner says, "Oh, that sounds hot! Let's try that!" instead of "I guess" with a shrug.

If you wait for an enthusiastic yes that sings with energy from you and your partner, you'll feel better about the sexual behaviors that you try. It is great if a partner says with enthusiasm, "I don't think that turns me on but I'd like to turn you on, so let's try it!" But that same sentence in a hesitant tone might indicate an unwilling, nonconsensual partner. Consent isn't about accepting the minimum-bar checkbox process; it is about moving enthusiastically toward something fun.

Chapter 3

CAN MY SEXUALITY BE GOOD?

OUR CULTURE HAS A LOT TO SAY about male sexuality. There are cultural beliefs about how our sexuality should be, what's wrong with someone when their sexuality doesn't fit the mold, and who is responsible for unacceptable sexual behavior. There are cultural beliefs about how men should feel, think, and act. There are cultural beliefs about what men can and cannot control about their sexuality. Because these ideas are so specific, there's not a lot of room for you to be the unique kind of man that you are. There's not much room for your sexuality to exist the way it actually does.

This chapter dispels some myths about male sexuality, starting with testosterone myths, which purport to use science to describe what men and our sexuality is about. It also reimagines male sexuality without violence, guides you in developing an awareness of your sexual desires, helps you remove shame about those desires, and creates space for you to be the kind of man you are instead of trying to cram yourself into the small mold of who you "should be."

THE REAL DEAL ABOUT TESTOSTERONE

A great deal of male behavior is blamed on—even excused by—testosterone, the hormone most associated with sex drive. This tendency to scapegoat testosterone has roots in our cultural history and our traditional narratives about men and masculinity. Let's look at how some of these myths have been updated to sound scientific by blaming testosterone.

OLD MYTHS	NEW MYTHS
Men must have sex.	Men are biologically driven to want sex because of their testosterone.
Real men have erections when they want them.	Low testosterone is the problem when a man has difficulty getting an erection. He can fix that with supplemental testosterone.
Young men have the good kind of sex—anytime, anywhere.	Old men need testosterone to be sexually relevant.
Boys will be boys.	Men are violent because of testosterone.

All these myths are contrary to science. We have a responsibility to learn about testosterone myths and the science that contradicts them—and to develop the skills necessary to navigate the biological reality of maleness, sex, and desire.

Testosterone Realities

Very high levels of testosterone in puberty cause the bodily changes associated with adult males, such as a deeper voice, facial hair, a broad chest, and a thicker bone structure. After that adolescent flood of testosterone, levels tend to drop significantly and then taper further as a man ages. Pubescent males and transgender men often go through a period of psychological adjustment to the new experience of having higher levels of testosterone. This can include experiences of anger-hostility, aggression, mania, and increased self-esteem.[1] Adjusting takes time; it's kind of like when your limbs grow in adolescence—at first you may be a little clumsy, but over time, you adapt to your new size.

It is unfortunate that many men are not guided through these experiences in adolescence. Essentially, we are told that, now that we've crossed into adult maleness, there's nothing we can do about our raging hormones. We're rarely told that we're expected to regulate our desires or how to engage in consent. But there is nothing that makes us incapable of learning the skills of consent now—and we should, for the benefit of ourselves, our lovers, and a rockin' sex life. Much of the remainder of this book is dedicated to these skills, but for now, we'll focus on the realities of what testosterone does and does not do.

Reality 1: Testosterone Does Not Create Desire

Ads on porn sites or any casual internet search for *testosterone* will reveal testosterone-replacement treatments that promise to return men's sexual desire to youthful levels. The research about testosterone contradicts this.

According to research, it is true that men with testosterone levels below the normal range—a condition called hypogonadism—can increase sexual desire by increasing hormone levels. But this condition is rare. In fact, absence of sexual desire doesn't predict low testosterone levels.[2]

In one study, of men who reported low sexual desire and other symptoms correlated with low testosterone, only 28.1 percent were confirmed to have low levels of testosterone. This means that for seven out ten men who reported these symptoms, other factors were the cause. Furthermore, for men with low to normal testosterone levels, increasing their testosterone did not increase their sexual desire.[3]

Another study found that "the effects of T[estosterone] supplementation on sexual function and desire may be modest and diminish over time."[4] In other words, once testosterone is within a normal range, it probably doesn't account much for different levels of desire, especially once the person has adjusted to the new level of testosterone. The takeaway from this research is that some testosterone creates a *capacity* to feel desire. Testosterone doesn't actually *cause* attraction, sexual comfort, or desire. Those experiences are influenced by psychological, *not* biological, factors. An individual's personality, the quality of their relationship with their partner, and the nature of the sexual opportunity are more important determiners of desire.

If you are doubting this and you're a straight person, just ask yourself how much testosterone you think it would take for you to be interested in having sex with a person of your gender. The capacity to be aroused and getting aroused by a particular experience are not the same thing.

Reality 2: Testosterone Does Not Create Erections

Often, when men come into my office for erectile dysfunction treatment, they are initially wary of the emotional vulnerability required to talk about their difficulties getting and maintaining an erection. More than one man has decided to stop treatment and try testosterone-replacement therapy after doing their initial assessment and treatment plan with me (usually a four-session process). Testosterone replacement seems easier than talk therapy. Most come back later reporting that they did get testosterone replacement, and their levels are now "normal," but they still aren't experiencing stronger erections. Testosterone treatment for erectile dysfunction is "marginally effective at best."[5]

To treat erectile dysfunction, it's important to rule out other medical causes, such as alcohol use, diabetes, or the side effects of medications. Then we look at erectile function during masturbation or nighttime erections as a kind of baseline because no one has the same erection strength for their entire life. If a person's erection strength is different between partnered sex and masturbation, there are three common causes: The first is a partner who the man in question perceives as invalidating, pressuring, insulting, or mean. The second is that he has sexual desires and fantasies that he hasn't brought to light or isn't able to bring to the sexual relationship with his partner. The third is that either he or his partner lacks skill in providing him pleasure during partnered sex. None of these erection challenges requires testosterone levels higher than the minimal amount to get an erection.

Reality 3: Testosterone Is Not the "Male" Hormone

Yes, men tend to have higher levels of testosterone than women. Even with that tendency, there's "about 10–15 percent overlap between men's and women's levels."[6] That means that some women have higher levels of testosterone than some men. Women's testosterone is mostly produced by their gonads (ovaries) and adrenal glands, just as men's testosterone is mostly produced in their gonads (testicles) and adrenal glands. So, there's nothing inherently "male" about testosterone or testosterone levels. Furthermore, like other neurological or endocrine differences between men and women, these differences may not matter very much.

Different people are affected differently by the same level of testosterone. This won't be that surprising to you if you think about it. One person finds cotton candy to be too sweet; another loves it. One person tastes a carrot and finds it sweet; another person can't taste those sugars at all. Relative to testosterone, this is referred to as androgen sensitivity. At a given level of testosterone, a person with low androgen sensitivity may experience low competition motivation (like depression), lethargy, and malaise.[7] Another person with the same level of testosterone in their bloodstream but who has medium androgen sensitivity may feel neutral. A third person with the same level of testosterone but high androgen sensitivity may experience testosterone as highly energizing and may want to compete and win at every opportunity.

This information helps us understand the irrelevance of testosterone levels when comparing testosterone levels across men or between men and women and make sense of men's behavior in comparison to women's behavior. A particular woman's sensitivity to her lower testosterone level may be higher than a man's sensitivity to his higher testosterone level. Her behavior might be more influenced by her testosterone than his, even though he has more of it. So, the woman trying to get her makeup, high heels, and dress to look awesome; the woman kicking butt as a lawyer; the man charging down the football field; and the man striving to succeed as a dancer might all be experiencing the same effective impact of their different testosterone levels: testosterone is helping them all strive harder in their respective endeavors.

This is a common factor to consider about many other sex differences. Although one biological difference may be detected—in this case, higher levels of testosterone in men than in women—the behavioral effects of that difference may be negated or diminished by another biological difference, such as the potential that a particular woman's higher androgen sensitivity may make her lower testosterone levels affect her more than a particular man with lower androgen sensitivity but higher testosterone levels.[8]

Reality 4: Testosterone Does Not Create Aggression

The strongest science concerning emotions and hormones suggests that testosterone is best viewed as a competition hormone—but don't confuse competition with aggression. In fact, the relationship between testosterone and aggression is weak.[9] What scientists refer to as competition covers a broad range of behaviors that may include physical aggression but may also include nonviolent competition, such as the mating dances of male birds, who may never fight one another.

Therefore, I prefer to refer to the motivation that testosterone creates in people as a performance motivation (not to be confused with performance demand, see page 4), instead of competition. Testosterone motivates us to perform to increase our social status. Testosterone increases in the presence of other performers, increases again when we're successful in outperforming others, and decreases when others outperform us. The decrease in testosterone may steer us away from challenge to reevaluate our strategy. That a social event can change our hormone levels shows that we can't deduce truths about ourselves from biology without considering how sociology affects biology.[10]

Nothing here suggests that testosterone inclines men toward sexual coercion, assault, or rape. It simply suggests that men (or any person significantly influenced by their testosterone) will be inclined to compete or perform to achieve their goals, and one goal might be sex. Other goals might be creating art, acquiring money, social status, social recognition, or cleaning house. None of these things are considered biological needs, though, and no one is entitled to them (except perhaps money, to secure the basic needs of security and dignity).

You may have similar feelings of energy and intense concentration when playing a sport, trying to succeed at work, hitting on an attractive person, or buying a new car or house—this might be testosterone influencing your performance. Nothing here suggests a biological imperative to violence. You know better than to punch a coworker competing with you for a promotion.

Professional athletes do sometimes engage in violence, but those instances increase or decrease according to the degree to which a sport condones or penalizes those behaviors. Hockey encourages fistfights during games, with both written and unwritten rules about those fights, including how and why they begin, how far they go, and whom a player should and shouldn't invite to fight. In basketball, contact between competitors is highly regulated. In the NBA, for example, players are ejected from the game, fined, and heavily penalized for punching. These rules influence how often violence happens in both sports. Even in professional sports, it isn't maleness that determines violence, but the social construct.

Culture Creates Violence or Safety

As we've established, nothing about testosterone suggests a biological necessity for men to coerce, assault, or rape. So why are those behaviors more common with men? There is a complicated link between aggression and a relatively high ratio of testosterone to cortisol, a hormone released in response to stress.[11] In other words, a combination of higher levels of testosterone and lower levels of cortisol has been found to correlate with increased aggression in men.[12] Higher cortisol levels encourage a person to feel fear and withdraw, but that doesn't explain why lower stress may be correlated with higher levels of aggression. One man wrote about an experience that exemplifies what the connection might be:

> I think I did it [touched a woman secretly without her consent] because she seemed otherwise out of reach for me; perhaps such one-sided contact was all the intimacy I could ever hope to enjoy with her. And yet, with so many elbows, knees, hands, and feet flying about, I also recall making an instantaneous calculation: Maybe I can get away with this.[13]

The correlation between low cortisol and increased aggression is due to the fact that when you think you can win easily or get away with something, aggression becomes a safe option for you. Humans, like all organisms, have a natural self-preservation instinct. When we believe that we will lose a conflict or will be punished (high cortisol), we become submissive. When we are less afraid of getting caught and think we will get away with whatever we are thinking of doing, we experience less stress (lower cortisol). A man who thinks he will get away with pushing boundaries, sexual coercion, assault, or rape is more likely to have less stress about it and more likely to respond to the inclinations of his desire by becoming violent.

Now we're back to the layer of culture. If men believe they will get away with it, they may be more likely to engage in violence. When men believe that they are culturally entitled to sexual acts from others, they believe the culture will support their coercion. When men are physically stronger and larger than an intended victim (as men often are, relative to women), they may feel more confident in their ability to physically overpower the victim in an assault or a rape attempt.

When we don't teach boys about the importance of consent, we imply to them that we don't expect them to regulate their sexual desires. When men get away with sexual coercion, assault, and rape, this increases the perception that men need not be stressed about that behavior. When men joke or tell stories about coercion, assault, and rape and are seen as funny or manly for it, these behaviors are reinforced. All these things create a low-stress environment during arousal (low cortisol), with high performance motivations (higher testosterone). In other words, culture influences biology by creating the conditions for sexual aggression and assault by men. Culture reinforces those conditions with other messages conveyed to women and other common victims of male violence including other men. The good news here, of course, is that culture can also influence biology by reducing the conditions for those same assaults.

If we continue to create a culture where all people are held accountable for acts of sexual violence, then all people, including men, will become afraid (higher cortisol) of punishment for sexual violence. As individuals in our culture, we shape how men view violence. When we speak out among other men disapproving of sexual violence, we change other men's endocrinology (higher cortisol) if they ever think about enacting sexual violence, and we make them less likely to do it. We can influence other men's behavior by discouraging sexual violence.

RECLAIMING MALE SEXUALITY, STARTING WITH YOURS

If men and male sexuality are good—but male sexuality some-times manifests with poor consent practices, coercion, assault, and rape—then we must examine where and how that good nature becomes distorted.

Some authors have attempted to identify the nature of male sexuality as the core problem. In the opinion piece "The Unex-amined Brutality of the Male Libido," the author equates harmful manifestations of male sexuality with the nature of male sexual-ity, as in the statement "the often ugly and dangerous nature of the male libido."[14] Some feminist authors describe male sexuality as divided and repressed in adolescence, as bell hooks does in *The Will to Change*: "During these formative years, when a boy's sexual lust is often intense, he learns that patriarchal culture expects him to covertly cultivate that lust and the will to satisfy it while engag-ing in overt acts of sexual repression. This splitting is part of the initiation into patriarchal masculinity; it is a rite of passage."[15] But hooks defines healthy male sexuality with the single word "inti-mate"—and, otherwise, by what it is not. To her it is not "fuck-ing," dominant, obsessive, addictive, or violent. She believes gay male sexuality also suffers under patriarchal culture and cites as evidence that "the images gay men seek are male, but males posi-tioned in the same way as the male and female bodies of straight pornography."[16] In this portrayal, gay sexuality—like much of male sexuality—is shamed and feared. This view of male sexuality does not see the developmental process of liberation taking place in gay sexuality and does not clearly imagine male sexuality that is free.

We need to define healthy male sexuality ourselves. We need to create a vision large enough to include the diversity within the community of men and flexible enough to allow for personal nar-ratives of sexual health, like yours.

What would your sexuality look like without the shame patriarchy puts on it? What would your sexuality look like if you had been given responsibility for it? The exercise in this chapter will help you answer these questions by giving you tools to describe your sexuality as it is now. You'll also learn tools for decreasing patriarchal shame about your sexuality and for taking responsibility for your sexuality.

To keep our desire powerful and positive, we have an obligation to ourselves and to our partners to develop the force of will required to regulate it. Regulating your sexuality just means being able to make good choices about how you will express your sexuality. Future chapters will teach you more about the nature of your desire, including how to regulate it, how to take responsibility for desire and other emotions, and how to build relationships, including sexual relationships.

For now, know that no one else can regulate it for us. If we don't self-regulate, then our sexual partners will live in fear of our sexuality instead of savoring it. It can be hard to stop our desire, but it is possible.

EXERCISE: Know Your Turn-Ons

Before you develop the capacity to regulate your desires, you must know what your desires are. This exercise will help you inventory your sexual desires. This self-awareness will make it easier for you to regulate your desires and to have consent conversations about them. Talking about what turns you on can be difficult. For this reason, I like to use nature metaphors and analogies for sexuality. Nature metaphors invite us to consider what exists in our sexuality, rather than how we *wish* it was or how we think it *should be*. Natural features aren't moral or immoral; they simply exist. For example, when we respect the nature and power of a river, we can safely play in it, work on it, and enjoy its beauty. When we respect the power of our sexuality as we do a river, we can follow it to pleasure and offer pleasure to our partners. Nature comparisons reduce the shaming and moralizing that may take place as we learn about our sexuality, including how it causes pain.

1. **Use the Erotic Landscape chart** (figure 3.1) on page 56 to create an inventory of your sexuality. You may also download a color copy of this form from my website.[17]

2. **Reference your answers** here as you read the rest of this book so that you know what to regulate, be vulnerable about, and get consent for. You'll be asked to refer back to your answers later on, so don't skip this task!

3. **Fill in the columns of this chart** with what you know about your sexuality as you read the following prompts. If you have trouble figuring out what to put in a column, just leave it blank. If all you're putting in the columns is one kind of information, like sexual positions, that's fine, too. That's a common experience, so at the end of this chapter, there's a little extra guidance.

This chart presents a metaphor for your sexuality—one side of a riverbed. On the left side, in the column labeled "Essential for Expression," imagine the deepest part of the river. Reading across to the right to the column labeled "Good for Vibrancy," imagine a shallower part of the river. The next columns are for the riverbanks ("Interested but Unnecessary"), the plains near the river ("Uninterested but Willing"), hills beyond the river ("Unwilling"), and finally high hills far beyond the river ("Gross-Out").

Essential for Expression (First Column)

This is the most essential part of your erotic river. If this part of a river didn't have any water flowing in it, there wouldn't be a river. Therefore, this is the part of your sexuality that is utterly essential. Think of it as the minimal experience required for you to feel that you are expressing your sexuality. Or, looked at another way, it's the last element of sexual expression you'd want to give up.

Start this column with information about your sexual orientation. Also write down the sexual behaviors, thoughts, or fantasies that are very common for you. Given how common masturbation is for men,[18] think about writing something about your masturbation habits if you, like most men, masturbate regularly.

Additionally, consider what sexual expression would look like for you in the extremes of life. For example, what would your sexuality look like if your partner was very ill or if you were dying? For many people, essential sexual expression focuses more on touch, simple kisses, and physical closeness than it does on sexual positions or penetration. Men commonly list orgasm and penetration in this column, but there are no requirements for what you list here—just be honest.

What seems essential now might change as you learn more about your sexuality, or as you age. This is common. Whatever you've written down and whatever changes, don't worry. You can move elements around whenever you want or when you discover new things about your sexuality.

Good for Vibrancy (Second Column)

This column represents a river that is full of water; it holds the elements of sexuality that go beyond minimal expression. This is your image of what your sexual expression looks like when you feel (or imagine feeling) content with your sex life and when it is helping you thrive.

If you haven't ever felt content with your sex life, don't worry. You're not alone. There are many circumstances that can inhibit sexual contentment (e.g., depression, emotional disconnect, a bad relationship, addiction, trauma, poverty, oppression, illness, religious restrictions, or threats to safety, just to name a few). For now, just write in this column what you imagine your sexuality would look like if you were content with it and it was helping you thrive.

Interested but Unnecessary (Third Column)

This part of the sexual landscape analogy represents the parts of the riverbank that flood seasonally. Sexually, this represents the things you enjoy sometimes as a bit of spice. Maybe you like receiving anal sex a couple of times a year. Maybe you like your partner to dress up in a sexy outfit on your birthday. Many people have some elements to their sexuality they like only occasionally, or when they're in the right mood. List those elements of your experience here.

This column can also include sexual experiences that you're curious about but that aren't important for you to try. For example, maybe you'd like to try role-playing with a partner, but if your partner isn't into that, it wouldn't be a deal breaker for you. Write these down, too.

Once you try something you have been curious about, you may change which column it goes in. For example, if you had a fantasy about a threesome, but the reality was not fun, you might move "have a threesome" to the Unwilling column. Conversely, if you have a threesome and it is awesome for you, the reality of a threesome might shift into the Good for Vibrancy column.

Uninterested but Willing (Fourth Column)

In the riverbed analogy, the fourth column represents the plains above the riverbed, where crops can be irrigated with water from the river. This represents the work it can take to do something sexually that you are less interested in. In this column, list sexual things you're willing to do even if it doesn't turn you on. Only list those things that a sexual partner is interested in or has expressed interest in and that you're willing to do for their pleasure. There's no need to list every possible behavior you might be willing to do.

Just because your partner is interested doesn't mean you have to list a behavior here. If participating in the experience would make you feel demeaned, belittled, emasculated, or resentful, it doesn't belong in this column. If you'd only ever agree to do it if you got something in return, don't put that here, either. This column is for behaviors that are possible for you to do for someone else when there's a basis of trust, generosity, connection, and intimacy.

Unwilling (Fifth Column)

In the riverbed analogy, the fifth column represents the hills above a river valley. There'd be a damaging flood if the water from the river reached this area. Sexual experiences you list in this column turn you off—for example, words you don't like, positions that hurt you, sexual behaviors that you have bad associations with, or things that are just on your no list because that's how you work. Focus on the things that feel relevant to you because they have come up in your experience. There's no need to catalog everything in human sexuality that turns you off.

Gross-Out (Sixth Column)

This column represents the highest hills above the riverbed—the ones so far above the river that it'd be catastrophic for the water to reach them. Sexually, this column holds the things that gross you out, or the extreme turnoffs. This category is not a way for you to shame your partner for their interests; it's about your subjective emotional experience. When you are grossed out, it's probably hard to even discuss the behavior, much less bring it into your sex life. Intense traumatic reactions to sexual topics or behaviors can be listed in this column.

Figure 3.1: Erotic Landscape chart

Turn-Ons ←—————————————————————

Everyday core aspects of your sexual expression—the minimal expression you'd want to maintain relationships and the last you'd want to give up.	Makes sexual expression fulfilling and vibrant; creates vitality, contentment, and thriving.	(1) Seasonal flooding, or "once in a while" experiences; or (2) things you are interested in but that aren't a big deal if they are off-limits for a partner.	Willing to do for a partner and you could be happy they're enjoying it, but wouldn't do much for you.
Essential for Expression	**Good for Vibrancy**	**Interested but Unnecessary**	**Uninterested but Willing**

→ **Turnoffs**

Not willing to do it, or not willing to try it.	Grosses you out and don't even like to talk or think about it.
Unwilling	**Gross-Out**

		Physical: Types of touch, behavior, acts, or verbs for bodies in motion.
		Emotions or feelings: May include your and your partner's feelings—consider before, during, and after sexual activity.
		Mental: Gender identities, roles, role-plays, kink dynamics, words, or the focus of attention.
		Spiritual: Meaning and purpose for sex, relationship style, and meaning-making rituals.

Quadrants of Sexual Experience

Prompts for Completing Your Erotic Landscape Chart

If you struggled to come up with what to put in each column, consider using the 4D Wheel described by sex therapist, researcher, and author Gina Ogden.[19] I've summarized that framework in the column on the far right-hand side of the diagram, inviting you to consider the physical, emotional, mental, and spiritual (or, as I think of it, the meaning and purpose) dimensions of sexuality as you complete each column. Here's a quick look at each dimension:

Physical. The physical dimension invites you to attend to what happens with the body. This can include sexual positions, types of touch, descriptions of how bodies move (e.g., "quick" or "slow"), or physical sensations, like temperature, texture, and pressure.

Emotional. Emotional dimensions of sex can include how you or your partner feel before, during, or after sexual activity. If you are including elements of sexual relationships, you might list general feelings in the relationship, such as "safe," "aroused," "free," or "accepted." You might want to specify some feelings for long-term relationships and others for casual sex relationships.

Mental. Mental elements of sexuality might include fantasies, gender identity (e.g., man), relationship roles (e.g., boyfriend or husband), role-play (e.g., doctor or fireman), kink dynamics (e.g., dominant or submissive), sexual words (e.g., "cock," "prick," or "dick"), or labels (e.g., "slut," "bad boy"). Labels or categories you list can refer to you or your partner.

Another mental dimension of sexuality might refer to where your attention is directed—that is, who is paying what kind of attention to whom? Finally, consider listing methods for preventing sexually transmitted infections or unwanted pregnancy. These belong in the mental dimension because you must think, plan, and remember to use them.

Spiritual. This dimension describes the larger context, purpose, or meaning for your sexual experience. This includes "an intimate sense of connection with one's self, one's partner, and/or a power beyond one's self."[20] This dimension can help you use the "Know Your Turn-Ons" exercise to express how you feel about different relationship styles like monogamy (a relationship agreement that allows one romantic and sexual partner dyad), consensual nonmonogamy (an ethical agreement that allows some form of sexual or emotional connections outside of a dyad), or polyamorous (a consensual agreement that there can be multiple loving relationships for each person).

This dimension can also help you identify how you feel about meaning-making rituals for a relationship, such as marriage, honeymoon, anniversary, couple vacations, separation, divorce, or makeup sex. Any one of these might go in different columns for different people, due to the different values and meanings people give to the practices.

■

How did your erotic landscape chart turn out? Don't worry if there are any blank or nearly blank columns. Don't worry if you didn't have much to write about one or more of the four dimensions. The important lesson from this exercise is to make sure that you understand the content of your desire. Knowing what you desire empowers you to claim your sexuality as it is, without shame. This allows you to share what you desire with vulnerability and to ask for consent for what you desire to build the sexual relationships that you want.

SEXUAL SHAME

If you feel that you want to hide what turns you on after completing the erotic landscape chart—or you skipped it altogether—that's a common experience. That experience is *shame*. Shame tells us that who we are or what we are is bad. Shame makes us want to hide the truth about ourselves or to withdraw from others.

Shaming our sexual nature is a part of the culture of the United States. Women's sexuality is repressed by telling them to be "good," "clean," "pure," and "innocent." If a woman likes sex or has sex others don't like, she is shamed with words like *slut*, *whore*, *tramp*, *nasty*, and others like them.

Men's sexuality is also shamed in our culture but in different ways. It is often equated with low value ("base desires"), disgust ("dirty"), animalism ("men are dogs"), mindlessness ("men just want to fuck"), and violence ("that's just the way men are"). If the positive impulse behind these labels is to guide men to be better, it falls short of the goal. Nothing good comes from telling people they are bad. If you believe you are bad, then you either must embrace being sexually bad, which gives you no motivation toward consent, or withdraw into isolation, including sexual self-repression.

When men embrace being bad, it sounds like destructive masculinity: "I just want to fuck some bitches"; "This is just how I am, deal with it"; or "I don't care about feelings." When men withdraw, it sounds like male isolation and emotional flatness: "I don't really have emotional needs, I'm pretty rational"; "I don't have many friends, but I don't need them"; or "I don't really like people."

But many of us men want to be good and want to be in relationships with others. So, we accept sexual shame from the outside and repress our sexuality ourselves. We work to be "good" by trying to be what we think society demands of us. The following table lists some of the ways men do this and why.

REASONS MEN MIGHT REPRESS THEIR SEXUALITY	SELF-REPRESSIVE BEHAVIOR
Fear of being perceived as gay	Pretending to be heterosexual
	Performing hypermasculinity even if you're straight
Fear of being perceived as feminine	Pretending to be cisgender
	Hiding your like for cute animals, pink shirts, or romantic comedies
Fear of being accused of sex addiction or pornography addiction	Hiding masturbation or pornography viewing
	Pretending you think masturbation or pornography is immoral
Fear of being seen as immoral	Denying or hiding sexual desires
Fear of being seen as degenerate	Denying or hiding sexual fantasies
False belief that not masturbating will increase testosterone	Restricting sexual behaviors like masturbation[21]
Belief that restricting sexual thoughts or behaviors makes you more spiritual, moral, or noble	Denying, restricting, or eliminating sexual behaviors
Belief that when you indulge in pleasure, the people who give you pleasure take your power or virility away from you	Denying yourself orgasms

Research is clear about this: trying to change your sexual orientation or your gender identity is damaging.[22] Fantasies don't mean we actually want to do, or will do, those behaviors. As sex researcher and educator Justin Lehmiller says of one woman's intense fantasy of forced sex, "This scenario is only appealing to her because it takes place entirely in her head, where she remains in control the entire time."[23] Although spiritual or cultural moral guidance about behaviors may have value, there's good reason to cast a somewhat skeptical eye toward our cultures' and religions' views about sexuality.

What about Religious and Cultural Values?

In the United States, there continues to be a strong push for abstinence-only sex education, which has a strong basis in many cultures and religions. This type of sex education stems from the widespread fear that if kids are taught scientifically accurate information about sex, it will lead to more teens having sex.

However, attempts to control human sexuality in this way just don't work. Research shows that accurate sex education lowers rates of teen pregnancy, causes teens to wait longer before having sex, and lowers rates of STIs in teens. The opposite is true of teens who receive abstinence-only sex education.[24] Put another way, people who are given accurate information about sex can handle the truth responsibly and make safer, healthier choices.

When it comes to sexuality and relationships, there may be some good reasons to conform to your culture or religion. For example, doing so gives you a process for entering a relationship—such as dating rituals and wedding customs—that your culture supports. Doing so may also help you develop the respect of your community and may help you maintain your community's support for your relationships.

However, when it comes to sexuality and relationships, there may also be some good reasons to question your culture or religion. For instance, many cultures and religions deny the existence of sexual orientation and gender diversity. These denials often state that apparent diversity is a choice. But neither culture nor religion has the capacity to decide what is true about our sexuality any more than they can decide that the sun revolves around the earth. Neither are founded in science. There are people from throughout history, in every culture, who weren't heterosexual or who defied gender norms.[25] Sexual orientation and gender identity diversity appears to be a cross-culturally and historically enduring aspect of human existence. Furthermore, "most people experience little or no sense of choice about their sexual orientation."[26] There is no evidence that sexual orientation is a choice. When culture and religion are wrong about the facts of sexuality, we should be skeptical of the moral meanings they make about the truth.

Some cultures and religions deny or ignore the benefits of sexual pleasure. Some cultures and religions believe that sex, arousal, or masturbation cause shame, and the harm caused by shame is used as circular evidence that the belief is correct. Contrary to these beliefs, science shows that partnered sex, arousal, and masturbation have physical and mental health benefits.[27] For another example, when a culture ostracizes queer people, that causes higher rates of depression within the queer population. The culture then cites the high rates of depression as evidence that queer folk are mentally ill. Again, this is circular reasoning. There's no reason to believe that having a queer identity causes mental health problems. Stigma and shame cause mental health problems.

So, yes, cultural and religious norms are important and can ease us into positive social experiences. But cultures and religions don't get to decide what exists in reality. Take cultural and religious guidance about sex and relationships carefully. If your culture tells you that your sexual thoughts, feelings, or actions hurt you or others, examine whether and where this is true. Sometimes the harm described comes from sexual shame, not from the thought or the act itself. Your sexuality is a part of your nature; it cannot be cut out of your life with shame or denial. For example, you can deny your orientation, but it will still exist. Attempting to cut sexuality out of your life has consequences.

The Consequences of Sexual Repression

If we don't accept human sexuality as it is, we hurt people, including ourselves. In the United States, we're learning this lesson about homosexuality. When individuals cannot accept their own sexual orientation, they're at an increased risk for suicide and for being diagnosed with a mental health issue.[28] Conversion therapy, which attempts (and fails) to change a person's sexuality, is damaging. Fortunately, it is also increasingly outlawed in the United States.

We're also learning these lessons about transgender people. As a society, we are becoming more open to concepts like bathroom of choice, pronouns of choice, and the freedom to self-identify gender.

We need to accept the nature of male sexuality, too. We need safe and consensual ways for male sexual desire to be expressed. If there aren't culturally or socially acceptable ways for men to express sexual desire, they will find other ways to do so. For example, if being gay is a crime, gay men will create secret ways of identifying and meeting each other in secret. If you shame men for masturbating, men will hide their masturbation. Some men may "successfully" repress themselves, but it will be a victory in name only. Denying your sexuality can lead to depression; suicide; anger; sexual opportunism, like affairs; compulsive sexual behavior; and unprotected sex. These individual problems then become social problems.

For men in the United States, this sexual repression has dangers. When sexual opportunism intersects with male entitlement, men can become abusive, demanding, and violent. Here is a simple explanation for how this plays out in our culture: It starts with boys learning from their parents, peers, and society that tender human connection is something girls and women do, and that emotional expression other than anger isn't acceptable for men.[29] So, they learn to repress their desires for connection, even though they are part of the human experience. This makes men hungry for authentic touch, connection, and a range of emotional expression. Society then tells men hungry for connection that sexual connection is manly. At the same time, society tells girls and women that they may not have sexual desire and must say no, or they will be sluts. When boys are told that girls will withhold sex from them—but at the same time boys are only allowed tender connection in sex—then *a girl's or a woman's no must be violated for heterosexual boys to connect to another person.*[30]

In this way, our culture twists the beauty of our sexual desire by restricting it. The culture tells men they can use sexual violence against women, transgender people, feminine men, weak men, or men of color to express their feelings. Being violent in this way isolates men and hurts people. The violence we witness in male sexuality is a direct outcome of our sexuality and sexual expression being split from us. To stop our violence, we need to stop shaming our sexuality, desires, and other feelings when they do not conform to the narrow definition our society allows for men. We need to reclaim our sexuality for ourselves.

In the next section, you'll read about reducing sexual shame around some common intense elements of male sexuality. As we continue through the book, you'll learn other ways to reclaim your sexuality, including how to regulate those desires, how to talk about them with partners, and how to ask for consent if you want to put them into practice.

Intense Desires Allowed, Hold the Shame

Go back now and reread your list of turn-ons from the "Know Your Turn-Ons" exercise (see page 51). Notice which entries you feel ashamed of. How many of those desires include an element that some might label as intense? Male desire may be intense, seek novelty, be visceral and embodied, and seek polarities (e.g., control or surrender). If we're honest about it, we're not afraid of sexual intensity. Women, transwomen, nonbinary people, lesbians, and many others may also want sexual intensity. What we're afraid of and what we often shame ourselves for is that we're not always clear where the lines are between sexual intensity and violence.

Let's review how male sexuality got twisted into violence, as described in the previous section. First, we were told that we had to be sexual to express ourselves. Second, we were told that others would try to stop us from being sexual (for example, because women aren't supposed to want sex, we're gay and aren't supposed to be gay, or our desire is bad). Third, we're not given tools for being aware of or talking about our feelings or needs. Fourth, we're given tools for violence, domination, and aggression and told it's our nature to use these tools. When you put these elements together, you can see why many men end up with a violent expression of sexual desire. The perversion of patriarchy is not that patriarchy made normal male violence sexual—it is that patriarchy restricted normal male sexual intensity unless it was violent.

Imagine a new sexual culture. First, as a man, you're allowed to have desires and feelings, and to seek connection. Second, other people want sex. Yes, women want sex; many even want intense sex.[31] Some people want intense sex with people like you. People, including men, are allowed to ask for the sex they want. People, including men, are allowed to say yes when someone offers them the sex they want. Simply put, you can express your desire, even for intense sex, without violence by asking for and getting consent. If that's true, there's no need for sexual shame. That's the culture we're building together.

REQUIRING CONSENT ISN'T REPRESSION

Many men start get defensive when I talk about repression but then transition to talking about consent skills. Some men will say that the demand that they ask for consent represses male sexuality. Let's use the checks on culture and religion that I've already advocated for to examine that fear.

The call for consent is not denying desire, identity, orientation, or any other truth about human sexuality. The call for consent isn't denying pleasure to any person. It is advocating for the pleasure of all involved. The call for consent isn't declaring any particular sexual behavior or desire immoral. Consent describes a process *to assist* the expression of desires. When advocates for consent identify the harm that occurs without it, they refer to statistics about sexual violence and the feelings of victims. These are not metaphysical abstractions. They are real facts and experiences.

In this way, consent culture fulfills the best elements of culture identified earlier: It provides guidance for how people can create desired relationships, how they can build and maintain community respect, and how they can get community support for relationships once they are formed. Here are some examples of consent culture in action:

- In BDSM communities, there are standards for how two people who want to get kinky with each other will behave. They talk about what they're going to do and not do, and what they hope to get out of the experience. Sometimes, they'll even write down the things they agree about. They identify how they'll slow or stop the kink activity if it stops being fun, like by using key words (a.k.a. "safe words"). After getting kinky, they'll sit with each other to calm down (a.k.a. "after care") and review how things went.

- In a group sex party, there may be rules about who can approach whom, how to start conversations, where to talk and where to have sex, and how to end a sexual encounter.

- On college campuses, consent culture includes guidance about who can consent (e.g., not people who are drunk or passed out) and what consent looks like (e.g., many campuses encourage "enthusiastic consent").

Notice that two of these examples come from very permissive sexual environments. Consent norms emerge when sexuality is not repressed because, rather than focusing on stopping sex, people can focus on making sex safe and enjoyable for all participants. Don't confuse calls for accountability and consent as restrictions on your sexuality. Accountability and consent are the cultural price of admission to a broad permission to express your sexuality.

BE A BETTER ASSHOLE

Many men have attractions they wish they didn't have. There might be an extramarital attraction, a significantly different arousal for young adult men than for a long-term husband, a kink, or a sexual orientation opposed by one's religion. Some seek therapy to eliminate these impulses. Others believe there's a moral flaw in these desires or that these desires suggest they aren't mature. Both impulses are misguided.

We don't choose our sexual impulses and attractions. They don't conform to relationship agreements we've made, social mores, or our values. They come to us without invitation. Rightly or wrongly, our desires point us toward avenues to express our sexuality. Our fantasies don't have a master, but we can master the expression of our fantasies. To do so, we need to acknowledge that, on some level, *we are all assholes.*

We need to acknowledge that the opportunistic nature of our sexuality is oriented toward short-term gains. Our sexuality doesn't consider other people's feelings. Our fantasies don't consider how, for example, our partner would feel if we hooked up with our coworker or the feelings of the coworker if we propositioned them. So, I use this colorful term *asshole* not to put you down but to help you accept that not all your desires are in line with your values.

Because we have fantasies and impulses that don't attend to other people's feelings, we are assholes. Because we sometimes (especially when faced with an ongoing opportunity) have a hard time resisting these impulses, we are assholes. We need to accept that this is the case and then strive to be *a better asshole.* This doesn't mean eliminating our desire—that's impossible. It means channeling the desire in positive ways that do conform to our sexual values. I'm talking about sexual self-regulation—that is, making conscious choices about when, where, with whom, and how to express your sexual desire. Chapter 4 will show that sexuality can be regulated and will begin showing you how. The next section shows how accepting the truths about your sexuality creates the capacity for self-regulation.

Even If Hidden, You're Still an Asshole

Even when we try to hide parts of our sexuality that we're ashamed of, there are often limitations to how well we can do so (see "Soothing Sexual Shame," in chapter 6). Semen-soaked underwear, your browser history, your emotional withdrawal when that colleague is mentioned, or that quiet stillness when an attractive person walks into the room all give away the existence of that part of your sexuality.

Shame about undesired attractions causes the desire to fester inside you. Your shame tells you that you're not lovable, so you act unlovable and withdraw—and consequently, your partner feels lonely, finds you hard to love, or feels disconnected from you. So, the desire that you hide to avoid hurting your partner can hurt them even if you don't admit it.

Admitting to yourself that you have this attraction changes the dynamic: "This desire isn't something I want to act on, but I do have it. I'm paying attention to the fact that I have this desire so I can regulate it." This is the beginning of integrity. No part of you is in denial about another part of yourself. Now you can begin to take responsibility for whether and how you express your attractions. When you admit this attraction, at least to yourself, you can better manage your experience. Sometimes it is helpful to admit these desires to your partner, though sometimes it isn't. You'll have to decide yourself whether your partner is the kind of person who can be nonjudgmental about your inner, private sexual life.

If you are wondering how you might share new elements of your sexuality with your partner, here are some scripts to help you get the conversation started:

- "I masturbate. It's an important part of my sexuality. It doesn't mean that I'm unfulfilled with you sexually; it's just a part of my sexuality that's always there. I want us to talk about it because I don't want you to be surprised or hurt if you catch me masturbating or find out that I did."

- "I want to let you know that I like looking at porn. I have a couple of specific things that I like watching and a few performers that I really enjoy. I'm telling you so that if someday you find my browsing history, it doesn't shock you or make me seem any less in your eyes. Can we talk about any concerns you might have about me watching porn?"

- "I'm attracted to a coworker. We're working together a lot right now. I don't want to do anything about this attraction, but because I'm feeling it, I wanted to tell you to help me protect our relationship."

- "I'm kinky. There are certain kinky behaviors that are important for me to express at least sometimes to have a full sense of sexual expression. Some of those behaviors are sexual for me and some of them aren't. We need to talk about this because what I've learned is that if I'm not able to express those parts of myself inside the relationship, with some regularity, then I express them outside the relationship and hurt my partners. I'd like to talk about it to find a way to express myself without damaging the relationship."

For some partners, these issues won't be a major concern, and they'll be happy that you're talking about it. You may find that your partner can easily accept (or already knows about) the thing you were so ashamed of. It might even become a source for deepened erotic energy in your relationship. Or you might find that your partner is hurt, angry, or grossed out—or now questions the relationship because you have shared these parts of yourself. So, it makes sense for you to be careful about sharing your inner erotic life with someone.

You may be thinking, "Whoa, I could never talk to my partner that way. I'd end the relationship with that conversation!" And you might be right; maybe you will decide not to share that aspect of your sexuality with your partner. You can do so with integrity if you admit to yourself the bargain you're making, which is multifaceted:

- I've decided that hiding this element of my sexuality is a cost I'm willing to pay in order to maintain this relationship.

- I believe maintaining this relationship in this way is better than ending it—or the risk of ending it—by naming that part of my sexuality.

- To make this bargain work, I accept personal responsibility for making sure that I regulate this part of my sexuality.

From there, you only have to do one more thing to make it work—you must be humble enough to admit it if you aren't regulating that part of sexuality.

Take a quick look back at your responses to the "Know Your Turn-Ons" exercise earlier in this chapter. If you have decided to hide part of your sexuality from your spouse, know that the closer the information is to the "Essential for Expression" column, the harder it may be for you to hide that part of yourself without consequences to your mood or relationship.

I Was an Asshole. Can I Save My Relationship?

When partners discover hidden elements of their beloved's sexuality, by discovery or admission, they often feel hurt or shocked. This is especially true when the aspect of your sexuality is something that appears contrary to the founding agreements of the relationship (for example, if you are polyamorous but this is a monogamous relationship, or if you are gay in a straight relationship).

After the shock wears off, most relationships go through an adjustment and reevaluation phase, where you and your partner may attempt to incorporate the new information into your relationship. You may discuss and decide together whether and how the information can be incorporated into your relationship. Even if you don't talk about it, pretend it never happened, and avoid the topic, this is still an example of the reevaluation and adjustment process.

One form of reevaluation and adjustment is reconciliation and forgiveness. This helps your partner heal and reestablish trust. Your partner will need to express the pain they felt when you hid important information from them. They will need you to acknowledge their pain, accept responsibility for it, and feel bad and apologize for having caused the pain. Then the two of you will need to identify why you hid the information and what you are going to do together so that you don't have to hide it in the future.[32]

When partners discover hidden sexual information, they may also have feelings of betrayal and mistrust. Your partner's sense of betrayal will be amplified if you were actively hiding or denying this part of your sexuality.

Even if you're able to completely hide that part of yourself, what you revealed may still be an essential part of your sexuality. If so, you'll likely be less fulfilled in your relationship when hiding it. We naturally want to be fully loved for our whole selves. When we hide a part of who we are, we limit the love we receive. Your partner will experience the sadness and loneliness you feel because you don't feel fully loved, and while feeling sad and lonely, you'll offer your partner less love and attention. In other words, even when you are 100 percent successful in hiding part of your essential sexuality, you are still an asshole because you take some of your attention, energy, or satisfaction out of the relationship.

Do Something about Being an Asshole

I don't condone cheating. Cheating hurts people. But as a realist, I know that humans often cheat. So, let's talk about what being a better asshole means, using cheating as an example.

A better asshole is aware of his attraction. He admits it and acknowledges to himself that it doesn't fit with his relationship agreements. He acknowledges that his attraction would hurt his partner and most of the people he might cheat with, as well as himself. Once he has acknowledged the potential for his attraction to cause harm, he chooses to do something different. He could tell his partner about the attraction before acting on it and work to prevent the attraction from being expressed. For example, he might try to eliminate time alone with the person he is attracted to. He might ask to be reassigned at work, if possible. He could talk with friends about his feelings. He might increase his masturbation practice (deliberately fantasizing about something other than the potential affair partner) to regulate his sexual desire. He might consider what it is about the desired person that he finds so attractive and seek an avenue to incorporate that desired element into his existing relationship, within the agreements of that relationship. In these ways, he might stop the potential affair from turning into an actual affair. But what if he's a bigger asshole that that?

A man who acts on his attraction when he's in a monogamous relationship might stop that behavior after one instance of sexual contact. That's better than multiple instances of sexual contact.

A man who is having an ongoing affair might do a number of things to prevent that from damaging his relationship more than it might otherwise. He might get regularly tested for sexually transmitted infections (STIs); stop having sex with the monogamous partner; use safer sex methods in order to prevent pregnancy and the transmission of STIs, even if there were clean test results; or tell his partner about the affair or stop the affair from continuing. Having an affair is certainly on the asshole end of the ethical spectrum, but it's easy to see that doing the things above is better than not doing them and would ultimately make you less of an asshole than someone who doesn't do them.

Okay, let's say that a man has an affair, doesn't admit it, and gets caught. Well, he's less of an asshole if he admits the affair as soon as he gets caught. He can then tell the truth about what has been happening and for how long, end the affair, and begin trying to repair his relationship if he and his partner want to stay together. That still makes you less of an asshole than the next option.

Imagine a man who has affairs repeatedly, gets caught, denies it, and repeats the process. This might be a lot farther out on the asshole spectrum. Even for that man, there's a way to be a better asshole. He can admit that this is his pattern, get into therapy to identify the causes of his behavior, and treat any underlying mental health issues.[33] Or he could work with his partner to turn his previously monogamous relationship into an open one, if his partner is open to that. Sadly, if there aren't any paths for an authentic expression of the man's essential sexuality inside the relationship, this might instead be the end of his relationship. But if a man doesn't take steps to make things right—if he blames his partner for being cold, denies the affairs, or tells his partner they are imagining it—then he is consciously making things worse. Being a better asshole is possible at any moment by just admitting the truth.

Embrace Diversity among Men

We men have all sorts of ways to put each other down. We call each other "dirtbags" for our authentic desires, "sissies" for what we find beautiful, or "softies" for what we care about. Here's the real lesson: when we accept our authentic selves, we realize that what we are ashamed of is not bad to begin with. In accepting ourselves, we realize that other men are not bad, either.

When we shame other men for "not being man enough," we restrict our own ability to deviate from destructive masculinity myths. Yet, we are all so varied and diverse that almost all men deviate in some way from the narrow definition of "a real man."

There are many kinds of male or masculine sexualities. Every man's sexuality can be better, more powerful, and more authentic when diversity among men is understood as the norm. When we affirm the sexual diversity inside of our community, it is easier to accept the sexual diversity within ourselves.

Older men can teach younger men that an erect penis may not be required to give a partner pleasure or have an orgasm. Transgender men can teach other men that our beliefs about testosterone may not be accurate. Gay men can provide models for celebrating unfettered, intense male sexuality. Straight men can teach the value of approaching your partner as someone with inherent psychological or emotional differences from you (a lesson that is true in every relationship, but gender differences may help heterosexual men expect those differences). Bisexual men can teach the value of seeing multiple perspectives across different ways of being in relationships. Men with children can teach the value of putting the needs of others before your own, and men without children can model the abundance of vitality and creativity that can come from authenticity. Younger men can teach the value and methods of accepting racial and sexual diversity that have become more common and more intuitive in their generation.

Men with small penises can teach men who are insecure about size that loving, sexual relationships can be had at any penis size. Men with thick or long penises can confirm that thick or long can hurt a partner and that care when interacting with a partner may be required to not cause harm. This diversity of experiences can help all men be happier with the penis they have. Men who cross-dress, perform in drag, or have jobs traditionally held by women can confirm that there's joy to be had in being freed from the strict confines of traditional masculinity.

There's more to the community of men than allowed within the narrow confines of "real manhood." All our ways of being men are real, valuable, and viable—and can lead us to love, connection, and hot sex if we accept them.

Chapter 4

CAN MY DESIRE BE REGULATED?

AFTER READING .THE PREVIOUS CHAPTER and completing the exercises, you now have a sense of what you desire. You also learned about some shame-shifting perspectives about desire, including that repressing sexual identity causes harm and that men aren't monoliths. That's all great, but you still want sex, connection, and love. But, as we've already established, if you don't self-regulate your desire, you can hurt your partner. Now it's time to learn more about how the emotion of desire works. In this chapter, Luis is our example as he tries to navigate a sexual experience with his new girlfriend, Isabella.

Luis and Isabella have been going out for three months. They have a special dinner planned. Their relationship has been deepening emotionally, and they've been getting more comfortable making out. Isabella likes to slowly develop a sexual relationship, and she's been clear that she hasn't been ready for intercourse. Luis has been respectful but also eager to have intercourse with her. Tonight, he thinks she'll be more open to sex based on some hints she's made.

We're going to follow Luis's thoughts and feelings as he inter-acts with Isabella. He's going to make some mistakes along the way, but he's going to learn. As he does, he's going to teach us both how desire works and how it can be regulated.

SEXUAL DESIRE ISN'T A NEED

Many of our culture's notions about sexuality come from drive theory, which was developed by Freud. In this theory, sexual desire is like hunger, a biological need; and if you don't have sex, it will lead to ill health and mental-emotional imbalance. This theory supports the false cultural belief that men need sex to prevent suffering. Drive theory creeps into our language and assumptions that men just need sex. Luis demonstrates that influence when he talks with a friend before his date and says, "How long can she expect me to wait, you know? I'm a warm-blooded man."

Modern sexual science, including the information revealed in this chapter, disproves drive theory, but first let's see how drive theory leads us astray. It is true that, on average, men as a group desire sex more frequently. When this fact meets the drive theory belief that sex is a need, it reinforces sexual entitlement. That is, it makes men think they'll burst or go crazy if they have don't act on their sexual desire. They won't, but we tend to behave how we're expected to behave. So, this false belief can make us think and act in harmful ways.

If we think a man's sexual desire is a biological need, then those who stimulate that need and don't meet that need can be labeled a cock tease or other insults and shamed for it. After all, the thinking goes, it's cruel to not feed a hungry animal. Therefore, we develop language that men "need to finish," that they "can't control" them-selves. Not having sex becomes something someone does *to you* instead of the absence of a behavior. This is how drive theory dis-torts our thinking, our emotions, and eventually our behavior.

For Luis, the influence of drive theory shows up early in their relationship in thoughts such as "She's holding out" and in emotions such as resentment of Isabella. For some men, these feelings and thoughts can feed on each other until resentment becomes blame and anger, and the thoughts begin telling a story that the partner who isn't having sex is cruel. Then they hurt the other person despite wanting, loving, and desiring the other person.

In fact, nothing negative happens biologically if men don't satisfy their desire. It's true that some men experience blue balls. This pain may occur if someone is highly aroused or erect for an extended period of time without ejaculating. The technical term for blue balls is *vasocongestion*, swelling caused by blood flow. This is the exact same term for a headache. Blue balls is just a headache in a different part of the body, and it is no more damaging than a headache. We wouldn't condone people being violent, coercive, demanding, or abusive because of a headache, so we shouldn't condone it for blue balls, either.

Furthermore, the pain of blue balls is easily cured by masturbating to orgasm, relieving the congestion. You may also take an over-the-counter pain medicine if your doctor recommends it. Very rarely, some men with delayed or inhibited ejaculation may have more complicated experiences and should seek medical assistance, but it's still not a damaging condition. Nothing negative happens to a man who doesn't have sex. Men will never get ill or die without sex. At worst, unfulfilled desire causes a headache or emotional disappointment. Therefore, unmet desire is never an excuse for abuse, coercion, control, demands, whining, pressure, assault, or rape. Sexual desire is not a need.

If you're disappointed by not having sex after getting turned on and you're inclined to blame your partner, there's something else you can do instead: Ask yourself why you've chosen to try to engage in sexual behavior with someone in a way that has negative consequences for you. Identify what different choices you'd like to make in the future rather than have this experience.

This is one opportunity for sexual self-regulation. Negotiating behavior, including the possibility for an orgasm, ahead of time (recognizing the risk you take because that consent can be removed at any time), is a way of taking control of your inner state. No one else can take control of your desire, anyway. If you don't take control of your desire, you may experience negative emotions and hurt your relationships. It is like blaming other people for not pulling the rip cord on your parachute. You can always choose not to engage with that partner in an activity that will prolong your sexual desire past your ability to cope with it. You can also masturbate prior to interacting with that person to relieve any vasocongestion or emotional tension. You can be in control of your sexual experience without trying to take control of another person. When men focus on taking control of their desire, they set aside entitlement and reduce the risk that their desire causes harm.

Let's check back in with Luis. As he drives to meet Isabella, Luis remembers he has been reading this book and pushes his drive-theory reactions to the side. Instead, he begins identifying some choices he can make. "I really want tonight to go well," he thinks. "Maybe I should just ask her if she's interested in having sex tonight. I can tell her that if she isn't, that's okay, but that I might cut the makeout session short because I didn't like how disappointed I felt when I thought we were going to and then didn't. "Yes," he tells himself, "I'm going to talk to Isabella about this. I really like her, and I want tonight to go smoothly. I'm not going to do stuff like my sister's old boyfriend did to her, pushing himself on her when she didn't want to. I like Isabella's values, and I want her to know it. I can always go to the bathroom and take care of it myself if I need to." He chuckles, thinking about that as he realizes how easy it is to do that and how ridiculous it is that men try to tell women not to let them down. Luis knows that Isabella has as much right to be free of pressure as his sister did, and he wants to be the better man.

DESIRE MOVES US TOWARD PLEASURE

The good news is that the drive narrative about desire is biologically and neurologically false.[1] Sexual desire is an emotion that arises when we anticipate pleasure. This is equally true of any desire. If we experienced ice cream before and it was pleasurable, or we *think* it will be pleasurable, we desire it. Desire is the emotion that motivates us to have positive experiences again. Desire encourages us to act in ways that we think will make positive experiences happen. Like buying ice cream. Conversely, if an experience is unpleasant or expected to be unpleasant, we desire to avoid the situation. In other words, men's sexual desire (and any neurotypical person's desire)[2] increases when we experience more sexual pleasure, and it decreases eventually when we have less sexual pleasure or negative experiences.

When Luis reflects on his experiences of making out with Isabella, he recalls, "The way she kissed me that night was electric. It went straight to my head, and I felt dizzy. I mean, I can't imagine what it'd be like to be inside her while she's kissing me. Just . . . wow!" Past experiences of physical intimacy with Isabella have combined in Luis's mind with his past experiences of sexual intercourse to create the powerful anticipation of a positive experience. He has strong desire, and his desire encourages him to do things that create the desired experience.

Luis's past sexual experiences also form contextual cues that suggest to him that Isabella is more likely to be ready to have intercourse with him. In Luis's experience prior to Isabella, the longer a relationship with a woman lasted, the more likely it was that they had intercourse. Unclothed makeout sessions also made it more likely that the next makeout session would lead to intercourse. Finally, in Luis's experience, special occasions were often the first time his past partners were ready to have intercourse. Since these context cues in the current relationship line up with his past experiences, his anticipation is higher, and he feels his desire even more intensely.

Another part of Luis's experience is less direct but also contributes to his desire. The messages he's received—implicitly and explicitly from his family, friends, community, and the culture around him—also contribute to his anticipation and therefore his desire. Luis's unconscious lessons from movies have taught him that sex at this point in a relationship is "normal" and that it would be "reasonable" for him to expect it. This increases his desire because it supports his anticipation of pleasure.

But the context for Luis isn't only positive. Luis remembers the experience his sister had of being pressured for sex. He remembers how tearful and scared his sister was. He doesn't want Isabella to feel that way. Because of his sister's experience, and because Luis knows how common it is that women have had negative sexual experiences with men, the context of a first sexual encounter includes some fear of negative experiences. Luis knows that two people may want different physical behaviors. He knows there's a risk a low-desire partner will feel pressured. He also knows that sex can trigger past traumatic experiences. Because Luis's *context* also includes cues to some negative experiences, he has a small amount of negative anticipation. Simply, this is fear or avoidance. Academics call it aversion. But aversion is only one kind of inhibitor, or barrier, to sex.

Some things make us want sex, and some things—inhibitors—stop us from wanting sex. In the psychology of sex, these two effects are often likened to the gas pedal and the brake. If the gas pedal is down—that is, if desire is present—that alone isn't enough for a person to act on their desire. A person's inhibitors—that is, the brake—must also be released. Inhibitors can be anything that causes you to not be ready for sex. For many men, cultural and personal training about sexuality lead to an easier release of the brake and a quicker acceleration of the gas pedal than for many women.[3]

Luis's sexual desire is a feeling that motivates him to move toward what he desires—to kiss, touch, talk, and act in the ways he thinks will help him have the desired experience. Luis's aversion is a feeling that motivates him to act to avoid or prevent what he fears—a pressuring, negative sexual experience for Isabella. Since these two feelings are in conflict, Luis has good reason to talk through what he wants with his partner. A conversation about consent as described in chapter 2, or in more detail in chapter 8, can help Luis and Isabella have an enjoyable night together whether they have sex or not.

DESIRE AND COMPETING EMOTIONS

People with competing feelings and competing motivations, like Luis, sometimes get paralyzed by this ambivalence. Most people easily and unconsciously resolve ambivalence by establishing one or the other motivation as the priority. Men in situations like Luis's will often prioritize following desire over avoiding fear because they believe that, if the feared situation arises, they'll know and be able to deal with it. They say to themselves, "I don't want to worry too much about a woman feeling sexually uncomfortable. That would stop the flow and make me look less confident. Women don't want that. Women want men who are assertive. Things are going well; she's really into me so far. If something's not going right, she'll let me know. I can tell if she's not into it." This false confidence underestimates the level of fear many people have about sexual activity and the pervasiveness of sexual trauma in our society. The healing path for men and their partners is to resolve this ambivalence by prioritizing avoidance of the fear and ensuring safety first. People who feel safe are more likely to engage in robust consent processes and have satisfying sexual experiences.

If you're focused on creating a positive experience for your partner, you'll try again and again to make sure this is the case. If you make a mistake, you'll adjust. But if your priority is your own orgasm or sexual achievement, you'll be focused again and again on reaching that goal despite information about your partner's feelings that may get in the way. The "win" isn't worth the risks you take or the harm you might cause. Your overconfidence is no shield against another person feeling pressured.

Therefore, you need to regulate and manage your sexual desire to create safety for your partner. You can downregulate your expectations by shifting your thoughts—such as "Will we, or won't we?"—to focusing on and emphasizing other values in time together—such as "My goal is to have a nice evening together." If you know how much anticipation of sex you can handle without risking an emotional crash if it doesn't happen, then you are responsible for stopping your anticipation before that crash. If sex isn't a possibility with this partner at this time and that is your goal, end the evening before you set yourself up for disappointment. Find more skills like this in "Gratitude: An Antidote to Entitlement" (see page 101).

Uncertainty Increases Desire

Since you now know that we tend to prioritize one competing desire over another, you know that you need to exit sexual situations before you reach your limits for prioritizing your partner's well-being. But desire is a tricky emotion; it wants us to keep trying and to succeed, so we need even more tools for self-regulation. Uncertainty increases desire. Gambling provides a good window into this experience. People don't gamble because they know they are going to win. They gamble because they don't know what will happen. The possibility of a big win would not generate as much motivation if it was certain. Instead, gambling would take on the chore-like nature of picking up your check from work.

This brings us back to Luis and his feelings of desire. Because Luis doesn't know for sure that he and Isabella are going to have sex tonight, he is uncertain, and this uncertainty increases his desire. In new sexual relationships, like hookups, the uncertainty is part of the pleasure. In Luis's case, he may consciously or unconsciously think, "If we don't have sex tonight, she may not be willing to have sex again for several more weeks or months." This desire to capture every opportunity is exactly what the gambler feels sitting at the slot machine: "If I get up from my seat, the next person will get the next chance on this machine, and if they win, I lost my opportunity." Their desire to win motivates them to take as many chances as they can while they have the opportunity.

This kind of process may be the reason why many stories of sexual pressure include the partner saying they don't want to have sex, which he seems to accept only to try again in the same encounter. It is like he is focused on taking more chances at the sexual slot machine instead of attending to the human experience, reasons, and motivations behind the partner's no. Realizing that you are being motivated by uncertainty in this way gives you a window of opportunity for self-regulation. Using a consent process can help you eliminate the uncertainty or can help you learn what might resolve uncertainty in favor of your desires. This will make you stop unwelcome pressure or make you more skillful in releasing your partner's brake and pressing their accelerator.

Desire Changes Our Perceptions

Another way in which desire can be a tricky emotion to regulate is that it changes what we perceive. When you desire something and you think you are close to having it or experiencing it, you begin increasing the value of near-term goals and you devalue long-term goals. In Luis's case, if he thinks he and Isabella are going to have intercourse soon (near-term goal), he might not pay as close attention to signs that she's hesitant and prioritize consent (long-term goal).

This highlights the importance of having consent conversations *before* things get too hot and heavy. Let's go back to Luis and see how he's engaging in self-regulation. Luis and Isabella have made out topless often enough that they didn't have a consent conversation about it on this date. Now, sex may be a possibility in Luis's mind though the context has changed. Luis is beginning to think he is seeing signals that Isabella is ready to have intercourse. But at this point, his anticipation and desire are increasing, and he notices his perception is starting to get clouded. If, for example, she turns away from him and is breathing deeply, he is interpreting that as arousal and anticipating having intercourse. But he knows better than this perception. She could be trying to calm her arousal because she still doesn't want to have intercourse. Since Luis understands the way desire biases his perception, he decides to pause the physical activity to have a conversation with Isabella: "Can we pause for a minute? I'm getting pretty eager to have you, but I know you've said you aren't ready, and I want to respect that. Can we get clear about where we're headed tonight so that I don't make assumptions and accidentally disrespect you?"

In other words, Luis recognizes that the heavy petting may be moving into new territory, something he does not yet have consent for. Because he knows that his perception has been diminished by desire, he decides to pause the activity to negotiate consent. That way, he and Isabella can talk with clear heads.

When you need to have a consent conversation, back away from what you desire so that it isn't close enough to cloud your judgment. You'll be better able to weigh your short-term and long-term goals wisely with a clear head. We'll cover this again in an easy-to-remember form in chapter 8.

But excitement isn't the only way that desire clouds our perception. Unfulfilled desire can also create frustration, sudden absence of desire, anger, and other negative emotional experiences. In our example, Isabella explains to Luis that she still isn't ready to have intercourse, but that she's ready to begin getting *ready* to have intercourse. She tells him she wants to have conversations about their future, their sexual histories, and how they'll have safer sex when they do. Despite his better thoughts, and his conscious attempts earlier in the day to regulate his expectations, he suddenly feels frustrated and angry that she still isn't ready to have sex. Luis isn't quite sure why he feels this way even though he knows "better." Luis also doesn't know how to get rid of these feelings.

To understand how the simple motivations, desire and aversion, accelerator and brake, relate to negative emotions like frustration, we need to understand that "the trouble starts in the *brain/mind*, not elsewhere."[4]

HOW OUR MIND MONITORS DESIRE

Desire and aversion are wired into the human nervous system. This system of evaluation and emotional feedback is called the incentive motivation system. Here's how it works. Our desire (motivation toward) increases when we anticipate pleasure (incentive). Our desire intensifies further (increased motivation) when we are close to our pleasurable goal (incentive is close). We try harder (increase motivation) when we think we're not moving fast enough (at risk of losing the incentive). We give up (motivation to zero) if we think we can't have our desire met (zero incentive). Our desire decreases some (lower motivation) if we think our desire will be met easily and we start desiring other things (search for other goals and incentives).

If we have an aversion (disincentive), we want to avoid it (motivation away). If we're making progress moving away, we feel relief (incentive). If we're not making progress moving away from our aversion, we work harder (motivation) by searching for errors, changing strategies, or defending ourselves. Don't worry if this doesn't make sense yet. I'm going to break it all down as we go through this section.

The following diagram shows how experience and anticipation operate in our incentive motivation system.

Figure 4.1: Basic incentive motivation system

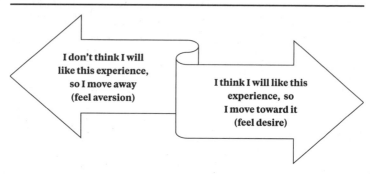

Whether we're moving toward or away because of aversion or desire, our mind is evaluating progress toward our goal. Sex educator and bestselling author Emily Nagoski refers to this process as "the little monitor."[5] Despite his conscious attempts to rewrite his culturally informed assumptions, Luis's little monitor thinks it "shouldn't" take this long for Isabella to feel comfortable having sex with him, and the monitor then creates his frustration. Luis is in good company; many men have this experience.

Based on experience and what we have been taught, we have expectations (usually unconscious) about how much work and how long it will take to complete a task. These expectations exist when we have positive goals that we are moving toward, such as mowing the lawn, doing a project at work, baking a cake, or in Luis's case, moving toward sexual intimacy with a partner. For desire, the little monitor turns the expectations into an evaluation: "Am I making progress toward my goal? Is it supposed to take this long to reach my goal?"

These expectations also exist when we're trying to avoid something, such as criticism at work, our partner's disappointment, or getting behind on our bills. For things we're trying to avoid, the little monitor evaluates like this: "Am I making progress avoiding what I dislike? Is this taking about as long as I expect?" Both questions can be summarized with the simple question, "Am I moving fast enough?"

The little monitor asks and answers the question about whether we're moving fast enough very quickly. Our mind immediately gives us feedback about our progress. The feedback comes as a feeling, such as the frustration that Luis is grappling with. Because feelings get us ready to act, they can help us respond quickly to changes in the world. That's been an advantage in our evolutionary history, but it can be a disadvantage in the quiet and intimate moments of our life.

Luis knows in his mind that Isabella has a right to take as long as she wants to have intercourse and that she even can decide to not ever have sex. But his frustrated feeling comes on faster than his conscious beliefs, so his frustration exists before he can stop it.[6]

Frustration isn't the only feeling the little monitor will give us as part of the feedback loop. Our little monitor has three answers to the question of progress: "yes," "no," and "yes, easily." Relief and contentment result when our monitor says, "Yes, we're doing a good job moving away from something unpleasant." We feel fear, guilt, or anxiety if our little monitor decides we're doing a bad job moving away from something unpleasant. If our little monitor decides, "Yes, this is good progress toward a desire," then we feel elation, eagerness, or excitement. A bad job of moving toward something we desire creates frustration, anger, and sadness. That's where Luis is stuck so far in our story. Finally, if we're achieving our goal easily, our little monitor *decreases* desire and goes looking for other goals.[7] More on this confusing decrease in desire will come in the section Desire in Long-Term Relationships (see page 94).

The moment that Luis feels frustration, he is motivated to act in a way that expresses his frustration. For a moment, he flashes on the thought of saying to Isabella, "What's wrong with you?"

Luis is frustrated because his little monitor says that he's not moving as fast enough toward his goal of having intercourse as he "should" be, given the time and effort he has put in. Luis's little monitor uses information created earlier in his life and by cultural scripts about sexuality that he no longer believes. His monitor is telling him that Isabella is the problem and that she is treating him unjustly. His monitor doesn't understand Isabella's feelings. It's only there to protect Luis. The monitor helps us find food and run away from lions. This situation is more subtle.

Figure 4.2: Emotional feedback from monitoring progress

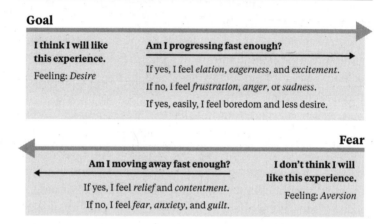

The problem is, even though Luis's unconscious process is a summary of personal experience and cultural messages, which is very complicated, the little monitor isn't very sophisticated. For example, the monitor asks the same question for avoiding a lion: "Am I running fast enough?" as it asks for whether you are making career progress: "Am I working hard enough?" The contexts are very different, but the evaluation process is very similar. For Luis, movement toward intercourse can't be measured in velocity, acceleration, or distance. Different people take different amounts of time to feel comfortable doing different sexual activities. Progress is subjective. But Luis's (and your) little monitor doesn't make much of a distinction between objective and subjective evaluations of progress.

For objectives like advancing in our career or moving toward arbitrary and personal sexual objectives, "fast enough" has no external measure. We measure progress against our expectations.

Those expectations are created by the intensity of our desire, experience, cultural messages, and our ideas about how effective our effort *ought to be*. These expectations are all in our minds. They aren't true, real, or right in the same way that our personal values are not true, real, or right. They aren't false, bad, or wrong, either. They're just our own. No one else has the same expectations about these subjective goals and how long they will take. Our expectations are unique. Our partner might have different goals. Even if our partner has the same sexual goals, they might have very different expectations about progress toward those goals, including the steps to get there, who takes what actions to achieve those steps, and how to assess whether the progress is "fast enough."

Despite our conscious thoughts, our little monitors are creating emotional feedback and preparing us to act all the time. In Luis's case, it created frustration that prepared him to verbally attack Isabella—an emotion-guided behavior, not a thought- or values-guided one. On the flip side, if Luis were more focused on his aversion to Isabella feeling pressured, and his monitor thought he was doing a good job in that process, he'd probably feel relief. His conversation with Isabella would likely confirm to his little monitor that he was on the right path. That is, if Luis were more focused on a different goal, his emotional reactions would be different. He'd either maintain his effort or maybe decrease effort a little by checking in verbally a little less often. If, on the other hand, Isabella told Luis he was pressuring her, he might have negative emotions, like guilt. Those emotions would signal to him that he wasn't avoiding the feared experience effectively. He'd be inclined to make changes to his behavior to become more effective.

If we continue to believe that we're succeeding in getting closer to our goals, then elation, eagerness, and excitement change to new emotions, such as celebration, anticipation, and preparation for experiencing our goal. If we don't think we're moving closer to our goals, then frustration, anger, and sadness can turn into increased effort, attempts to fight or control others, or giving up.

If we believe we are continuing to avoid our fears, then our relief and contentment turn into attempts to maintain or even decrease effort. We decrease effort to conserve energy and to monitor other goals. If we don't think we're avoiding our fears effectively, we prepare to be attacked, search for our errors, and may prepare to be submissive.

Figure 4.3: Emotional feedback when our effectiveness (or lack thereof) endures

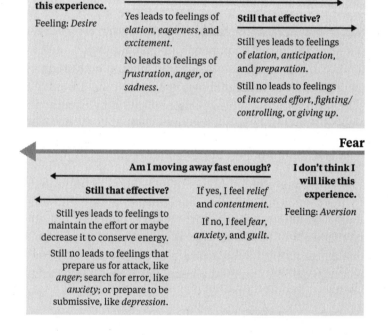

Keep in mind that, since Luis has two goals, the emotional signals can be mixed. He can feel relief that he isn't pressuring Isabella and also frustration at not having sex. He can change which goals are informing his emotions more by keeping his conscious

attention on one or the other. He has a choice. Other men who are not as reflective, empathetic, or ethical as Luis could feel some guilt about making Isabella feel pressured and feel elated to be getting closer to having intercourse.

Perceptions Change Closer to Goals

Because Luis thought he was very close to having intercourse with Isabella, he became very focused on the short-term satisfaction of desire. This is the same thing that all people do when they're close to a goal. Our focus decreases our awareness of other motivations, especially long-term goals, including both aversions and desires. This is one reason why people can have sex with people they don't like very much or even find gross. The short-term goal of having sex on a particular night outweighs the long-term goal of not partnering with people that you don't like very much. Focusing on maintaining integrity is harder when you get focused on the short-term goal.

Figure 4.4: We tend to ignore consequences when we're close to what we want.

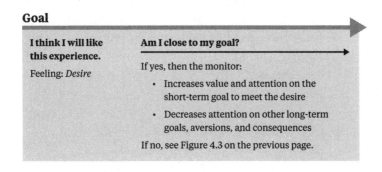

attention on one or the other. He has a choice.

Goal

I think I will like this experience.	Am I close to my goal?
Feeling: *Desire*	If yes, then the monitor:
	• Increases value and attention on the short-term goal to meet the desire
	• Decreases attention on other long-term goals, aversions, and consequences
	If no, see Figure 4.3 on the previous page.

As Luis thought he was getting closer to having intercourse, he decreased his attention on his aversion to creating feelings of pressure for Isabella. He felt frustration, and his little monitor prepared him to attack because it doesn't know that attack won't help. That could be a problem if Luis didn't know how to manage it. Fortunately, he does.

Although Luis's flash of anger at Isabella almost caught him off guard, he has self-regulation skills. He immediately takes a deep breath (soothing the physiological manifestations of anger). In other words, he brings his long-term-partner goals of respecting Isabella back into focus (changes his goals). He reminds himself that there's no right amount of time to wait for sex (changes his expectations). Then he puts effort into communication instead of manipulation or control (changes his effort to match his goal). He says, "Isabella, I'm sorry. I was trying to manage it, but I think I did have hope we'd have sex tonight. I had to reset my expectations for a second, but I'm good now." Luis notices that Isabella releases tension in her shoulders and relaxes as she smiles at him. "Let's have those conversations about getting ready to have intercourse," he says. It may take an ongoing effort before he can completely override the unconscious expectations and goals this culture has taught him; but Luis can be in control of his behavior, self-regulate his desire, and bring his behavior in line with his values.

Later in his life, when Luis helps create his son's beliefs about sex, he will tell his son that intercourse with the right person is worth waiting for. He'll help his son know from an early age that there's no set amount of time for having intercourse or any other sexual behavior, and Luis's son's reaction will be different because he was taught beliefs about sex at an early age that will more closely match his lived experience in the world. If Luis's son has an experience like Luis had with Isabella, Luis's son's little monitor will give him feelings like confidence and contentment.

Desire in Long-Term Relationships

If Luis and Isabella get used to having intercourse on a semiregular basis, Luis may experience what a lot of people do when sex is easy to have: decreased desire. When we evaluate that our progress toward our goal is happening easily, it's as if a little monitor in our mind says, "Great! Conserve resources. Decrease desire! Release emotional contentment! Throttle back effort! Widen scan for other goals!"

When we're meeting our goals, our emotional response gives us the motivation to stop trying so hard and use our effort on other things. When something is easy to get, it doesn't make sense to keep working hard for it—except, as I mentioned before, the little monitor is complex but not very sophisticated. It doesn't understand that your partner's relationship satisfaction may rely in part on whether they feel sexually desired by you, and their little monitor might assess that goal based at least in part by how frequently you have sex.

To maintain sexual desire and connection in long-term relationships, we must overcome the romantic and sexual myths that if we really love each other, the relationship and sex will come easily. We must put effort into maintaining our connection and doing some things that add a little spice, variety, or challenge to our long-term sexual relationships. The challenges brought in by introducing new elements, even if that is as simple as the effort to be more mindful, can reengage our little monitors to focus on helping us desire our goals again.

These systems govern human desire regardless of your gender and regardless of what you are desiring. We have goals to move toward what we desire and away from what we don't. There's a monitor in our brains that assesses whether it *thinks* we're making the right amount of progress. If the little monitor *thinks* we're making good progress, we get positive emotions and encouraging motivations. If the monitor *thinks* we're not making good progress, we get negative emotions and discouraging motivations. So much for the old internet meme showing one glowing light that only reads "on" for male sexuality.

Figure 4.5: Why we lose desire for things that are easy

Goal		
I think I will like this experience. Feeling: *Desire*	**Am I close to my goal?** If yes, then the monitor: • Increases value and attention on the short-term goal to meet the desire • Decreases attention on other long-term goals, aversions, and consequences If no, see Figure 4.3 (page 92)	**Yes, easily** If you are reaching your goal with ease, then the little monitor: • Decreases the intensity of your desire, because this resource is abundant and I can get it any time. • Decreases your motivation to exert effort to reach your desire to help you conserve resources. • Begins scanning for another goal that might be harder to reach. This helps you spend more effort getting scarce resources.

EXERCISE: Understand Your Monitor

This exercise will help you understand how your desires create emotional experiences when you are or aren't progressing in the way you expect. Take a few minutes to write down the answers to the following questions:

1. What is a sexual situation in which you had positive emotions like elation, excitement, or celebration? What were the pleasurable experiences (goals) that you had or anticipated in that situation? What effort did you have to put in to create those pleasurable experiences?

2. What is a sexual situation in which you had negative emotions like frustration, anger, or sadness? What were the pleasurable experiences (goals) that you hoped for in that situation but didn't get? What effort did you put in to create that pleasurable experience? What expectations did you have about the effort or time that would be required? How did that match or not match your experience?

3. What is a sexual situation where you were afraid of something negative happening? What did you want to avoid? What feelings did you experience when you did or didn't avoid that outcome?

4. Review your answers to the previous three questions. If you can, identify the assumptions your little monitor has about what kind of effort it takes to fulfill your desires or to avoid feared sexual consequences. The following form may help.

    When I'm trying to _____ [*sexual goal*], I expect that I'll need to _____ [*what you need to do*] for at least _____ [*amount of time*] but probably not more than _____ [*longer amount of time*]. If these expectations are violated, I feel _____.

    When I want to avoid _____ [*negative sexual consequence like unwanted pregnancy, STI, or a partner feeling pressured*], I need to regulate my desire for _____. To avoid negative outcomes, I also need to _____ [*what you need to do*]. When I succeed/fail in avoiding the negative outcome, I feel _____.

As you go through the rest of this chapter, refer to your answers. These are the experiences you need to self-regulate with the lessons in the rest of this chapter.

DETERMINING THE RIGHT GOAL, EFFORT, AND EXPECTATION

The reason why I've spent all this time describing a complex cognitive-emotional process is that this system holds the keys for regulating your experience. Emily Nagoski writes:

> There are three potential targets of change, right?
> - Is this the right *goal* for me?
> - Am I putting in the right kind of *effort*, as well as the right amount?
> - Am I realistic in my *expectation* about how effort-ful this goal should be?[8]

The incentive motivation system is a beautiful evolutionary development for our cognitive and emotional psychology; it is like a complex system of train tracks that points to many different emotional destinations. The first question Nagoski asks gives us the opportunity to self-regulate our desire by questioning whether to start the train down a track in the first place. Men are not taught to ask themselves this question. We're encouraged to pursue sex from the people that we desire, to be persistent in pursuing them. We're encouraged to be resilient to, or flat out ignore, the other person's lack of desire for us. This can easily create frustration because we're told that if we just plow ahead, we'll get the sex we want. We aren't encouraged to ask whether this is a person we should be pursuing. But now, you can change that.

For couples in which one person wants more sex than the other person, the high-desire partner rarely asks themselves if their efforts to initiate sex are the right kind or amount of effort *for their partner*. The high-desire partner's most common initial response to declined offers is to increase the effort to have sex. This is exactly what the model of desire predicts. If you aren't making progress, increase effort. This increased effort, usually expressed unskillfully by repeating requests, creates pressure for the low-desire partner that kills their desire entirely. The wrong type of effort and wrong amount of effort kills desire in a couple. You can now self-regulate your desire by asking both yourself *and your partner*, "Am I putting in the right kind of effort, as well as the right amount?"

In the long term, the high-desire partner often eventually gives up because their efforts aren't effective, just as the incentive motivation system predicts. Nagoski's third question can be helpful here: "Am I realistic in my expectation about how effortful this goal should be?" Remember the romantic and sexual myths that say if we love each other, sex will happen and be easy. You can now self-regulate your desire by updating your expectations. Maintaining a sexual relationship takes effort. What kind of effort varies by partner and phase of life. Skillful effort looks different for different partners and at different times of our lives. In this way, we empower ourselves with self-regulation. These questions allow us to control ourselves instead of trying to control our partners.

YOUR RESPONSIBILITIES WHEN IT COMES TO DESIRE

As mentioned, some elements of the incentive motivation system take place unconsciously. But "unconscious" doesn't mean "outside of our control." Our culture and experiences inform our expectations, but we decide which desires we will turn into priorities. Our little monitors aren't very skillful, and they don't have all of our conscious values in mind. If we act based only on the emotional feedback of our little monitor, we'll easily become entitled sexual terrors to our partners. If Luis had allowed his frustration to take over, he could have shamed Isabella and damaged or broken his relationship with her. We can value being kind to our partners over all other goals, just like Luis did. We can also prioritize protecting ourselves from harm over sexual pleasure so that we avoid sexual encounters with partners who won't treat us with kindness.

Luis recognized that he had two goals. One was a desire to move toward intercourse, and the other was an aversion to pressuring Isabella. In the moment he got angry that Isabella wasn't ready to have sex, he recognized that the frustration came from not making progress on the goal to have intercourse. But he reminded himself that intercourse wasn't his highest goal. When he reminded himself of his highest goal, he took steps to calm himself down, and he regulated his frustration.

Once he was back in alignment with the right goal for him—not pressuring Isabella—Luis was able to easily meet that goal of not pressuring her. He saw her relax as he told her that he had regulated his reaction. With her relaxation, he began working on his secondary goal of having intercourse when he said, "Let's have those conversations about getting ready to have intercourse." Luis's behavior also shows that he believes having intercourse with a woman like Isabella is worth this investment effort and time.

Our goals and our expectations create the emotions that prepare us to act. Whatever our emotions are, we have choices about whether and how we will act on those motivations. We also have choices about whether and how we will express, soothe, amplify, or reduce our emotions. If we have accurate information about the process of desire (an emotion, not a drive) then we have a responsibility to not act entitled. If we have the capacity to self-regulate, then we have a responsibility to do so. If we don't live up to these responsibilities, we can and should be held accountable for our behavior.

GRATITUDE: AN ANTIDOTE TO ENTITLEMENT

Managing expectations can be used in many different situations to manage or prevent negative emotional reactions. Almost all people cultivate expectations about themselves, others, and the future. The pervasive nature of sexual violence in our culture shows that men have a particular need to learn to manage sexual expectations. When expectations are combined with sexual desire, the results can be traumatic. A few simple truths about relationships can shift of lot of negative expectations men have about sex and relationships.

Truth 1: The universe doesn't have to give you what you want. We weren't guaranteed to be here at this time of history. We weren't guaranteed the privilege of living long enough to be having this conversation. We weren't guaranteed to have literacy, any information about our sexuality, or accurate information about our sexuality. We are lucky to be here together at all. If we take that base as a ground for our gratitude and recognize that the blessing to wake up another day is a gift, the mere chance at sexual activity can become a source of gratitude.

Truth 2: You aren't entitled to partnered sex. No one else is, either. You are not entitled to continue a sexual activity at all, much less until orgasm. This is as true during a hookup as it is in a long-term relationship. This is as true when you have your first kiss as it is when you are in the middle of an orgasm. If you can make peace with this reality, it opens space for gratitude.

Gratitude for the sexual openness and generosity of a partner is an antidote to entitlement. If no one is required to engage sexually until your orgasm, then someone agreeing to support your pleasure is an amazing gift. It's awesome that your partner agreed to participate in your pleasure and agreed to let you participate in theirs! This doesn't make you a lowly supplicant; it makes you an equal because no one else is entitled to your sex, either.

Truth 3: Your sex is a gift. Just in case you are feeling that this recommendation toward gratitude feels like you're begging for something, consider this: you're also giving that powerful gift to your partner, and you can also be the focus of their gratitude. Your ability to pay attention, to feel desire for your partner, to give pleasure, to receive pleasure, and to share in the intimacy of sexuality with your partner is a gift you give them. You can open up to being *grateful for the opportunity* to be generous with your sexuality.

Gratitude changes the entire framework around expectations. If you know you aren't guaranteed any sexual connection, then there's so much less disappointment if it doesn't happen. Suddenly instead of prioritizing penetrative sex, any sexual connection can be a source of joy. Finally, genuine gratitude for a sexual experience is a turn-on for your partners and will be more likely to create more chances for sex and gratitude in the future.

HOW TO REGULATE YOUR DESIRE

You may be thinking that you already know how to regulate your desire. You aspire to be a "good guy," so you know better than to openly express sexual interests in a professional setting. You've taken the human resources–mandated antisexual harassment training. You know not to tell your coworker she looks pretty, not to make sexual jokes, and not to hit on a fellow employee. These are external behaviors.

In my experience, most men do not know how to regulate anything more than their mouths and their hands. *Most men don't know that they need to regulate the content of their mind and their attention.* This section will introduce six skills for regulating sexual attention: empathy, cultivating appreciation, shifting the focus, meeting your needs, falling in love skillfully, and holding your desire accountable. If you've ever been accused of being creepy or of making people uncomfortable, you may want to pay special attention to these skills.

Empathize with Coercion and Pressure

Many men experience relationship coercion or pressure, but they downplay these experiences. Have you ever had someone insist, cry, and try to convince you that you should be in a relationship with them? Have you ever felt trapped in a relationship conversation longer than you wanted to because you were afraid of the emotional consequences if you ended the conversation? These are examples of relationship coercion. When you fear that someone won't regulate their reactions to your honest answers, it can be hard to give those answers.

Have you ever had the experience of being in the middle of a process on your computer or phone and your partner just comes up and starts talking to you? Did your partner then get upset and accuse you of not paying attention? And all this even though you said "Mm-hmm" at the right breaks in their monologue? If so, congratulations, you have a good basis for understanding the effects of male sexual entitlement.

These experiences can help you develop empathy. But be very careful, as some men make a false equivalence between these experiences. A man might have a hard time knowing how to respond or feel overwhelmed when his partner brings up emotions. However, this doesn't compare to the violation of physical sovereignty when a man uses his partner's body for sexual pleasure without consent. Emotional overwhelm isn't the same as a man using his power in a company to get away with sexualizing female coworkers. Relational coercion can be a basis for empathy, but feeling uncomfortable emotionally is not equivalent to sexual assault or rape. These are not the "same" or "just alike."

If you recognize that it is hard to tell the truth about your lack of relationship interest because of emotional consequences, you may get a hint about why it can be difficult to say no clearly to a man. It is difficult to tell a male partner no when you fear he'll be grumpy, irritable, or passive aggressive. A partner may fear being broken up with. A casual date may fear being shamed or labeled a "cock tease," "bitch," or "slut." Most women and many other partners of men fear violence, threats, assault, and rape. These rational fears chill authentic communication.

It doesn't matter if you have never or would never do any of those things. A significant number of people *have* experienced those behaviors from men at least once (and not just cisgender heterosexual women). Even people who haven't had the direct experience have a coworker, friend, sibling, parent, or relative who has. Because of those experiences, many people attracted to men also feel afraid of men for good reason. To make sure that clear messages are heard through that fear, we need to be attentive to no in all its forms.

Knowing this about women's experiences, how would you speak and act to set women at ease around you? This question is applicable whether you are attracted to women or not. How can you consciously create in women a feeling of safety? Consider efforts that go beyond the absence of sexual coercion. Here are some examples:

- Walking up the stairs behind a woman, put your eyes down to the side and stay several stairs behind.

- Walking behind a woman at night, cross the street to the opposite side. Don't make her cross.

- Use the social roles to focus your interactions. If she's a bartender, do ask for your drink, pay, and tip. Don't hit on her. A bartender's role isn't to be hit on. If she's your boss, do listen to her directives, give her the information she needs, and do the tasks she assigns you. Don't question her authority, tell her your unsolicited input, or tell her what she already knows, given that she's your boss.

Take a Cue from Art Appreciation

Sexual entitlement around people you're attracted to can be countered by directing an initial sense of desire or attraction toward appreciation and away from acquisition.[9]

Practice this by looking at a beautiful landscape or a place in your urban jungle that inspires you. Take a deep breath and appreciate it. While feeling appreciation, remember that you can't take it home. Notice that even a picture won't really "capture" a landscape. Noticing the fleeting nature of the scene while also feeling your appreciation increases your feeling of appreciation. The temporary nature is part of the beauty.

Attractive people who are off-limits to you are just like this beautiful landscape. You can appreciate the person and feel your desire without those feelings tipping into the motivation to take, own, possess, do, or use that person.

As an intermediate practice, notice the flower in a neighbor's yard, or the latest tech gadget that you can't afford. Now, don't pluck the flower. Don't steal the gadget. Easy, right? Even though you appreciate the thing a whole lot, you can move on without stealing it. How do you do that? Every day, without even thinking about it, there are probably thousands of things you desire in some way but that you leave undisturbed. You probably don't even think about it beyond the initial observation: "Damn, wouldn't it be nice to have that?" Then you move on.

Now extend this simple courtesy that you already have for property to the sexy and attractive humans around you. Accept the natural and cultural constraints on sexual desire, like you already do for other types of desire.

Finally, cultivate appreciation by saying to yourself, "Wow, she's gorgeous!" Then look away, internally give thanks (gratitude) for the presence of beauty in the world, take a deep breath, remember that their beauty isn't yours, and go on about your day. You say this to yourself because just like you cultivated empathy for women in the last section, you now recognize that male desire can be threatening to other people because you know that men are more often violent than other genders.

It is not possible or socially acceptable for you to possess all that you desire sexually. It is expected that you manage your desires, and you can manage your desires.

Find an Unpleasant Focus

If you're having a hard time redirecting your attention away from someone you find attractive despite the inappropriateness of those feelings, try finding an unpleasant focus. No one is perfect. Play a mental game to find the flaw in the person that you are feeling so attracted to. Here are some possibilities:

- Find a personality flaw in them, such as being mean, negative, Pollyanna-ish, or overly confident.

- Look for which eye is open wider than the other (everyone has one).

- Find a hair out of place.

- Listen carefully to their words, and find a misused or misspoken word.

- Find a scuff on their shoe or a small stain on their attire.

- Notice their mole, freckle, or blemish.

- Identify one characteristic this person has that falls short of your ideal partner or beloved current partner.

Once you've found this unpleasant focus, stop looking at the person (no one needs you ogling the mole on their neck all day). Concentrate on the negative quality or trait. Whenever your attraction comes up, focus your mind back on the undesirable quality. Most of the time, this process can mitigate desire.

Make Sure Your Needs Are Met

If you find yourself fixating on someone with whom you can't have a relationship, or to whom it would not be appropriate for you to express desire, it may be because you haven't accepted some element of your sexual or relational nature. For example, maybe you're fantasizing about a new person because you imagine they would fulfill sexual desires that you haven't brought up in your current committed relationship. Or maybe, you're focusing on a certain man who isn't available because you are ashamed of being gay, and you've unconsciously decided that being frustrated and gay is better than being in a loving gay relationship.

Once you know and accept your sexual and relational nature, you're responsible for finding avenues in your life for expressing that nature in ways that are within your values. Look for more tips on meeting your needs so that unmet needs don't take over your process or redirect your attention in chapter 5. You'll also find more guidance about identifying and living within your values in chapter 7.

Fall in Love Skillfully

Desire is a great part of falling in love. But it can also be a uniquely destabilizing process, and we need to self-regulate the desire and other emotions that come up when we fall in love, just like we regulate other parts of our desire. English is so imprecise that it uses the same word *love* to describe love of our friends, love of our family, and love of our dog. We say we love this food, and our new romantic partner, and a partner we've been with for many years. I'm focused here on the "falling in love" kind of love. For that reason, I'm going to use the word psychologists use for that experience: *limerence.*

You probably know the symptoms of limerence: dizzy and float- ing feeling when together, sick to your stomach and bereft when apart, impulsive, obsessively thinking about the other person, and preparing for and reviewing interactions that you have with the person. In limerence, your attention is drawn away from the oth- er's faults or you reframe them as quirky, innocuous, or cute traits. The loved one's strengths are amplified by focused attention. Some- times, feelings of metaphysical import accompany limerence and you feel the relationship was "meant to be" or "destined."

When a person doesn't skillfully regulate the experience of limerence, they may become dangerously obsessive, jealous, pro- tective, disconnected from reality, or even violent. Remember the statistics from chapter 1: men are disproportionately prone to the violent expressions of limerence than women. This is why many partners of men are cautious or afraid of men in the state of lim- erence, even if they have similar feelings.

Even if you're not personally prone to expressing limerence in this way, managing your feelings will help you make the best choices to support your new relationship. The next exercises can help.

EXERCISE: Manage Limerence

Grab your notebook and get ready to write down responses to the following prompts:

1. **Know yourself.** Write down what you know about your emotions and thought processes when you start fall- ing in love. For example, do you fall in love quickly and intensely? Are you a person who doesn't fall in love easily, but when you do, you become rapidly committed? When in love, are you more prone to obsessive thinking, jeal- ousy, or wanting to escalate the sexual relationship? If you haven't had this experience yet, ask the members of

your family or friends what they experience when they are in limerence. You may recognize similarities. Write down what you think you might be prone to.

2. **Check yourself with friends.** Tell your trusted friends and family how limerence has made you think, feel, and believe (or what your relatives reported). Ask your friends how they could help you with these experiences or what they'd recommend that you do. Write the answers down. Then—and this is very important—if you find that you're falling in love, you must follow their recommendations and accept their help to stay balanced. If you are in a relationship, introduce your friends to the person you are feeling limerence for. Ask them what they see in the person. Ask what blind spots you might have about this person. Write down their answers. Their perspective can help you end an unsustainable relationship early and decrease future pain. On the other hand, if your friends are supportive of your relationship, their confirmation can help you embrace and support a promising new partner.

3. **Identify and counteract your impulses.** If you recognized some problematic impulses in answering the first prompt, write them down in a list on the left-hand side of a page. On the right, opposite each one, write something you can do to counter that impulse. For example, if you start obsessing, you might write "Spend time focusing on my hobby." This can help you maintain your responsibilities even when under the influence of limerence. If you aren't eating, eat. If you aren't sleeping, exercise more and improve your sleeping habits. If you aren't spending the time that you usually do with your friends, that's dangerous because you need them right now (see number 2).

4. **Make certain behaviors off-limits.** When you're under the influence of limerence, don't make big life decisions that pertain to the person. This includes moving together, quitting your job, getting married, buying a dog, deciding to have a baby, or ending friendships. Because of how common men's violence is, there are some behaviors you should avoid. For example, don't show up at your partner's house in the middle of the night unexpected. Don't blow up your partner's phone with texts or demand that they respond by a certain time. Don't make violent threats under the veil of "expressing my feelings." If you need help managing these feelings, go back to number 2 or seek therapeutic help. If the person you have limerence for tells you that something you're doing is scaring them, believe them even if you didn't intend it that way. Stop doing what makes the person scared. Don't defend or justify the actions. If they are open to dialogue, ask them how to help them feel safe. Then start doing that, even if that means leaving them alone. Write down a list of "off-limits" behaviors.

5. **Soothe your fear of uncertainty.** It's natural for you to be afraid that your partner isn't as interested in you as you are in them. That's a painful experience. Try some of the following: Take deep breaths, take a cold shower, talk to a friend, write in a journal about it, take a long walk (far away from where the focus of your attention lives), or get a dog (for yourself). Complete this thought: "When I feel fear of uncertainty, I should do the following . . ." Make a list of the activities that help you work those feelings out.

EXERCISE: Talk about Limerence to Manage Limerence

If you are in a relationship with the person whom you're feeling limerence for, you can always have a consent-based conversation about the relationship and the feelings. Here are the concrete steps to such a conversation:

1. **Inquire about your partner's feelings, and share your own.**

2. **Repeat back to the other person what you have heard.** Consciously amplify disconfirming evidence: "It sounds like I'm feeling more invested than you are, and I need to slow down a little so I don't get ahead of you," or "Maybe we aren't quite on the same page. I'm still interested, but I might pull back a little so I don't overinvest when it isn't reciprocated."

3. **Paraphrase back any elements that might be contrary to your desire.** Get confirmation from the other person that, as far as they can tell, you have heard them accurately.

4. **Ask if you can share your feelings about the relationship.** If they agree, share your general relationship goals, not specific fantasies with them: "Eventually I'd like to get married and have kids with a partner."

5. **Summarize any differences between the messages.** "You like our dates, but you're concerned that I'm getting more emotionally invested than you are, and you don't see much long-term potential, either. Am I getting it right?"

6. **Make choices together about how to address any discrepancies.** This might mean ending a relationship if you're not on the same page. It might mean taking a wait-and-see approach.

If you are heartbroken that your limerence isn't recipro-cated, don't ask the other person to help you manage the feelings. That's not their job. Spend less time with them, and distract your thoughts away from them. Get that support from your friends and community. Do encounter other potential partners in social situ-ations. Do grieve and soothe the pain of unrequited feelings (see "Expressing Sadness," page 199).

Check Desire Before Expressing Desire

Not every desire should be acted upon. We know this when it comes to wanting to buy something in a store but passing it by. But as a group, we often lack the ethical muscles to apply the same principle when we desire people. This section gives you tools for checking your desire before you act on it.

Perpetrators of physical and sexual violence are overwhelm-ingly male, so your gender may remind potential partners of per-petrators of violence. There is a high chance that your partner (regardless of their gender) has a history of trauma at the hands of men.

You can do a lot to create a positive experience when you approach a potential partner. It starts with assessing the situation, which means acknowledging any privilege you hold, considering the power dynamic that exists or could exist, and checking the environment. It continues by being empathetic and communi-cating skillfully. Here are steps to take when you want to express desire for a potential partner:

1. **Ask yourself, "Do I have any power over this person?"**
   Before approaching someone to invite a sexual or roman-tic discussion, consider whether you have power over them in any way. If the answer is yes, don't approach them. For example, don't hit on employees, volunteers who report to you, or people who rent property from you. Their ability to honestly accept or decline your approach

is fraught with the power differential. Employees might fear losing their jobs. Volunteers might fear losing their ability to be of service. Tenants might fear eviction. Even someone serving you when you are a customer at their business is beholden to you for a good review, positive feedback, or a tip. Don't hit on people whom you have this kind of power over.

2. **Ask yourself, "Is this an appropriate context?"** Before you engage a potential partner, consider the environment. Do you have reason to believe that the person is open to being approached where you are? For example, if you found their profile on a dating site or spotted them at a singles mixer, then approaching the person is not only appropriate but also the purpose of the venue. If you spotted them at work, it is not likely the context for picking someone up. You risk your reputation by approaching them when you're in that situation. There are also several ambiguous situations where it may or may not be appropriate to approach the person and where you'd have to do some inquiry or sequential steps in an approach. For example, at the party of a mutual friend, it might or might not be problematic to express interest in another guest.

3. **Ask yourself, "Is this person free to leave if they feel uncomfortable?"** Know that your advance can make a person feel trapped if there's no easy way out, either in the short or long term. Asking a person out in an elevator, for example, could create a lot of discomfort because the person is not free to decline and then go about their business. Asking someone out at a concert may be okay, but the person next to you might feel awkward if you ask them out and there are hours left in the concert. The freedom to leave and decline is important because the history of men's violence, rage, and coercion makes every advance

114 CHAPTER 4

by a man a potential threat. If the person can leave, it may make your approach less scary.

4. **Ask yourself, "Will this person feel safe?"** When the other person can easily leave, an encounter can feel less threatening to them. Equally important is whether the person will feel safe afterward—not just while you are making an advance. For example, approaching someone on a dating app can feel safe because the other person can simply block you. But approaching someone at their workplace could have lasting negative consequences, creating an unsafe feeling for them at work. If you approach someone at the party of a mutual friend, leaving might be possible but also inconvenient or socially awkward, not to mention how that might create tension when you see each other in the same social circle again. At such an event you might say, "I'm leaving, but I enjoyed talking with you, and I'd be interested in getting to know you better if you're open to that. Here's my number. If you're interested, call me, but there's no pressure. Bye."

5. **Ask for consent to open a conversation: "Are you open to talking with me?"** This begins the conversation with consent. When you ask the person if they would be open to a personal conversation, don't just listen to their words. Notice body language, too. Have they turned their shoulders and face toward you (likely more comfort) or away (likely less comfort)? Have they tilted their upper body toward you (likely more interest) or away from you (likely less interest or caution)? Have they smiled or maintained a neutral face? If in any doubt, ask, "Is this making you uncomfortable?" and state your intention: "I don't want to make you feel uncomfortable." Stop if there's any hesitation or ambiguity in their response, "I'm sorry, maybe this is awkward. That wasn't my intention.

I'll move on. Have a good night." Notice that this skill isn't about sex—it is about a conversation—but what you've just learned is how to have a consent conversation that seeks enthusiastic consent.

6. **Check explicitly for ongoing consent, and create exits.** Make more of your assumptions and interpretations explicit as a way to check them: "You seem open to this conversation so far. Are you willing to continue?" or "Are you feeling comfortable talking with me?" Remember to maintain an awareness of the person you're talking with. A good time to check in with the person you're chatting up is during any transitions. If you were chatting at the bar but then their friends arrived, you might say, "Hey, I'm really into you, and I'm glad we could chat for a few minutes. I see that your friends are here. Should we bring this to a close and let you shift to visiting with them?" By actively offering to end the conversation, you give the person a graceful exit if they're the kind of person that finds it hard to say no.

∎

Yes, your sexual desire can be regulated. It was never a need. You won't die if your desires aren't fulfilled. But to regulate your desire, you must understand it. Because our desire is monitored, the encouragement or setbacks we perceive along the way toward our goals create emotions for us. By understanding what those emotions tell us about our expectations, we learn to regulate our desires by changing our expectations. The core expectation that we men need to change is that we aren't entitled to have our desires fulfilled. This realization can create some grief. Since desire is one of the few emotions destructive masculinity allows us, it can feel like something has been taken away from us when we find out we aren't entitled to fulfillment. Express that grief, but have hope. The next chapter begins the process of giving back to you all the parts of your healthy self that the patriarchy took away. Once you've healed more of the wounds of the patriarchy, you'll be more prepared to express that desire skillfully.

Chapter 5

IF NOT SEX, WHAT DO I NEED?

TO BALANCE AND REGULATE your sexuality, you need to balance and regulate other aspects of your life. People with strong positive relationships with friends and community are more likely to behave ethically. People who take care of their physical health are more likely to treat others with respect. You are more likely to treat your partners with kindness when you treat yourself with kindness.

To bring your best self to your sexual relationships, you need to take better care of your needs. If you don't have good work-life balance, you may not have time for sex. If you aren't taking care of your physical health, you won't be able to maximize your pleasure. If your mental well-being and emotional well-being aren't managed, you won't have the resilience to be grateful, mindful, or present enough to enjoy the sex you have. This chapter offers a multidimensional guide, illustrated in figure 5.1, to pursuing wellness in six different dimensions of health that make healthy sexual expression easier for you to achieve.

Figure 5.1: Six dimensions of wellness that support a healthy sex life

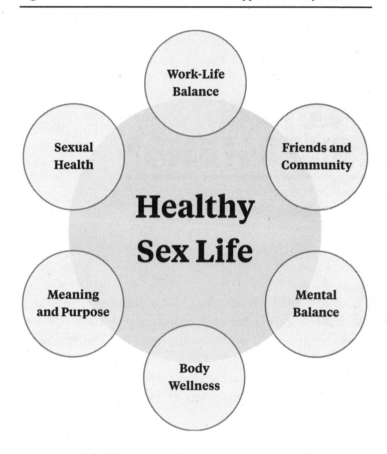

WORK-LIFE BALANCE

Work-life balance doesn't just mean being at home from work. Sitting zombielike in front of the TV, too tired to engage with our family, can create a painful experience of disconnection for them. For partners, children, family, and friends to enjoy our company and for us to enjoy their company, we need to have the mental and emotional energy to pay attention and engage with them. That means that, though we expend energy at work and during our commute, we must reserve enough energy to engage at home. This is also true of our desire for great sex. We'll only have energy for consent conversations and the sex that can follow them if we have emotional and mental energy left for them at the end of the day or week.

But how do we preserve that energy when work demands so much? Let's tackle that question in two parts. First, we'll ask whether those work demands are accurate. Second, we'll assume that work does demand a lot and ask what to do about it.

Does Work Really Demand Too Much?

Silicon Valley workaholic millionaires make up a fair portion of my clients. These men, despite wealth, success, or financial security, still feel driven to earn or achieve more. Some of that tendency may come from those outdated ideas about masculinity discussed in chapter 1, which say that men are only worth what they earn. But even when we feel otherwise, work may not be demanding so much of us.

Instead, we may not be keeping work *regulated*. We say yes to every task put in front of us. We try to get every promotion. We agree to every offer of overtime that is available. We don't know how to prioritize our values over the value of our work. Here are some ways to say no at work:

- "No, working more hours than this would reduce my quality of life."

- "No, I already have more work than fits into my forty hours a week."

- "No, I can't do that. I'm already too stressed with the tasks I already have."

- "I can't complete that task on time without help."

Just because you can achieve or earn more, doesn't mean you have to. It is okay for your job to just be a job. It is okay for you to prioritize parts of your life that aren't work.

Commitments beyond our careers bring meaning to our lives. We can achieve all that we want, but we also need people with whom to share and celebrate our successes. Here are more questions for you to consider as you ponder whether, or how to create, more balance at home and work.

- If you only work, earn money, and achieve, does it feel like a good life?

- If a physical accident, a lawsuit beyond your control, or a technological disruption rendered your work obsolete, what would bring meaning to your life?

- If you succeed at work but your partner leaves you and you are separated from your children, how would your heart feel?

Don't get me wrong, if you love your work, that's great. Work that does good in the world is a reason for deep gratitude. But don't confuse the mental stimulation of a rewarding career with the warmth of relationships built over a lifetime that will bring loving and supportive people to your deathbed to bid you farewell.

Yes, My Work Does Demand Too Much

Sometimes, work really does demand too much. Not all men have the freedom to make choices about how much they work because economic inequality keeps many people at or near the poverty line. Some people, especially those with service jobs, must consistently work unsustainable amounts of time to support themselves and their families.

This may help you recognize the importance of creating an economic system that allows all people the freedom to work in amounts that allow them enough free time to balance other elements of their lives, including their sexual expression. To support sexual health in our culture, we need to create economic justice.

If your job is very demanding, you may leave work in a fugue-like state. It can be hard to transition from the logical, goal-oriented, command structure, and competitive ways of talking on the job. But at home, with friends and family, you need to use emotional, process-oriented, equality-based, and cooperative communication methods. If you try to interact with your family in *work mode,* you'll probably start using logical arguments when empathy is needed and working hard to get "the job" of family done—but you'll forget to be kind to your family members in the process.

Here are some simple ways to dial back from a demanding job or transition to home-mode when work really does drain you:

Go slower. Consciously go a little slower at work. You'd be surprised how much energy you can save and how little efficiency you lose if you slow down a bit. Most people won't notice, but you will feel the difference.

Take one deep breath, often. If your job allows you to have a cell phone on during business hours and you can afford a smartphone, try downloading a mindfulness app. Set it to notify you at semiregular intervals. When it goes off, take one deep breath.

Avoid screens when you get home. TV is an easy, passive way to keep your attention off your stress, but it won't recharge you. Recharging requires an active approach. Instead, take a walk or warm shower, sit in a chair and stare at the ceiling (doing nothing with your mind actively recharges it), or talk with a friend. TV is great after you're refreshed.

Switch to home-mode in two steps. First, establish a five- to fifteen-minute routine where you rest when you get home, breathe deeply, and attempt to shed the stressors of work. Do this without a phone, tablet, computer, or TV. I recommend silence, above all, but if you need something to block out noise, listen to music without words. Second, do something with your body that gives you energy: splashing cold water on your face, ten push-ups, or a quick run around your apartment building.

Vote, donate, or volunteer to increase income equality. Measures to raise the minimum wage are a good example of what to vote for. There are organizations like Poor People's Campaign and Jobs with Justice to support. At first, this might sound absurd. How will volunteering help you with how tired you are from working too much? Working for justice, especially for yourself, can be energizing. Bring the family along while you are at it. You'll make your partner or children proud of your values in the process.

FRIENDS AND COMMUNITY

One myth of masculinity is that we don't need other people. We stand alone and are a "rock." This is a lie. Study after study confirms that for every metric of physical health,[1] mental health,[2] and mortality,[3] men, like all people, need other people.

Beyond these medical perspectives, this book demonstrates our need for connection. We cannot regulate our emotions without having other people to talk with about our feelings. You've already seen how I recommend using friends to manage emotions in chapter 4, for example. I'll return to this idea in chapter 6 and 8 as well.

Seeing the world from only your perspective is not a virtue. It's myopic. A narrow perspective won't just have a negative effect on your personal life. As the business world relies more and more on soft skills,[4] the ability to form, maintain, and nurture relationships through supporting and valuing different perspectives will become a necessity for career success. If men don't catch up with their capacity to develop those soft skills, they will be left behind.[5]

Here are some quick tips for how to find friends and improve your community:

- Join a community that meets regularly.

- Say nice things to the people you meet.

- Create events like parties, games, or dinners, and invite potential friends.

- Ask for help, or offer someone help with a skill or chore.

- Tell people about important, vulnerable things going on in your life.

Using these tips can help you build a community around you. I also recommend psychologist Marisa Franco's book *Platonic: How the Science of Attachment Can Help You Make—and Keep—Friends*. Finally, I'd never want to discount friend connections through the internet, but make sure that your community passes the test I ask my clients: "If you were sick, who would bring you soup?" If you don't have an answer, you don't have enough community yet.

MENTAL BALANCE

If we haven't refreshed our minds, it is hard to be present, creative, and emotionally balanced in relationships or the bedroom. Our lives, workdays, and phones are so full of demanding stimuli that, sometimes, we just need a mental refresh. Hobbies and mindfulness are two ways to build mental balance into your life.

Hobbies

A great tool for mental self-care is a dynamic or creative hobby. A lot of work today is either highly abstract cognitive work or highly repetitive and mindless labor. The first is draining, the second numbing. Our work used to be more diverse. My grandpa, a farmer, had animals to feed, fences to mend, a garden to tend, tractors to maintain, and a home to beautify. It can feel good to have small goal-oriented tasks that we can accomplish with our hands or bodies.

Tasks like this allow our minds to be engaged but not taxed. When we complete a task, our minds get a little reward, and that builds our self-esteem, too. That's why hobbies can have such a positive effect on mental balance. In contrast to our difficult, unending work and life tasks, our hobbies give us discrete achievable tasks. Hobbies also connect us with community and help us make friends, which you already know is important. Here are some ideas of tasks that fit the bill for mental rejuvenation:

- Write for creativity, with no purpose or goal.

- Paint, draw, or make decorations for your home.

- Paint, draw, or write badly in a secret journal, and never show anyone.

- Do woodworking or make furniture or accessories for your home, garden, or friends.

- Tinker with or wash a car.

- Garden. No garden is too small. Patio or window gardens in apartment homes can refresh your mind just as well.

- Dance, practice a martial art or yoga, or join a cycling or exercise community.

- Play board games.

- Cross-stitch, embroider, knit, sew, or crochet.

ability to stop, slow, or change the sexual activity to prolong sexual activity.

Mindfulness can help men in relationships by slowing us down and helping us observe: we perceive what our partner said or did, we interpret those experiences, and then we have feelings about them. Let's use the example of Sanjay and his wife, Arthi, to illustrate the benefit of mindfulness in a relationship. Sanjay and Arthi are supposed to meet up at a party. Sanjay gets delayed at work but doesn't tell Arthi what happened. People at the party express concern to Arthi, and one of her friends takes her aside to ask if everything is okay in their relationship, which is embarrassing for her.

Sanjay finally arrives, and they have a good time for the remainder of the party. But when they get into the car, Arthi yells at Sanjay, "What happened? You didn't call or text. I kept telling people that you would be right there." Sanjay, taken off guard, uses his mindfulness. He notices that his body is tense, so he relaxes his muscles. He notices that he's stopped breathing, so he takes a deep breath. He looks at Arthi's face, where he notices hurt and confusion. He waits until his defensiveness shifts to compassion. Finally, he speaks softly, "I'm sorry that I left you alone at the party so long. I didn't know that I had made you worried or embarrassed. Can we talk about what happened to make it better and make sure it doesn't happen again?" Because Sanjay responded with compassion, Arthi's anger melts. She apologizes for her outburst, and they talk it out.

There's nothing about Sanjay as a man that *requires him* to be less reactive to his wife's yelling. But men like Sanjay *can* protect their relationships against negativity. It only takes one person to offer peace. Mindfulness can help you have that strength to offer peace in your relationship.

EXERCISE: Get Mindful in Five Minutes

If you happen to have a smartphone, there are many mindfulness apps, from simple timers to more complex apps for guided meditation. If you don't have another way to begin mindfulness, search "mindfulness" in the app store to see what pops up.

If you don't have a cell phone or prefer more connection, search for a mindfulness-based stress reduction (MBSR) course. Find a certified instructor, and take the eight-week course for a secular introduction to several different mindfulness practices. If you're interested in Buddhism, search for a *sangha* (which means "community") near you to learn and practice meditation. If you're looking for a Christian mindfulness practice, look for a centering prayer retreat.

However, given its simple nature, you can practice mindfulness at home without any fancy cushions, instructions, lessons, retreats, or teachers. What follows is a simple introduction to mindfulness meditation. For some people, mindfulness meditations create anxiety. If this happens for you, just stop. This meditation isn't the only form of beginner mindfulness practice, and if this one doesn't work for you, try finding someone with experience and more meditation methods to help.

1. **Sit down comfortably.** If sitting is uncomfortable for you, try lying down. If you fall asleep easily when lying down, try putting your knees up.

2. **Set a five-minute timer.**

3. **Close your eyes.**

4. **Pay attention.** Start by noticing your breath. Be aware of how it feels moving in an out. You'll soon begin to detect other internal experiences. Notice anything else that happens inside your mind, your emotions, or your body. Then, name what you feel: "That's a thought," "That's a feeling," "That's an itch," or "That's a sound."

5. **When your mind wanders and you forget to engage in conscious noticing, congratulations!** You are experiencing what people who meditate do—it's hard to keep noticing what's happening in your mind. Just bring your mind back to noticing your breath, in and out.

6. **When the timer goes off, open your eyes, take a deep breath, and go about your day.**

Once you feel comfortable sitting like this, you can expand the number of times a day or the length of time you do it, or both. As simple as this skill is on the surface, you may notice that the simplicity of the practice doesn't mean it is easy.

BODY WELLNESS

When it really comes down to it, you'll be using your body to have sex, and body wellness comes into play. We don't need to be athletes to have great sex, but maximizing our body health within our capacities does help us have better sex. The fact that a man's average lifespan is lower than a woman's can, at least in part, be blamed on the fact that we men don't take as good care of our bodies.[7] But the only one who can give us equality on that score is ourselves.

Sleep

Emotions take place in the body. If you aren't taking care of your body, you will be irritable, moody, selfish, and impulsive. These negative side effects of an out-of-balance body have negative sexual and relationship consequences.

Sleep is one of the easiest keys to turn in order to unlock your mental health potential. Yes, you can probably survive with six hours of sleep, but the research is clear that mental capacity is greater with more sleep. Less sleep creates a host of problems including irritability, difficulty concentrating, loss of patience, negative thinking, and vulnerability to depression. If you have mental health challenges like ADHD, bipolar disorder, depression, or addiction, sleeping better helps you regulate these experiences.

You can begin regulating your sleep by not taking naps; going to bed and waking at the same times every day (yes, even weekends); making your sleeping room dark; and eliminating caffeine, nicotine, and alcohol. For more ideas about how to improve the duration and quality of your sleep, search online for "sleep hygiene," or read sleep researcher William Dement's *The Promise of Sleep: A Pioneer in Sleep Medicine Explores the Vital Connections Between Health, Happiness, and a Good Night's Sleep.*[8] These suggestions are summarized from that book, but there's so much more that you can do to take charge of your sleep.

If you experience sleep apnea, intense snoring, ongoing insomnia, or chronic early waking, you may need a sleep study, a therapist skilled in these issues, or other medical support to improve your sleep. Be the better man by getting the help you need to get better sleep.

Exercise

Exercise is one of the most elusive elements of physical health for many people. This is due in part to our work and commute schedules, which leave little energy for exercise. The paradox, of course, is that exercising provides energy once you're engaged in a regular habit. It also helps improve the quality of sleep and improves mood.

EXERCISE: Increase Exercise

Do thirty minutes of mildly aerobic exercise in the morning to improve your mood. A brisk fifteen-minute walk away from your home and the fifteen minutes back is a good example of simple, inexpensive exercise. Even in a small apartment in a neighborhood not conducive to walking, you can march in place gently for fifteen minutes to get your heart and breathing rates up.

If you can't fit thirty minutes of mild exercise into your day, you're not alone. If this is the case, do one to two minutes of brief body-weight exercise (e.g., push-ups, squats, or planks) between any two elements of your day, like before getting in the car for work, between meetings, on a work break, or after getting up from dinner and before clearing the table. Almost everyone can do one minute of exercise. Now that you have one minute of exercise, during a break in the day, try adding a couple more. You'll be surprised by how much positive impact those few minutes have on your emotional self-regulation and body confidence.

Diet

Diet also has a major impact on mood and emotions. If we don't regulate what we eat, it can be very hard to feel sexy in our bodies, or energetic enough for the sex we want. But for many people, class and money are barriers to eating well. It is easier to eat better when you can spend more money on better food and have the time to get and prepare it. Because of those factors, I recommend focusing on your portions, which can be done no matter what your socioeconomic background is.

EXERCISE: Regulate Portions

Here are some quick ways to effectively reduce calorie intake:

1. Eliminate sodas. Sugar is just empty calories. Choose water instead.

2. Cut out the fries, onion rings, chips, or whatever else you might add on. Most of the standard sandwiches or burgers at restaurants have enough calories for a meal.

3. At a restaurant, take half of the meal from the beginning and wrap it up to go. If it is already wrapped, it'll be easier to stop when you're full. At home, you can apply the same idea by using a smaller plate or bowl. The extra time and

effort to get another portion may help slow you down and give you more chances to stop eating.

4. If you are ordering in a restaurant and sides come with the meal, ask for a salad.

Medical Care

Maybe the only thing that men avoid more than emotions is doctors. If you're trying to take care of your body wellness, you'll need to get regular checkups for your body, dental care, and vision.

Medical care is something we tend to put on the back burner because it requires that we face many elements of ourselves that fly in the face of patriarchal masculinity. We must admit our fallibility, put ourselves in the care of someone else, be evaluated and told what to do by someone who knows more than we do about something—and then we might, especially as we age, face the nature of our declining strength and mortality.

Receiving medical care serves our families and communities. We can't work if we get sick. We can't give meaning to the lives of our families and loved ones if we don't receive from them the care and support that we need when we need it. We can't teach the next generation to take care of themselves if we don't model it. We can't be loving if we're dead. Stop reading this book right now and schedule your next physical, dental appointment, and vision checkup if you haven't had those in the last year. Do it right now.

In the United States, affording medical care is an issue for many men. If you struggle to afford care, look for low-cost community clinics and make an appointment there. All of us men need to take care of each other and make sure this basic need is available for all people. I don't mean to minimize those challenges with flippant, quick ideas. Some people certainly need more help than I've offered here to help maintain physical health. The important message here is to be conscious about and maintain your physical health. Doing so is a good first step in affirming your inherent value.

MEANING AND PURPOSE

A sense of meaning and purpose from living according to your values is important to most people. For some, this comes from their spirituality or religious tradition. For others, it comes from an internal motivation to do meaningful work. A sense of meaning and purpose unites today's effort with larger life goals. This seems especially appealing to the men in my practice. However, few people name their values, prioritize them, vet them with their community, and then align their daily lives to support their values.

Having a sense of meaning and purpose helps you figure out how you want to act when life throws you a curve ball. Without a sense of meaning and purpose to guide your behavior, it is easy to chase short-lived pleasure like money, video games, danger, alcohol, drugs, or sex to make each day feel "worth it."

EXERCISE: Identify Your Values

Your values can help you make decisions when there aren't obvious right answers or when you don't know the consequences of your choices. Values also can make you resilient to criticism and help you deviate in meaningful ways from your cultural norms. Take a few minutes to write down your answers to the following questions:

1. What makes life feel good for you? What gives you a sense of life satisfaction? (Example: Financial security, time with friends, my family, or downtime. Not: Feeling happy, healthy.)

2. What are the values you have that give those experiences meaning? (Example: I value security, friendship, feeling bonded, and relaxation.)

3. What do you need to do to work toward those values? (Example: I need to work diligently, nurture my friendships, spend time with family, and prioritize downtime.)

If you have trouble with this exercise, keep trying over the next few days until you can pinpoint your values. If you can't identify the values that give meaning to life events, you can feel like life is pushing you around and not giving you any choices. Without clear values, it's easy to become fixated on specific ways you want life to go, then grow disappointed because life rarely goes exactly how you want it to. For example, if you lose your job, you could get depressed because now you don't have financial security. But if you know you value financial security and that you must work diligently to maintain it, then you become motivated to begin searching for your next job.

EXERCISE: Identify Your Sexual Values

Values can also guide us in sex or relationships. Look back at what you wrote down for the "Know Your Turn-Ons" exercise from chapter 3. Write down answers to the following questions with those responses in mind and close at hand:

1. What makes sex feel good for you? What gives you a sense of satisfaction in sex? (Example: Orgasms, giving my partner pleasure, feeling close or intimate.)

2. What are the values you have that give those sexual experiences meaning? Identify three to seven sexual values that resonate with you. Feel free to use the following list for inspiration, but if you have a value that isn't on the list, that's great!

Adaptability	Generosity to partners
Adventure	Independence
Community building	Kindness
Connection	Learning
Consent	Losing self-consciousness
Freedom	Maintaining fitness
Fun	Novelty
Generativity	Playfulness

Pleasure	Sensuality
Relaxation	Stress relief
Safety	Sustainability
Self-discovery	Vulnerability

3. What do you need to do for sex to live up to those values? What kinds of conversations will you need to have with partners so those values guide the sex you have? (Example: I need to communicate what gives me an orgasm and ask my partners to support me in having an orgasm. I need to find out what gives my partner pleasure, do those things skillfully enough, and be vulnerable and encourage my partner to feel vulnerable.)

4. What kinds of behaviors would undermine this value for you or your sexual partner? How can you communicate with a partner to make sure that you both avoid behaviors that would undermine this value?

Awareness of your sexual values can help you stay focused on the big picture. For example, having sex but not orgasming during penetration doesn't take away the meaning or purpose during sex if your value is connection. Similarly, it isn't important for your partner to orgasm during penetration for you to be generous. Penetration without an orgasm might be pleasurable for them, or they might like it if you are generous enough to help them orgasm another way. If intimacy is your value, then you might not need to have sex at all. Talking, taking a shower together, cuddling, or sharing an activity can also create intimacy.

■

Whether we're talking about life values or sexual values, it's important that you check your values with your community. Here's an example of a man checking with his partner about values related to a job: "Honey, I have an opportunity to make a career change. It makes a lot of financial sense, but it means that I'll have to spend less time with you and the kids. What is important for you in this situation?"

Here's an example of a man checking with his partner about his sexual values: "Hey, it seems like you haven't had an orgasm yet. Is that true? [Partner says yes.] Okay, well, one of my values in sex is being generous, so I'm willing to keep trying to give you more pleasure and, if possible, help you have an orgasm. What's important for you to make this a good experience?"

Your values give your behavior meaning and purpose. They define what kind of man you want to be. Once you know what kind of man you want to be, you'll know what kinds of actions move you closer to being that better man.

SEXUAL HEALTH

In addition to the values you defined for yourself and vetted with your community in the last section, you may want a guide to determine if your sexual behavior is healthy. But how do you do that without imposing someone else's bias on yourself? You can use the six sexual health principles from Doug Braun-Harvey and Michael Vigorito, which they distilled from the World Health Organization's definition of sexual health: consent, nonexploitation, protection honesty, shared values, and pleasure.[9] Let's take a look at each.

Consent

In chapter 2, I presented legal and operational definitions of consent. In this section, we're talking about health-oriented aspects of consent. That is, if you're not getting consent, then you won't feel sexually healthy. By now you know that consent means that the people involved in the sexual activity have agreed to participate in it. In my experience, when we move the discussion to sexual health, it's helpful to review concrete examples of a few situations.

Imagine that you are watching pornography on your computer

in a common area of your home and someone walks into the room and sees you. The actual sexual activity was taking place on the screen. Presuming ethical production processes, those performers consented to be in the activity. Consent? Check. You were the other participant in the sexual activity in that you were watching sexual material for your own pleasure. You *wanted* to look at it, and you *were* looking at it. Consent? Check. At this point, though, some men get too literal about what participating means. Witnessing sexual activity is a kind of participation. You consented to participate in witnessing the performers. The person walking in on you also had the right to consent or not consent to witnessing both what was on your screen and you viewing it for your pleasure. If they didn't consent and you were in a public area, you violated their consent by bringing sexual material into a public space.

Consent applies to public sexual acts like having sex in public, masturbating in public, or exposing yourself in public. People in the United States don't expect to see sexual activity or sexual material when they are out in public. The norms for public sexual material and behavior are different in different cultures. Some cultures allow some sexual behaviors in some public settings at some times.

Consent is a very broad term encompassing many aspects of participation, witnessing, and consequences. For example, imagine a man who ejaculates into the used underwear of his partner without their consent. For some partners, this would be just fine. For others, it might feel like a violation. Consent isn't just about what's done to a person or with their body. It also includes elements of privacy, autonomy, and health consequences that are hard to define.

EXERCISE: Keep Sexual Expression Consensual

Grab your journal and review your turn-ons inventory from chapter 3. Do you see any behaviors in the first four columns of the chart that might bring up the consent concerns highlighted in this section? For example, it would be common for people to be turned on by the idea of sex in public or sex where they could be caught. Make a list of these behaviors.

For each turn-on you list, write down how you could ensure consent while trying to express that desire. For example, if you have public sex on your list, you might write down that going to a sex party with your partner is a way to express this desire while ensuring any witnesses are consenting.

If you can't figure out how to express any of the behaviors while ensuring that all participants are consenting, you may have a challenge. This is a great situation to talk about with your partner, therapist, or a trusted friend.

Nonexploitation

Sexual exploitation is "leveraging one's power and control to receive sexual gratification from another person."[10] Not all consent is equal. The principle of nonexploitation broadens the principle of consent to state that, unless consent is given freely, it is not actually consent.

Most people immediately understand that nonexploitation is about the coercive use of money or power. You probably understand by now why it is problematic for a boss to proposition a subordinate at work for sex. Like power, money can be used to coerce someone into consenting. If one person is unable to maintain their basic needs for food, clothing, shelter, and medical care, and another person offers that person money for sex, they may agree. However, the person with money has used the power of money to gain consent for sexual activity. It is easy to see how this is exploitation.

I want to add a brief caveat here. Money as part of a sexual exchange isn't *necessarily* exploitative. I once saw a meme on social media that asked whether I'd eat tacos every day for a year to get $10,000. My immediate reaction was, "I'd eat tacos every day for a year even if you didn't pay me; the money would be a bonus." Some people like sex that much. Some people like giving others pleasure and like receiving pleasure. Some people—yes, even some women—would choose sex work and feel happy and fulfilled by it. Like workers in any industry, sex workers might not like some aspects of their jobs, but the presence of money in the exchange isn't necessarily exploitative. Advocates for sex workers (who usually are or have been sex workers) have more complete guides to sex workers rights, but the simple guide is this: anything that's good for other workers and moves other work toward nonexploitation also moves sex work toward nonexploitation.[11]

In addition to power and money, knowledge can also be used exploitatively. For example, when one member of a couple is having an affair yet maintaining a relationship with a committed partner, the betrayed partner has not consented to the relationship in the context of the cheating. They can't consent to it because they don't know about it. The cheating partner is using the power of withholding information to exploitatively gain ongoing consent from their committed partner.

Any hidden sexual behavior that's not in line with the relationship agreements can create exploitation. If your partner would say, "If I had known you did that, I wouldn't have had sex with you afterward," then hiding that knowledge is exploitative. Phrases like "It is a victimless crime" or "What they don't know won't hurt them" reveal that our culture sanctions exploitation when using the power of knowledge.

Exploitative behaviors hurt both the people exploited and the people who are doing the exploitation. People who are sexually exploitative may lose their job, suffer accusations of exploitation, get outed in a #MeToo process, damage their self-esteem, or rupture their relationships. And that's why sexual exploitation diminishes your sexual health.

Men who are ready to take charge of their sexual health need to attend to how they will make nonexploitation a guiding principle of their sexual health and how they will use their influence among other men and boys to spread that principle to the rest of the male community. Here are a couple of situations where exploitation may or may not be taking place, with some questions for you to consider about how you'd respond.

- Your brother invites you a party and tells you he hired two strippers. How do you assess the possibility for financial exploitation of the stripper? What would you say to your brother to maintain your sexual health relative to exploitation and to support his sexual health, too?

- Some pornography is produced with standards of care for the performers. A lot of porn is produced without that care. If you view pornography, how do you make sure you aren't supporting exploitation?

I intentionally chose to illustrate situations without a right answer. These are instances where it is hard to figure out exactly how to take responsibility for yourself and your own behavior, stay true to your values, and hold men accountable without trying to control them.

Protection from STIs, Unwanted Pregnancy, and HIV

You likely took driver's ed to learn how to operate a vehicle safely. Likewise, sexual activity has health risks—such as STIs, unwanted pregnancy, and HIV—that can be mitigated with accurate information and best practices. Here are some ways men can take responsibility for sexual health:

- Use a condom (and don't complain about it).

- Take pre-exposure prophylaxis (PrEP) if you are at a higher risk of HIV.

- Get tested for STIs proactively and regularly, when appropriate.

- Have proactive conversations with partners about pregnancy prevention.

- Consider a vasectomy as a low-risk, minimally invasive, and effective option for preventing pregnancy if you decide your child-rearing years are over.

These are basic protective methods, and they don't cover everything. Men who prioritize protection take the time and energy to familiarize themselves with whatever methods are available and appropriate for their sexual expression, such as lubrication, gloves, dental dams, kink safety, other fertility management methods, and more. Talk with a doctor, sex educator, or sex therapist if you don't know how to uphold this principle given your current sexual behaviors or those that you are considering doing.

Maintaining this health principle also requires maintaining the principles of consent and nonexploitation. Many of my clients who have sex with men report being coerced or pressured to let go of their own limits about sexual safety because their male partners grumble about those limits. Sexual health requires that the most cautious person feels protected.

Honesty

There's always a challenge when we talk about honesty. We know that there's a difference between answering questions honestly (being truthful) and volunteering relevant information even if we haven't been asked (being forthcoming). Honesty as a principle means a little bit of both and more. Here are three ways of thinking about the principle of honesty in relation to sexual health.

1. **Honesty is about giving information so others can make informed choices.** It's about telling other people what they need to know so they can make choices related to sexual consent with you. For example, a person you are picking up for sex in a bar will usually want you to be

honest about whether you are married. If you are planning on picking someone up at a bar for sex, your committed partners will usually want you to be honest about that plan. Their assessments of the emotional and health risks of having sex with you are based on this information. If you get their consent without honesty, you may fail to uphold the principle of nonexploitation.

2. **Honesty helps remove sexual shame.** For example, you may want to admit to your partner that you masturbate because hiding it would create fear of discovery and shame. Being honest about this also allows your partner to consent to a relationship knowing your sexual behavior. Honest information about sexuality with our closest friends can help us reduce shame and make better choices to become better men. For example, you may want to tell a close friend that you're tempted to have an affair before you do so he can help you stop.

3. **Honesty has a limit.** There's a difference between secrecy and privacy. Everyone is entitled to a little sexual privacy. Does your partner have a right to your honesty about all your sexual fantasies? Some of them might believe they do. How will you decide whether honesty with them is healthy for you or not? These are the questions you'll have to ask yourself as you move toward honesty as a part of your sexual health.

Exactly where you will draw the line between what you share with others about your private sexual life is up to you. This principle doesn't require telling everyone everything. It does mean that you are thoughtful about how honesty supports the other health principles.

Shared Values

In the "Meaning and Purpose" section, you identified your sexual values. Knowing your values prepares you for finding shared sexual values in a relationship. If you don't know what your sexual values are, you won't be able to have a robust discussion about whether those values are shared with your partner.

When a tough conversation arises that shows differences between your sexual values and your partner's sexual values, you may be tempted to just agree with your partner's values to avoid conflict. You might say, "Sure, I don't have to masturbate. I'll stop." Hastily made, unsustainable promises are easily broken if they are against your values.

Imagine a guy named George and his new sexual partner, Maxine. George values sex as a means to establish and maintain an exclusive relationship. Maxine values sex as stress relief. If they have sex without establishing shared values (or meanings), he might feel disrespected, and she might feel pressured into a relationship. Neither person is wrong, but both can easily get hurt if they haven't worked to create shared values in their sexual relationship.

When I cover this principle with my clients, I invite them to also consider an extended scope of shared values. It invites them to consider social contracts, too. This gets complicated, though, so an example can help. Imagine you're visiting some friends. They give you their Wi-Fi password. These friends are religiously and sexually conservative. One expresses disdain for sexually explicit themes in TV shows that you find unremarkable. The other has mentioned the pornography "crisis" in the United States. If you then watch pornography in their guest bedroom on your phone using their Wi-Fi, how do you think they'd feel if they checked their router logs and saw the sites you visited? If you don't have shared values with them and they find out about your behavior, how could your sexual health be affected? What if you shut your Wi-Fi off and used your cellular data instead, but you are still in their home?

There's a special caveat that I always like to add to the discussion of shared values. In the United States in the past and in many countries to this day, homosexuality and gender diversities are outlawed. Those laws are not effective in stopping people from being gay or preventing gender diversity. They exist contrary to the reality of human sexual diversity and create trauma via their existence and enforcement. Despite the possibility that those laws reflect the shared values of their communities, they outlaw something that's naturally occurring. The harm comes from laws that deny reality, not from the identity. We can see this because in the absence of those laws and with community acceptance, homosexuality or gender diversity violates no sexual health principle.

This is an important caveat for the male community, and not only because we count in our number gay and trans men. Male sexual behavior such as masturbation (common for men of all orientations and identities) can also be the focus of control in sexually repressive communities. Although it's important that we pay attention to the shared values of our community, we also have a responsibility to speak up within our communities for the right for male sexuality to exist. We have a right for the shared sexual values of our community to reflect our existence. This also shows that, when we work to make our communities safer for our gay and trans brothers, all men are safer.

Pleasure

The "pleasure" that this principle refers to is not a euphemism for orgasm. Pleasure means that the people engaged in a sexual activity (witnessing is one way of engaging) are doing so for their own benefit or out of their own motivation. To explore this value, let's start with an individual example.

The principle of pleasure means that, if a person wants to masturbate on their own in private, for their own benefit and in their own way—presuming that nothing about the method of masturbation violates the other health principles here—then it can be healthy for that person to do so.

Pleasure within a couple doesn't mean that everyone has a right to orgasms. It does mean that both members of a couple engage in shared sexual behaviors for their own reasons. The pleasure gained might be the altruistic fulfillment of giving their partner pleasure. Some people feel pleasure from comforting touch with little sensual interest. For others, pleasure refers to a hot, rollicking sexual extravaganza. The point is that the principle of pleasure identifies each person's pleasure, enjoyment, and positive emotional experience as a central metaprinciple of sexual health. When there's pleasure (and the other principles are upheld), we can say that the behavior has the markers of health.

■

The difference between the principles I describe here and the values you identified in the previous section is important. The sexual health principles here apply to everyone. The sexual health principles represent the minimum bar for healthy sexual behaviors, and you can use them to assess the health of your own behaviors. Review the health principles alone or with a therapist, partner, or a close confidant. If you are trying to bring your behavior in line with the sexual health principles, then you are becoming healthier. Trying to behave in a sexually healthy way is more productive and effective than trying to stop sexual behavior that you think isn't healthy for you. Moving away from unhealthy behavior creates shame. Moving toward sexual health builds self-esteem.

Your sexual values point you toward your aspirations about the kind of sexual man you want to be. Personal sexual values help you create shared values for a sexual relationship. Trying to act in line with your sexual values is a never-ending process. For example, if generosity is a sexual value for you, even if you were generous in your last sexual encounter, you can almost always imagine being *more* generous. That's why sexual values are aspirational.

Each encounter, we try again to move toward this vision of the lover we want to be. There's no achievement, just learning and growing toward our value.

Masturbation

Statistics on male masturbation suggest that most men masturbate.[12] Many cultures and religions have historically, or still do have, stigma or taboos around masturbation. This includes many of the cultures and religions present in the United States. For that reason, no discussion about male sexual needs and health is complete without addressing masturbation. Let's take a look at some common questions.

Is Masturbating Healthy?

Physically, medically, and psychologically, no harm is done by masturbating in most circumstances. Although some people do injure themselves during masturbation, the same can be said of any human activity. Injuries during masturbation are most often caused by lack of experience, lack of lubrication, or lack of knowledge about safe masturbation practices. Most boys navigate those risks without injury and go on to a lifetime of masturbating. This suggests that masturbation is not *unhealthy*. In fact, given that masturbation is also associated with other aspects of sexual health, there is every reason to believe that masturbation is healthy for many men.[13]

But Some Men Masturbate Too Much, Right?

Research evidence about masturbation cannot identify a number under which it is healthy to masturbate and over which it is unhealthy to masturbate. Prior attempts to classify a certain number of times per day as healthy or unhealthy were unable to avoid sample and researcher bias.[14] Some men feel that masturbating more than once a week is too much for them. Some men find they can masturbate several times a day and that's just fine for them.

But Married Men Don't Masturbate, Right?

Nope. Married men and men in relationships masturbate, too.[15] Most men continue to masturbate through their entire life-span, and being in a relationship doesn't change that. Masturbation is a time when people can focus on their own experience.

Should I Tell My Partner I Masturbate?

Some partners want to know about their male partner's masturbation habits, some don't, and some don't want their male partners to masturbate at all.

If your partner wants to know about your masturbation habits, you might want to ask why and what they want to know. Maybe they find it sexy. Or maybe they want to watch you so they can learn from you. If that excites you, that's great, have fun! But you might also have a right to privacy.

You wouldn't be the first man who didn't want to report to their partner about their masturbation. Some men find that reporting to a partner reduces the pleasure of their masturbation. If that's your experience, you might say, "I don't feel comfortable telling you about that, it's for me. It kind of ruins the experience if I'm reporting back to you. Is there another way I can meet your need for honesty on this issue?" There's room for privacy inside of honesty.

If your partner doesn't want you to masturbate, tread carefully. If you *absolutely never* masturbate, this might not be a problem. But 94.3 percent of men aged twenty-five to twenty-nine have masturbated.[16] So even if you masturbate once a year or less, to maintain honesty in this relationship, you probably need to admit that. A rich discussion can help you understand what your partner's sexual values are and why those values create a request that you don't masturbate. There may be other ways to meet the needs. The request that you never masturbate may also come from the idea that, if a man masturbates less, he will have more frequent sex with his partner. In reality, men who have emotional intimacy and pleasurable sex want to have more frequent sex with their partners (and will still probably masturbate sometimes).

The request that you never masturbate may also come from the false equivalence of masturbation and orgasm. Not all men orgasm every time they masturbate. For example, some men masturbate to create sexual desire, don't orgasm, and then bring that desire to their partner. Educating your partner about how your masturbation keeps your sexuality vibrant may change their perspective.

In any case, be wary of people who try to control your masturbation or orgasms. Limiting your pleasure is a form of control, shaming, and violence against you. Set whatever boundaries on your behavior support your values, but don't forget that one element of sexual health is pleasure, and masturbation falls under that.

Are There Different Ways to Masturbate?

Yes. Most men masturbate to orgasm in just a couple of minutes and describe the process as functional in terms of the depth of enjoyment and pleasure they get from it. Some men masturbate while edging, a process of masturbating and getting close to orgasm, then slowing down enough to delay the orgasm only to repeat the process several times. This often creates intense orgasms. Many men view pornography when they masturbate; many don't. These ways of masturbating are all just fine. There's also another way to masturbate with some different benefits.

When men masturbate most of the time, it is a functional, fast, and minimally satisfying process. Men rarely masturbate in a way that includes a deep emotional process (instead of just being numb or focused on media), vivid internally directed fantasy (instead of watching something else), or deeply satisfying orgasms (instead of just a release). When men lack the skill to generate their own deep sexual-emotional pleasure, they're unnecessarily dependent on sexual partners to experience this kind of satisfying and soothing release. To be clear, this is not the reason why men commit sexual assault. However, it does reveal a pattern in which society fails to prepare men to accept the duty of maintaining their own pleasure and their own emotional stability. That pattern may be one of the causes of abuse, coercion, and assault.

EXERCISE: Whole-Person Masturbation

To maintain our own pleasure and emotional stability, we need to know how to knock our own socks off. This exercise can help you develop that capacity. In the "Know Your Turn-Ons" exercise in chapter 3, we used the physical, emotional, mental, and spiritual framework to help explore your erotic landscape.[17] You can use the same framework to approach masturbation beyond just genital stimulation until you trigger a reflex.

Physical. Pleasure can be experienced in your whole body, so include your whole body in the process of solo pleasure. When taking a hot shower or bath, allow yourself to take care of your body intentionally because you respect and love yourself.

When you are in the bathroom, look at your body in the mirror and acknowledge what a lover would admire. If you think of yourself as skinny, realize that someone likes how "lean" you are. If you carry a few extra pounds, realize that someone likes your "hot dad bod." If you are an older man, remember that "love handles" are called that because some people love them. Look at your body and affirm in your mind that you are physical lovable.

Consider the space where you are going to masturbate. How does it give your body what it needs? Covers on or off? Is the temperature high or low enough? From soap, deodorant, massage oils, and lotions to incense and candles, include the fragrances that you like while you are masturbating.

When you begin to masturbate, involve your whole body. Touch your neck, chest, nipples, or (properly lubricated, of course) anus or prostate.

What happens if you slow the movements down? What happens if you focus on your breath? What muscles do you tense up as you become aroused, and what happens for you if you relax those muscles instead? How can you draw out or intensify your pleasure, instead of just focusing on getting to an orgasm?

Emotional. Create a safe, low-stress environment. Lock the door. Make sure you're alone in your home, or create a clear expectation that you need alone time. Instead of masturbating to create relaxation, consider trying to relax to create enhanced masturbation. Meditate, listen to music, or just lie down and rest a little, before beginning.

Mental. During solo pleasure, the mental component of attention becomes very important. Here are some ways to focus your attention during whole-person masturbation:

Focus on your body and your breath. Stay present, here and now. If you begin fantasizing, gently bring your mind back to what you are doing and how you are feeling in that moment.

Use internal observations to support your attention. For example, think to yourself "That feels good," "I like that," or "I'm going to keep doing that but slower." In this way, you can become an expert in your own pleasure, and these observation skills support dirty talk with a partner if they happen to be into that.

Consciously build a detailed fantasy. If this appeals to you, identify what you want to fantasize about before you begin. Consider fantasizing about elements other than sexy bodies and what they do. What kind of relationship would make you feel like you had won the lottery of life? What would your partner say to you while having sex? How would they touch you? How would the emotional bond reflect what happens in the bedroom? Now, as you begin moving toward touching yourself and seeking physical pleasure, keep your real self a character in your fantasy.

Meaning and purpose. When you reach whatever conclusion you desire for this masturbation session, remind yourself that whatever positive experiences you had during this time were created by you for you. You love yourself, and you can express it. You are worthy of this time and attention for yourself. You are in charge of it, and you can spend the effort to improve the feelings you're able to give yourself over time. No one else can give you the same instantaneous feedback loop between how the touch feels and how it needs to change to escalate or slow your reaction down.

This is one way that masturbation can help men become more sexually fulfilled, less needy, less dependent, and more skillful lovers. When you are an expert in giving yourself pleasure, you'll be less dependent on your partners for sexual release. Being less dependent will make you more confident and less demanding, and that will make you sexier to potential partners.

Pleasure, Porn, and Ethics

MILFs or DILFs, mature or young adults, amateur or professional, vintage or uploaded today, free or pay, video or live cams, humans to cartoons—if it is a human behavior, thought, or art style, there's porn related to it. We can't contend with sexual health or relationship agreements in the modern age without addressing this nearly ubiquitous and easily accessible expression of, mostly male, sexuality.

David Ley's excellent book *Ethical Porn for Dicks* is about pornography for a male audience. I highly recommend this book. I focus here on the elements that are most related to consent and stronger relationships.

When porn fills in the gaps in our cultural sex education, it can create the idea that porn is what sex looks like. Porn is a fantasy. Many people have fantasies that they have no desire or intention of ever living out. You may be aware that the pornography you watch is created by men to depict male fantasies for men to watch. But if you watch heterosexual porn, it may not occur to you that most sex depicted in porn is a fantasy of heterosexual sex. It does not reflect the actual sex that most heterosexual couples have most of the time. Notably rare in pornography are women's fantasies of sex. If you have sex with women and you want to create pleasure for them, you probably need to leave aside assumptions about sex that porn might have created for you.

It's possible, in theory, that the person you're in bed with also watches the same kind of porn you watch. It is also possible, though significantly less likely, that they are interested in enacting some of those behaviors with you. There's a higher overlap between what's depicted in gay porn and what takes place in gay men's bedrooms than there is in heterosexual porn, though it still tends to skip the preparation, PrEP,[18] consent conversations, and relationship maintenance that goes on before the hot-and-heavy scene takes place. But given how varied porn is and how diverse sexual desire is, how likely could it be that you find someone who is into the same fantasies *and* wants to put them into practice in the same way?

It is safe to say that it's more probable that your partner's fantasies, whether depicted in porn or not, won't match you on all of those variables. The problem isn't porn. The problem is that many men get myopic about their porn in the following four ways:

1. **Men negatively compare the sex they have with their partners to pornography.** Most porn performers are skilled stunt performers who happen to have bodies that work well for their stunts. You wouldn't say you had a bad weekend if you didn't jump off an exploding building even though you watch action movies. But many men do lament not performing some imagined essential sexual act that they like watching in porn. After watching a Cirque du Soleil performance, you wouldn't come home and criticize your partner for not being a contortionist.

In those action movies and circus acts, we recognize the exceptional nature of the performers, and we don't compare our lives to them. Sometimes, we forget to apply that same logic to porn.

2. **Men forget that all sex requires consent, preparation, planning, and cleanup.** Most porn doesn't depict these experiences, so men's fantasy scripts don't include them. Then they don't understand that bringing fantasies into reality requires a willing partner, a lot of communication, preparation, and cleanup. That's all required for the porn, too, but those behind-the-scenes experiences don't make the final cut. Since we often aren't taught about preparation elsewhere, and most of us don't see other people having sex except in porn, we have the illusion that sex depicted in porn is all there is to see.

3. **Men can get so focused on the fantasies they see in porn that they neglect their partner's fantasies.** Maybe you should ask what kind of porn your partner watches or what erotica they read. Maybe they don't do either, but they do have fantasies that they're willing to share. Even if you find that you're not interested in enacting those fantasies or able to become a horse-riding billionaire chef with abs forever, learning about your partner's fantasies may give you some empathy for why your partner may be as reluctant to enact your fantasies as you are to enact theirs.

4. **Men forget that they must talk about and abide by their relationship agreements about pornography.** Because many men begin watching pornography before they begin a relationship, they may skip over the awkward conversation in which they acknowledge watching porn, ask their partner how they feel about porn, and identify

what the boundaries of fidelity are *for their partner* when it comes to pornography. How to have those conversations is the focus of the rest of this section.

What Are Your Relationship Agreements about Porn?

In chapter 3, you learned the importance of accepting your sexual nature. This includes your porn habit. If you watch pornography, then you need to admit that fact to yourself and share it proactively with your partner. Use the discussion about honesty (see page 141) to help you navigate the difference between secrecy and privacy. You may decide that your search terms, favorite performers, or favorite acts to watch are private. Sharing those details might be appropriate or even sexy in some relationships. In other relationships, it might be inappropriate or detrimental.

Whatever you do share, it's unwise to wait for your partner to find out that you watch porn or to ask questions about it. Tell your partner early in your relationship. Ask your partner how they feel about pornography and how they feel about you watching pornography. Apply the principle of shared values (see page 143) to establish some relationship agreements about pornography. For example, many people feel one way about their partner watching live cams (where the audience is watching and maybe chatting with the performer live) and another way about their partner watching premade videos. Some people feel differently about porn performed by people versus drawn or computer-generated images. How your partner feels about porn is hard to predict. You must talk about it to find out.

Just because your partner has some requests for relationship agreements about pornography doesn't mean that you have to agree to them. In some cases, I'd advise against it. It's your responsibility to meet your own needs, so it's important that you not abdicate your rights to manage your sexuality as you see fit within your values. Your personal masturbation practice belongs to you.

As we've discussed earlier, we're used to being shamed for the nature of our sexuality. When it comes to pornography, your partner may endorse those judgments. Your partner may try to tell you what will or won't work in your relationship with them. That's awesome if they can clearly articulate that. Then you must take an honest look at the history of your sexuality, the ease of access to pornography, and the frequency of your desire to masturbate to pornography. You need to admit to yourself and your partner whether you really want relationship agreements that limit your sexuality in these ways.

Look back at how you filled out the chart in the "Know Your Turn-Ons" exercise. If you didn't list where pornography and masturbating to pornography fit in, consider adding it now. You might list certain types of pornography in one category and other types of pornography in another. Now consider the relationship agreements about pornography that your partner is proposing. Sustainable agreements allow you to maintain behaviors closer to your "Essential for Expression" column. Sustainable agreements more closely adhere to your existing practice. They leave you the autonomy you need (and different people need different levels of autonomy around this issue) to watch porn when and how much you want to.

That is either the moment of integrity or of becoming a bigger asshole. If you're conflicted about your partner's request to limit or eliminate your porn viewing, try saying something like this:

I really want to make this relationship work because I see a future together. I want to just say "okay" when you ask me not to watch porn so we can stay together. But I've never curbed my watching in this way. Can we talk more about this?

Maybe your partner would be willing to read *Ethical Porn for Dicks* by David Ley with you to help dispel some of the myths (e.g., porn doesn't break your capacity for an erection) and help you identify some of the real possible negative consequences (e.g., if you masturbate with a tight grip, it may make it harder for you to ejaculate when penetrating your partner).

Finally, remember that making a relationship agreement doesn't mean that you don't have the right to renegotiate that agreement. Anyone can renegotiate their consent at any time, regardless of what they agreed to earlier. Similarly, you have the right to renegotiate the sexual agreements in your relationship at any time, regardless of what you agreed to earlier. For example, if you make an agreement to not look at a certain type of pornography, you may find that the prohibition increases the desire, pleasure, and shame when you watch it. This is a common experience for people who try to limit their sexuality. You might need to renegotiate that agreement and tell your partner how the prohibition increased your desire for it.

Does Porn Oppress Women?

Let's start by narrowing the question. Porn is a vast field of media. Queer, feminist, and lesbian porn by and for lesbians and porn with an intended audience of female-identified people is still porn. Porn can be created by women and for women with the aim of increasing the representation of women's desire and of liberating women's sexuality, orgasm, and love styles from oppression. Gay porn is also still porn, even if it doesn't include women and it isn't implicitly or explicitly teaching gay men how to treat women.[19] So, porn isn't one thing.

Nevertheless, many people of all genders find some porn violent, distasteful, gross, oppressive of performers, or degrading. It isn't surprising for someone to be concerned about the well-being of porn performers or what it means when their partner likes watching porn that they find disturbing.

What we're really grappling with as a culture is whether porn targeted at a heterosexual male audience—the vast majority of porn—oppresses women or supports male oppression of women. Instead of engaging your partner in a theoretical debate about the pornography media landscape, make the conversation with your partner about porn and oppression personal. Here are some prompts to help:

- **Is your partner concerned about whether porn oppresses the performers?** Share with them how you try to make sure the porn you watch isn't oppressing the performers you watch.

- **Is your partner concerned about what you watch and how that affects your view of your sexual partners?** Talk about how you understand the difference between the fantasy of pornography and the reality of sex with your partner.

- **Is your partner concerned that watching pornography will make you misogynistic, violent, or degrading in the relationship?** Then tell your partner about your values related to gender equality, your risks to violence, and your behavior. Ask if your partner finds you misogynistic, violent, or degrading. Listen and believe them if they say yes. Discuss what it means for each of you that the porn you view does match or is very different from your behavior.

- **Is your partner concerned that the porn you watch means you don't value consent?** Ask your partner if they've experienced you violating their consent or devaluing it. Repeat back and believe them if they say yes. If they haven't experienced that from you, talk with your partner about how you view the fantasies in porn of not having to ask for consent, or of violating consent, and the reality of consent with them.

- **Is your partner concerned about your porn viewing because their sexual desires aren't being met in your relationship?** The cause of low sex frequency in a relationship is almost always conflict, too much stress, sex that isn't pleasurable, not enough energy, or a mental health issue. In most cases, it is much more effective for the couple's sex life to focus on those issues rather than porn.

I have had men in my office who watch kinky porn and understand it as they understand their own kink scenes—consensual sexual pretend-play among adults that lets them access pleasure. They'd no sooner use the language of a porn video with a person on the street than they would walk into a parking lot and begin smashing car windows. I've also had men in my office who had a hard time separating the fantasies they found in porn from the partners in their beds.

The problem these men experience with porn is located *in them*, not in the content on their screens. The problem, in my opinion, isn't that porn oppresses women. Porn, like any industry, may oppress the workers. With less stigma and more performer-inspired regulations, the industry could oppress women and all other performers less. The problem is that specific men oppress women, and there are many of them.

Why Porn Instead of Sex?

Partner concerns about men viewing pornography are often based in fear: if he watches pornography, then their sex life will suffer. Research says the opposite is true.[20] Aside from the ethical or practical concerns about pornography, partners often just want to understand why the man in their life watches porn.

Simple answers like "Because it's pleasurable" or "Because men are more visually focused and prefer images and videos over written material" do little to create that understanding. Partners will argue back, "Isn't sex pleasurable? Let's do that instead." Those arguments don't help men or their partners understand why masturbating to pornography might be uniquely desirable. In my experience, the one answer that does create understanding is this: porn is easy to watch.

How long would it take you to view pornography from where you are right now? People with smartphones can view porn in seconds. Sex with a partner is much harder to create. Sex in a long-term relationship may include negotiation, interpersonal communication, an effort to connect emotionally, an effort to eliminate the stress of managing a household or parenting, and emotional labor. In short-term sexual relationships, the effort is usually front-loaded so you prepare your home and your safer-sex plan; wash and prep your body; choose a venue to meet a potential partner; and then you have to get up, go out, work up your courage to connect to potential partners, face rejection, be resilient enough to try again, have consent conversations, and learn each other's needs quickly. After either kind of partnered sex, there's also cleanup, cuddling, or aftercare with the partner. This is all great stuff, but it tells a simple truth: real sex requires effort.

In long-term relationships, that effort builds intimacy and long-term connection. In short-term relationships, that effort can create high-charged erotic experiences. But arousal and orgasm are so amazing that they have many more capacities than that.

A partner viewing porn for arousal and masturbation might be seeking a natural stress reliever, a sleep aid, a natural energy boost with fewer side effects than coffee, the opportunity to pas-sively appreciate beauty or a fantasy, or an erotic boost to bring into the relationship at another time. Porn brings the promise of all these benefits and requires almost no effort in return. As with any coping skill, if viewing porn is the only one you have, you may not have *enough* coping skills. But that doesn't mean the one coping skill you have is a problem.

Porn is to partnered sex what potato chips are to eating fruits and vegetables. For evolutionary reasons, we're naturally inclined to eat fats and salts often. Even if we like eating fruits and vegetables, they take a little more effort than just opening a bag and eating. To get the right balance for ourselves between chips and fruits and veggies, we must be clear about what is supporting one process and discouraging the other. In this case, partnered sex takes a little more effort. Chips aren't the problem; they're just tasty. Porn isn't the problem; it's just easily accessible and very pleasurable.

Chapter 6

HOW DO I MANAGE MY EMOTIONS?

THE POPULAR CULTURAL MESSAGE about men is that we aren't as emotional as women. Is it any wonder? We discussed in earlier chapters that, from a young age, boys are teased or shamed for expressing vulnerable emotions.[1] This means that we aren't taught what our emotions are, how to express them skillfully, or how to soothe them. When it comes to navigating sex—one of the most emotionally evocative experiences of our lives—is it any wonder that we have a problem as a group with how we handle those experiences? This chapter fills that gap in your emotional education and teaches you how to understand and take care of your emotions.

FEELING LOVE, BEING LOVING

Chapter 4 included an exercise on managing limerence (falling in love). We also need to manage other feelings of love, such as an attached sense of devotion. There are two important truths that will help you regulate your experience of attached love. First, even if you feel love in your heart, your actions may not make the other person feel loved. Second, love hurts.

When you say "I love you," you're describing how you feel. You're saying that you feel a bond with the other person, that you want to be close. Feeling that way doesn't mean that you are treating the person well or that you'll create in them the feeling of being loved. Treating the person lovingly means knowing what it takes for the person to feel loved.

In her book *All About Love*, bell hooks describes the difference between feeling love for someone and being loving toward them.[2] Being loving means that you must put the other person's well-being first. If your actions are intended to make *you* feel better, then your loving feeling will be expressed selfishly. If your love is in service to the other person, based on their description of their needs, then your feelings of love will become loving actions.

So often, people give love the way that they want to be loved. A person who likes back rubs offers back rubs. A person who likes to be helped around the house offers to do things for the person they love. A person who likes attention and conversation offers that to their partner. This is well intentioned but selfish.

Men often fall into this trap with romantic and sexual gestures. We offer sex or acts of service when our partners want attention or support. We engage in acts that we think are romantic or devoted, but the behavior might feel creepy or obsessive to our partner.

Skillful loving means acting in ways that help the other person feel loved. Instead of thinking that you already know how to be loving to them, you need to find out by asking what the other person wants and what will make them feel loved. Once they tell you, being loving means following their requests.

If you really understand the difference between feeling love and being loving, then this next point will be easy to understand. When you feel love, you're almost certainly going to experience a gap between that feeling and the real world. For example, you may love someone who doesn't love you back. Being loving toward that person means sitting in the pain of that difference. You may want to express your love to someone in a way that they don't want to be loved. Being loving toward that person means experiencing the pain of not expressing your love the way you want to. It may also mean experiencing the dissonant pain of learning to love them the way they want to be loved despite it not feeling natural to you.

You might be lucky enough to love someone and be loved by them. However, how they express their love to you will almost certainly fall short of your hopes and dreams about how to be loved. Love may feel perfect when you're in limerence, but once a long-term relationship and attaching love develops, love includes this type of pain. The pain is part of what makes the moments of connection we build with intention so special.

All kinds of love cause us pain. When we get a dog or a cat, we know we will most likely bury them. When we have children, our devotion to them is often asymmetric, and they leave us to live their own lives. If we buy a car, it needs repairs and maintenance, and taking care of it causes us headaches and stress. To love is to open yourself to vulnerability, pain, loss, hurt, and grief.

Accepting this truth is a way to manage the feelings of love. With acceptance of the pain, we can stop trying to avoid this inevitable part of loving. With acceptance, we stop trying to coerce others into loving us in the way we think they ought to magically love us. With acceptance, we can stop trying to make others accept the love we want to give even when it doesn't feel good to them, and we begin to learn how they want to be loved. When we can sit with the pain, we can tolerate all the love we have in both the beautiful and painful aspects.

SOOTHING REJECTION

The experience of rejection is one inevitable pain of love. Because other people are not here to fulfill our desires, at some point in our life, someone is bound to tell us no. When we feel rejected, the pain can be intense. Because men have been so taught to equate their sexual performance with their identity and self-worth, men often feel that having our sexual offer declined is to be rejected as a person of value. There are different ways to manage rejected feelings in a relationship versus in hookups or dating. Let's handle rejection in a relationship first.

Whether we're talking about sexual rejection or having your offer to spend time together turned down, having your invitation declined is not the same as your partner rejecting you. They are declining what you're offering, when you're offering it, or maybe the way you're offering it. They may still love you, want a relationship with you, or want pleasurable sex with you.

Rejection is an emotional experience we have when we *interpret* the declined offer as a rejection of *me*. We have all experienced this kind of pain. That suffering really hurts, but your partner may not have felt hurtful toward you. Here are three ways to soothe feelings of rejection.

Are You Really Being Rejected?

Before you conclude that your feeling of rejection is the only possible explanation, examine how your emotion came to exist. Before you made your offer (sexual or otherwise), you had enough self-confidence to believe someone might want what you offered. After they declined your offer, your worth didn't change. You're still whole. You have the same gifts, skills, and attractive qualities that gave you the confidence to make the ask.

Before your partner declined your offer, you found them attractive, sexy, and desirable enough to want to want to share something with them. After they declined your offer, their attractiveness didn't change. They are still whole. They have the same gifts, skills, and attractive qualities that increased your desire and helped you to feel safe and turned on enough to invite them to have sex with you.

So, if your nature is unchanged and their nature is unchanged, what does it mean when your partner repeatedly declines your offer for connection or sex? Ask your partner directly what's happening when you feel rejected: "When you declined my invitation, I felt rejected. What is the right way for me to think about why you're saying no?" Listen carefully to what your partner tells you in response. If your partner is having a hard time answering your direct question, here are five possibilities:

1.   **They don't ever want to be with you again.** This is a very vulnerable and scary topic. If your partner does not want you, you may never know unless you ask. When you ask directly, you give yourself the ability to make conscious choices about how to respond with the full information. It is rare that a partner says they never want to spend time or have sex with you again. But even if it's true, those hard realities are better faced by knowing what's going on.

2.   **They don't want what you offered when you offered it or because of the way that you offered it.** Some people prefer morning sex to evening sex. Others prefer sex on the weekends to weekdays. Some people prefer time together on vacation. Some women prefer cuddling, sex, and active quality time at different times of their menstrual cycle. You might need to learn about those timing preferences and adjust your offers accordingly to increase the chances that your partner will say yes. Similarly, if you plead, beg, or ask for connection in negative ways, then your partner will probably decline your offer. Your offer can be skillful or unskillful, and that may affect your partner's answer. If you talk about this, you can find

out what's not working and begin making more effective offers.

3. **They don't want the kind of connection you are offering.** Maybe your partner is kinkier than you are. Your offer of missionary penetrative sex (again) isn't exciting, but trying something kinky would really generate some excitement. Maybe your partner experiences knee pain when playing tennis, but that's the only kind of date you offer. They might be open to nice dinners, theater, or a beach vacation, but you don't offer that quality time. You'll never know unless you ask. Genuine, nondefensive curiosity can be a powerful tool in learning new things about your life with your partner.

4. **The circumstances aren't right.** Last weekend when you asked your partner for sex, your parents were sleeping just outside your bedroom door. Last night when you asked to go out on a date, your partner had come off a hard week at work, and today they need to go to bed early so they can volunteer in the morning. If you keep thinking that the problem is that "they just don't want to invest in the relationship," you'll try to get your partner to change, and blame them for the problem. On the other hand, if you work with your partner as a team, you may be able to put connecting time on the calendar. This is a common strategy for long-term couples, and done skillfully, it doesn't need to eliminate spontaneity. Maybe the two of you need to work together to try to eliminate some of life's stressors.

5. **They have a barrier to connecting that has nothing to do with you.** A partner's experience of sexual trauma, mental health issues, sexual shame, or other stressors may simply have nothing to do with you. You can offer to help your partner and vulnerably share your sadness or

grief at missing this connection with them, but unless and until they ask for your assistance, you can't change what's happening for them. You must accept your powerlessness and get support from your friends and community.

The previous list is not exhaustive, but I hope it illustrates that your interpretation that someone is rejecting you should be questioned. For more information about what might be inhibiting your partner's desire, see chapter 4. If you can manifest genuine curiosity, you'll be more likely to begin a collaborative approach to healing your sexual relationship with your partner.

Use the Feedback You Get

Take what your partner tells you about barriers to intimacy seriously. Bad breath turning your partner off? Invest in a tongue scraper, mouthwash, floss, a dental visit, or maybe medication. Does your partner need a clean home before feeling ready to accept an invitation for a stroll in the park? Then clean up in the days before you'd like to take that walk. Take your partner seriously, then do your best to eliminate any barriers to intimacy that are in your control.

The very worst outcome of this process is that you act, show your partner you took them seriously, and then they still turn you down. In that case, you get to downshift the conversation with your partner: "I know you said this was the problem. I took care of that, but you're still not ready to feel close. Is there something else?" This allows you to show your partner that you take them seriously and encourages them to consider their reasons for declining your offers more carefully.

The best outcome is that you take your partner seriously, and it resolves the problem. Yay! You not only paved the way for connection but also reinforced for your partner that communication is effective in your relationship. This will help them be more open in the future.

Why Rejection and Not Disappointment?

Consider these two men with different approaches. Jordan says to his partner, "Hey, I'm feeling sexy. Want to join me?" The partner says, "No, thanks, I'm tired." Jordan gives his partner a kiss, says, "I'll miss you," goes into the bedroom, and enjoys masturbating till his toes curl.

Dan says to his partner, "Hey, I'm feeling sexy. Want to join me?" The partner says, "No, thanks, I'm tired." Dan, feeling rejected, stands and walks to the bedroom, his mood ruined by the rejection from his partner. He reviews in his mind all the other times his partner rejected him and nurses his resentment by ruminating on all the things he does in the relationship.

Why did Dan feel rejected but Jordan got to have a great solo session? Assuming that everything else is equal in the two relationships, Dan may be more vulnerable to feeling rejected than Jordan.

Unmet relational needs like connection, reassurance, comfort, closeness, or quality time might be underneath your feelings of rejection. Maybe Jordan spends more time with friends. Maybe Jordan is the kind of person who naturally focuses on the positive. Dan doesn't need his partner to change; he needs to examine his unmet relational needs and take control of them in the rest of his life.

When you find another way to meet your relationship needs with friends, family, or community, you can reduce the likelihood that your whole sense of social well-being rests on whether your partner says yes to you. If you can meet the need in another way, you're more likely to feel a less intense emotion, such as disappointment or mild sadness. Remember, sex isn't a need, but sexual expression is. You can meet that need for sexual expression yourself using the exercises in the "Masturbation" section of chapter 5.

Vulnerability, the Antidote to Rejection

Maybe you've done everything that you can to examine whether you are being rejected, to use feedback, and to meet the underlying needs of your partner, but you're still feeling rejected. You may still feel the emotional pain of disconnection and disappointment. Many men hide their emotions because that's what we've been taught. But we can't keep getting hurt and stay emotionally available, so we slowly withdraw over time.

Perhaps you not only initiate connection less often but also harbor a resentment about having received "unfair" treatment from your spouse or partner, like Dan did. You may say to yourself, "She puts all of her energy into the kids and doesn't make me a priority anymore," or "All he cares about anymore is his career," or "I've tried everything, and it doesn't matter—they're just cold and don't want sex."

The problem with these narratives is that you begin to blame the other person for the absence of sex. This is a common psychological defense when we have no awareness of how to escape the pain we're in. We preserve our ego by blaming others. Unfortunately, this is disempowering.

When you blame your partner for their feelings, you stop looking for a way to change the experience. Blame also kills the very intimacy that was desired because your partner won't be attracted to you if you're blaming them for your feelings.

Vulnerability is the solution to the disempowering and relationship-killing effect of disappointment and disconnection. You need to share your emotional experience with your partner. If you are feeling rejected, talk at a predesignated time when sex is off the table, like on a long walk or sitting down at a quiet coffee shop. Turn to your partner and say, "I've noticed that our sex life isn't as fulfilling for me as I'd like. I have tried initiating sex with you, but my memory is that you sometimes decline. Could we talk about why you are declining, how you're feeling about our sex life, and whether there's anything we can do to invigorate that part of our relationship?" Or if this about connection, try saying, "I've asked every weekend for a date for the past three weeks and you keep declining. I'm not sure what else to do about that. I've tried asking to do things you say would interest you. I've tried spending time with friends without you. I'm still missing you. Do you have any ideas about what to do?"

This process identifies your own experience rather than labelling your partner. It presents your own memory tentatively, not as an accusation. It asks for consent to have a conversation (more on this in the next chapter), acknowledges that you partner's experience of your sex life may be different, and brings humility to the process rather than painting your partner as the problem.

If you've talked about it and your partner doesn't have answers and continues declining your offers for connection, then you can rest assured you've done everything you can to improve the relationship. This empowers you to make the choice that remains: leave a relationship that isn't satisfying your desire for connection, or stay.

Managing Rejection While Dating or Hooking Up

So far, I've focused on emotional experiences of rejection in long-term relationships. The tools for handling rejection in short-term relationships are a little different. In a long-term relationship when your spouse says, "I don't want to have sex tonight," it probably doesn't mean that they never want to have sex with you. However, the person at the bar who says they're not interested in you probably means just that. Don't wither at the first sign of rejection as if your whole ego depends on it. You don't want to be the guy who doesn't take no for an answer and ruins someone's night, or makes them scared because you can't take no for an answer.

When you're approaching a person online, at a singles event, or in a more casual social situation, manage your potential feelings of rejection by preparing ahead of time with the following tips:

- Set your expectations: no one is obligated to respond to your invitations for connection—sexual or otherwise.

- Be prepared to move on if you don't get a welcoming response.

- Remind yourself what you have to offer in a relationship. Your friends can be a good source of this confidence. Ask them what they like about being your friend. Those are probably the same reasons why someone would want to date you.

- Remind yourself that people who decline your offers are only guilty of not wanting what you're offering.

This advice counters what pickup artists tell you to do. Just as I highlighted in the chapter on desire, you must decide what your highest priority is—to get another notch in your belt or to be a better person.

USING ANGER FOR JUSTICE, NOT CONTROL

When people don't manage rejection or other vulnerable emotions, those emotions often turn into anger. Skillful anger helps restore justice or boundaries. Anger to restore justice is the energy to tell others, "That is not right! I will not stand for being treated that way! I insist on being treated more humanely!" That's good. Revolutions for justice the world over, including in the United States, are formed out of anger.

Anger also brings the energy to restore relationship boundaries. It makes sense to be angry if your partner cheated on you. Anger helps you respond rapidly to what hurt you to prevent further injury. Your anger will let you be decisive and clear: "I want you to end that relationship, move out tonight, and tomorrow we can talk about whether and how we might repair this relationship!"

The problem is that as men, when we experience other negative emotions (e.g., sadness, disappointment, or shame), we haven't been taught how to soothe ourselves. So, we try to control other people with threatening anger so they don't make us feel sad, disappointed, or ashamed. This results in using anger unjustly and to violate boundaries.

But anger can be hard to manage because it rises rapidly. If your finger is slammed in a door, you quickly grit your teeth, draw down your eyebrows, tighten your stomach, and shout as you push back against the door to protect your finger. Anger arises rapidly to protect us from physical threats without needing to think about it. But muscle flexing is not helpful for resolving emotional wounds. Punching a lion that pounces on you is great. Punching your spouse because they surprised you with information that makes you feel insecure is abuse.[3]

Managing anger requires questioning the anger, being in control of the anger, and expressing the anger skillfully. Skillful anger helps you restore justice without committing an injustice in the process. Your reason for being angry may be perfectly appropriate. *How* you express that anger is your responsibility. The next five exercises are designed to help you check, regulate, and express your anger.

REGULATE ANGER EXERCISE 1: Review Incidents

Anger management sounds great in theory, but how do you remember to use it when it arises so fast and so forcefully? One way is to review instances of anger, then identify and practice ways to change the script.

Take out a sheet of paper and fold it in half the long way. Review an experience of recent anger and write down in the left-hand column the last moment when everything was okay and there was no anger or rising tension.

Continue writing in the left-hand column the sequence of events, conversation, behaviors, feelings, and thoughts that escalated the anger. Describe the event until you reach the resolution of anger. When there is a significant change in your level of anger, up or down, note it on a scale from 0 to 10. In figure 6.1, the left-hand side shows what someone might write down at this stage.

Use the right-hand side to identify ways to regulate anger. Write down something that could prevent the escalation or that could de-escalate your anger at that stage. The right-hand side of figure 6.1 shows what someone might write in this part of the exercise.

Figure 6.1: Example of a completed anger management tool

EVENT AND ANGER LEVELS	WAYS TO REGULATE ANGER
We were sitting around on Saturday morning watching TV. I was pretty relaxed (0 out of 10).	(a) Since relaxing was so important to me, I could ask ahead of time for her to respect that time and not bring up any needs or stressors while we watch TV, or (b) I could plan my relaxation with my partner explicitly ahead of time.
My partner said something like, "When are you going to do that yard work you've talked about?" I interpreted that as a criticism of me hanging out and relaxing.	If she does interrupt my relaxation, I could (a) ask to come back to those needs questions after my show, and (b) ask if she is criticizing me.
I felt angry (3 out of 10), defensive, and surprised.	I could acknowledge my rising anger and pause the process by stepping away for a minute to observe my anger and regulate it (e.g., with a deep breath or meditation).
I paused the show and said defensively, "Can't I just enjoy a little relaxation for once without you telling me how I'm not measuring up?"	I could reply without generalizing.

EVENT AND ANGER LEVELS	WAYS TO REGULATE ANGER
My partner's eyebrows furrowed, and her mouth tightened. I thought, "We're gonna have a fight," and got angrier (6 out of 10).	I could apologize then and there; acknowledge that I attacked her; and ask to step away, cool down, or restart the conversation.
She said, "I was just asking. Why are you so angry all the time?" (anger: 9 out of 10).	I could ask if she is criticizing me.
Lots of yelling back and forth. I eventually went outside to start the yard work, all the while slamming doors and tossing yard tools around (anger: 10 out of 10).	In a way, going outside did pull me out of the argument, but consciously cooling down before doing the chore would be better than slamming things around.
As I worked over the next two hours, my anger subsided (2 out of 10).	Maybe work is a good way for me to calm down, and I should do it intentionally sooner in the process (try testing it out).
When I came in, I apologized, and she said I'd done a good job on the yard work and asked me if I wanted to finish the TV show (anger: 0 out of 10).	Ending the conflict was good, but we could have reviewed how it started a little more together to both identify how we could prevent it in the future if she's open to helping me with it.

Reviewing several incidents with this table will help you identify your escalation process, the communication gaps that lead to it, ways that you can interrupt the escalation process before your anger rapidly rises, and ways to stop your anger when it's in process. Now take those tools out, make a list of those processes, and review them daily. Here's what the previous example would look like as an intervention list.

Figure 6.2: Sample anger intervention list

1. Proactively communicate my needs, and plan with my partner to meet them.
2. Gently protect my needs by saying something when she's interrupting my needs.
3. If I'm feeling criticized, say that right away. Ask if that's what is intended.
4. Walk away and cool down as soon as I feel criticized.
5. Stay concrete about what is bothering me right now (don't overgeneralize).
6. Cool down (try an activity, but not if I'm so angry that I'm slamming things around).
7. Apologize as needed.

Reviewing your intervention list regularly will help you recognize when your anger is escalating and help you use the tools to change the process.

REGULATE ANGER EXERCISE 2: Identify the Injustice

If your anger isn't out of control, then you can check whether it is justified with this exercise. Remember, skillful anger helps you to restore justice. So, for anger to be the appropriate emotion, an injustice or boundary violation must have been committed. What is it? Here are some common examples:

- **Your partner made an explicit relationship commitment to you and broke that agreement.** A common example would be a partner cheating despite a relationship commitment of fidelity.

- **Something about your partner's behavior took away your autonomy or choice.** Be careful before you leap to this conclusion, because most of the time when people *feel* controlled, the other person isn't being controlling. A common example of controlling behavior is someone telling the other person what to do without negotiating to be the leader. A common experience when people *feel* controlled but aren't is when a partner becomes emotional, and you feel like you *have to* comfort them.

- **A violation of a boundary.** Common relationship examples include sexual pressure, spending "our" money without being consulted, treating the other person in a harmful way, or disrespecting an important value (like a partner who says negative things about the other person's religion).

If you believe you're the victim of an injustice or a boundary violation, test that assessment by describing your perception to your partner and seeing whether they agree. Check with your family, friends, and community, too. Do they agree with you or your partner?

If there is an injustice or a boundary violation, then your anger makes sense. Your anger is coming to protect you from that violation. Sometimes, though, our anger is masking other emotions and preventing us from doing our own emotional work.

REGULATE ANGER EXERCISE 3: Question Your Anger

This exercise can help you ensure that your anger isn't masking another emotion. As men, our cultural script says we're allowed to be angry but not to express other emotions. We need to undo that training and reclaim our other emotions in order to express them and to preserve the good qualities that anger can have.

Common emotions that men turn into anger are pain, helplessness, shame, fear, sadness, surprise (in the form of violated expectations), disappointment, and loneliness. Emotions are complex. Sometimes, a triggering event will cause a primary emotion like pain, but then because we don't express that emotion, it turns into anger. In this case, anger probably isn't needed; it is a mask preventing others from seeing our vulnerable feelings. In other situations, more than one emotion arises at the same time. Here are some questions to help you tell the difference between anger as a first reaction and anger masking another emotion:

- **Did you express the other emotion?** If you felt hurt but only showed anger, then anger may be masking the other more vulnerable emotion for you. Replay the experience in your mind. Was the volume, tone, body language, and pacing when you expressed anger different from when you were vulnerable? If not, you may be saying vulnerable words, but your angry way of expressing them may be masking the pain.

- **When you expressed your anger, what was the goal of your anger?** If your goal was to hurt the other person, threaten them, or force them into doing something, then your anger is probably masking another emotion. At the very least, it isn't skillful. If the goal of your anger was to establish safety, declare a boundary, or get someone to stop causing harm or violating boundaries, there's a greater chance that has a valuable role to play. It is easy to confuse controlling behavior with an effort to establish safety. A boundary is telling a person how to act *to be in a relationship* with you. Control *demands that this person behave how you want or else you'll hurt them.*

- **Are you capable of soothing and tolerating the other emotions that come along with anger?** Imagine a man whose beloved father dies. He's sad and grieving, but he doesn't talk with anyone about it. He goes through the motions of the funeral arrangements but never cries. When the caterer is late, this man starts yelling at people. Anger masks other emotions when we don't know how to experience or express those emotions.

REGULATE ANGER EXERCISE 4: Calm Your Anger

This exercise helps you modulate your anger to productive levels for relationship and expression. If you tend to stay angry for a long time, or if your anger goes away while you're distracted but then comes back strong once you're reminded about what made you angry, this is the exercise for you.

Since anger responds to a range of challenges, including unlikely ones such as being attacked by a bear, anger can show up at levels of intensity that aren't helpful in relationships. To skillfully express anger in relationships, modulate your anger appropriately to the situation.

You can modulate your anger by physically practicing a de-escalation process. It is good to talk about this exercise with the people you live with so they know what you're doing and how to respond when you're practicing it.

Start by going to a place in your home where you've gotten angry in the past. Imagine the physical feelings and the emotions that signal the beginning of your anger, such as tightness in your chest, lowered eyebrows, and shallow breathing. Now follow these steps:

1. **Say calmly, "Time out" or "I'm getting angry. I'm going to go cool off."** This cues you to begin your de-escalation process. It also lets the people around you know what you're doing.

2. **Move to a safe space.** If you have room in your home for it, go to a place where you can be alone and close a door. This might be a bathroom or closet. Go outside your home if necessary. Lock the door if applicable. This isolation helps you feel safe enough to calm your anger.

3. **Physically soothe your anger.** Try stretches, short-burst cardio like running up and down stairs or wind sprints (not punching a punching bag or practicing martial arts),

or strong sensory experiences like smelling a strong odor (mint, lemon, and lavender are common ones). Strong, intense physical activity can help the primitive parts of your brain believe that you "fought off the bear" so you can calm down now. Since smell is closely associated with memory and emotion, strong smells are a powerful way of changing emotional experiences. Strong physical experiences can also help. Try holding ice cubes (do so for two minutes, taking a two-minute break between cubes), a hot shower, or even snapping a rubber band on your wrist. Repeat these efforts or try different ones until your muscles are relaxed, your breathing is deeper and more even, and your face has relaxed to neutral.

4. **Emotionally soothe your anger.** Ask yourself, "What need isn't getting met? How was I vulnerable there?" Write down the answers to these questions. When you reconnect with family later, share the answers with them so that they understand your needs. Check your entitlement in the process. Just because you have a need doesn't mean other people (even people who love you) are responsible for meeting that need. You want to be careful that you aren't telling your family, "Meet my needs or I'll unleash my anger on you."

5. **Mindfully soothe your anger.** Practice mindfulness meditation, yoga, or deep breathing. There are plenty of apps on the market now to guide you through this process if you have a smartphone. There are also tutorials and videos online or free meditation classes in some meditation centers if you qualify for a scholarship.

6. **Socially soothe your anger.** Reach out to a friend. If you have a friend outside of the family who is willing to be a support for you, reach out to them. Feeling like you're not

alone and that you have help is a great way to reduce the feelings of helplessness, being trapped, or hopelessness that may create anger.

Many people, especially in the smartphone age, like to use technology to distract themselves enough to calm down. Using distractions—like watching cat videos, playing app games, or getting on social media to calm down—functions a little like changing the channel on your emotional TV. You shift your attention away from what made you upset, and as long as you're focusing on that distraction, you won't feel the anger. Once you remember the thing that made you angry, you may get angry all over again. If your distractions are effective but your anger comes back when you think about the inciting event, I recommend trying one of the other self-soothing methods mentioned in this section. Then start thinking about the anger-causing event again and see if that helps you stay calmer.

REGULATE ANGER EXERCISE 5: Express Your Anger Skillfully

If you feel certain that your anger is justified and that you don't generally have an anger problem but that you need help with expressing your righteous anger skillfully, this is the exercise for you.

Once you've weathered the acute manifestation of your anger, it would be easy to apologize for reacting and not talk more about it. The needs and vulnerabilities that brought out your anger still exist. Don't take the destructive path of avoiding your anger. At best, avoiding anger leads to resentment. At worst, you'll train your anger that it only has a very small window in which to effect change, so it'll become more intense and more unmanageable in order to better protect you in those moments.

If your anger has a strong message that says you need to be protected, listen to that message. If you really believe that your partner has committed an injustice or violated a boundary, consider what you are asking for. Let's imagine that you caught your partner having sex with another person and you had a clearly defined monogamous relationship. Anger might be appropriate, but how are you going to express it? There are five ways to express anger skillfully:

1. Physically express your anger in a moderated way, which might include a slightly raised voice, muscle tension (but not physically threatening or menacing postures), and turning or moving away from the other person.

2. Declare your feelings: "I am so angry with you!"

3. State the injustice: "You have just broken our relationship agreements!"

4. Request what would restore justice for you: "I'm not about to pretend that everything is okay with us. Please leave the house tonight, end that relationship, and get an STI check." If the person refuses to grant your requests, decide how you will keep yourself safe. This prevents your anger from being controlling, abusive anger.

5. Declare what you need to keep yourself safe: "I won't talk with you about our relationship until you can tell me that you've done all of those things."

In other words, this expression of anger is about making your feelings clear with nonverbal and verbal expression; sharing your perceptions; and asking for your needs to be met while maintaining control of your own behavior without physically, emotionally, or conversationally controlling or threatening the other person.

DEFUSING JEALOUSY

Although jealousy is a form of anger, the manifestations of this emotion in our culture and in men's sexual violence in particular merits special consideration. The root of all jealousy has two parts: (1) entitlement and (2) denial of what is and is not in your control. Polyamorous author Deborah Anapol describes five types of jealousy.[4] Let's look at them now, but notice that entitlement and denial of helplessness are at the root of each manifestation.

Possessive Jealousy

Possessive jealousy is the desire to have something for yourself. When it comes to relationships, this could refer to your partner's attention, flirtation, sexuality, or many other things. Jealousy arises when you believe something belongs to you that doesn't. You get jealous when your partner notices the sex appeal of another person because deep down you believe you alone are entitled to your partner's sexual attention.

What if your partner cheated despite a relationship agreement of monogamy? That's a case of injustice. You might be feeling anger rather than jealousy (see page 175). In contrast, possessive jealousy denies your choices. Jealous people tend to focus on what their partner did, what they might do, and what they fear. But your partner is totally free. You have no control over them; and they can cheat, flirt, or violate your boundaries if they want to. When jealousy causes you to focus on your partner's behavior, you give up your power to soothe your feelings and restore a sense of security. In that way, possessive jealousy motivates you to tell the other person how bad they are because of their behavior instead of acknowledging that you can't control their behavior.

- To regulate feelings of jealousy, it is crucial to pause and ask yourself: *What am I going to do?*

- If your partner broke your relationship agreements: *Do I want to try to repair my relationship with a partner who damaged it?*

- If your partner is denying the validity of your jealousy: *Can I relax into trusting my partner? Can I identify what I need to do for myself so I can feel secure?*

These questions can help you regulate the impotent rage of possessive jealousy by disputing the entitlement behind it, then redirecting your attention to your responses and your behaviors.

Fear Jealousy

This type of jealousy manifests when you are afraid that your partner's interest in someone or something else threatens your place in their life. You might think that you'll "lose" your partner. You imagine that, having lost your partner, your life is "over" or "wasted," or that you'll "never find someone else."

Fear jealousy exhibits entitlement because it reveals that you think it's your partner's job to give your life meaning and value. It shows that you don't think very much of yourself without your partner, yet despite your low estimation of your value, you think your partner should stay with you forever. A temporary balm for this type of jealousy is asking your partner for reassurance. Please do ask your partner for that balm. But most likely, because the root of fear jealousy is your insecurity, a feeling of helplessness to hold their fidelity, the jealousy will return.

The antidote to the entitlement behind fear jealousy is making yourself independently vibrant and alive so that you know what you bring to your partner, and have confidence in your ability to attract a new partner if your current partner leaves you for someone new and shiny.

Keep in mind that losing or keeping your partner has never been in your control. No matter how loving you are or how devoted a coparent, your partner could leave you. They are free. They could also die suddenly. Yes, being left by your partner for someone else brings feelings of sadness and pain (see page 165). But jealousy motivates you to try to control the other person (which you can't) to prevent feeling helpless instead of figuring out how to land on your feet.

If this is your type of jealousy, use the following questions to develop a plan for how you would cope if your partner suddenly died or left you. For each time frame, identify three responses. Don't spend too much time focusing on the practical details. Focus on the emotional coping.

- First day or two. Who would you call, and how would you grieve the shock and sadness?

- First couple of weeks. How much time off work would you take, who else would you call and lean on, and how would you begin the early adjustments to your housing situation?

- First couple of months. What would you do to give yourself time to grieve while you maintain the requirements of work and family?

- The long term. What would you need to do to begin living fully?

When you have confidence in your capacity to put this plan into action, you will have more capacity to face your fears instead of being jealous and trying to control others.

Competition Jealousy

This type of jealousy focuses on the fear that someone might be better than you in some way. But, of course, someone out there *is* better at something than you! Even if you happen to be a gold medal–winning athlete, being the top athlete in the world is only going to last so long. Someone else will almost certainly be smarter; and more successful, emotionally savvy, and attractive than you because none of us could ever possibly be the best at everything all at once and forever.

You are afraid of competition because deep down, given your flaws, you believe you are not worthy of love. This jealousy exhibits entitlement because it motivates you to control another person's attraction to manage your insecurity. To compensate for feeling unworthy of love, competition jealousy motivates you to earn your partner's attention or to get confirmation that you have it. This puts you in a never-ending cycle of performance, because no external achievement will make the shame behind your insecurity go away.

If you're experiencing competition jealousy, use a modified version of the unpleasant focus exercise (see page 106). Notice something about the person you're jealous of that they don't have and you do. If they're younger and more attractive, maybe you have wisdom and experience. If they're more successful, maybe you are better at maintaining relationships. Reassure yourself that everyone has strengths and weaknesses, and what you have is something that someone wants.

Whether your partner wants you or someone else is not in your control. However, you *can* control your reactions. Instead of focusing on what you don't have, find security and confidence in what you do have.

Ego Jealousy

Ego jealousy describes how you feel when you aren't necessarily upset that your partner is attracted to someone else, but you are upset by whom your partner is interested in. You might think, "I don't know what they have that I don't; they're such an idiot." Ego jealousy focuses your attention on what other people will think about you and how their negative judgments might make you feel. Ego jealousy exhibits entitlement because your jealousy motivates you to control your partner so you won't be judged by their behavior or their desire.

One antidote to this type of jealousy is deciding that you'll protect yourself from that vulnerability. Fill in the ego gaps causing you to be scared about what other people think. For example, you could learn to say to yourself, "It's true that Jim doesn't have a college degree like I do, but he's kind and respectful. I share those qualities with him, and that's why my partner is attracted to both of us."

Another antidote is learning that someone else's behavior isn't a reflection of you. How we value others is about the person. For example, you can respect someone even when they live in a country whose government you don't agree with. You can like someone even when you don't like the company they work for. Someone can like you even when your partner does something they don't respect. Your partner's behavior isn't a reflection of your worth.

Stay focused on how you will respond to your partner's behavior. If people associate you or your worth with your partner's behavior, decide how you will insulate yourself against that person's judgments. Don't try to control your partner to avoid taking responsibility for your behavior in these circumstances.

Exclusion Jealousy

When you feel insecure because you're left out of a part of your partner's life, that's exclusion jealousy. You can also call it fear-of-missing-out (FOMO) jealousy. It's when you get upset that your partner takes a work trip, engages in a hobby, or goes to a social event without you. There may not even be another person in the picture; your partner is just not exclusively focused on you.

Exclusion jealousy exhibits entitlement because it reveals an underlying belief that you are entitled to be a part of this aspect of your partner's life. Your partner is an independent person with a life, interests, and capacities of their own, some of which you cannot share.

Exclusion jealousy denies your responsibility in a couple of ways. First, rather than building a full and engaging life of your own, you focus on limiting your partner's full and engaging life. Second, your jealousy blames your partner's behavior for "wronging" you without your identifying what your needs are, how they weren't met, and how to seek a resolution with your partner.

Instead of saying, "You should have invited me on your work trip with you," taking responsibility sounds like this: "That work trip sounds like a lot of fun. I'm sad that I missed it. I'd like to come with you next time if that's possible. Don't worry, though. I know you're really focused on your career there. If I can't come, maybe I'll throw a big guys' weekend. Then when you come back, we'll both have some fun adventures to share."

■

The cultural root of the entitlement inside of jealousy is the myth that your partner belongs to you. Yes, a kind and loving partner will seek to meet your relationship agreements, but a kind and loving partner is still a separate person. You cannot stop, legislate, or control their internal experience. Yes, a kind and loving partner will seek to treat you so that you don't feel insecure and jealous, but a kind and loving partner may trigger those insecurities despite being committed to you. You must work through some of your insecurities on your own. Instead of doubling-down on the cultural myth that your partner is supposed to be *everything* to you, soothe your own emotional experiences of vulnerability, and communicate those vulnerabilities with kindness.

Jealousy is the emotion that leads to many of the violent behaviors that men commit against their loved ones and partners. Even if you don't go that far, if you don't root out the entitlement and emotional control at the base of this feeling, you may still hurt your partners and damage your relationships.

MANAGING GUILT

Despite our best efforts, we sometimes hurt our partners and damage our relationships. When we notice that, we can experience guilt. Unmanaged guilt can cause us to emotionally implode, which hurts ourselves, our partners, and our relationships even more. So, managing guilt is an important process.

First, let's distinguish between guilt, shame, and fault. I can feel *guilty* if I was in a car accident and someone got hurt. I recognize that actions I took (e.g., driving) caused someone to get hurt. I can be at *fault* in a car accident or not. I feel *shame* when I believe that I'm bad and my bad nature caused the car accident.

Guilt is the negative feeling we experience when we acknowledge doing something that hurt someone else. Guilt motivates us to repair the relationship with the person who got hurt. Guilt makes us want to take actions that prevent people from getting hurt in that way again. In the car-accident example, this might mean I apologize, take a defensive-driving course, or drive slower in general.

Fault is when we could have known better, could have anticipated how our behavior would affect the other person, or made choices that we now recognize were flawed. We can see choices we made or didn't make that caused the harm. In the car-accident example, I would be at fault if I were speeding and I think that's what caused the accident. Fault is a cognitive assessment. Guilt is a feeling.

Acknowledging fault in a relationship is helpful for repairing trust. It allows you to tell your partner that you see the choices you made that hurt them, and what you're going to do differently next time.

Sometimes we have guilt without fault. Especially in new relationships, we can easily cause hurt by joking about something the other person is sensitive to or not meeting the other person's needs because we don't know them yet. Guilt motivates us to improve how we navigate the relationship. Guilt helps us to take responsibility for improving our actions. We hope that taking this responsibility will elicit forgiveness from the people we hurt.

Shame is an entirely separate emotional experience. Guilt is feeling bad for what we did. Shame is feeling bad about who or what we are. In the car-accident example, I might say, "I'm such an idiot! I'm always doing stupid things. This car accident shows again that I can't do anything right." For more on managing sexual shame, see page 60. Now that we've separated guilt and shame, let's turn our attention to managing guilt.

EXERCISE: Manage Guilt in a Current Relationship

One common cause of guilt is when you realize you did something wrong in a relationship. To manage this type of guilt, follow these four steps:

1. **Manage your own emotional experience.** Write in a journal, spend quiet time alone, or reach out to a friend (see "Expressing Sadness," page 199). If you don't do this step thoroughly enough, your feelings of guilt (and not the hurt person's pain) become the focus when you engage with that person again. You won't be able to repair the relationship because you'll be asking the person you hurt to take care of you. This is like hitting someone and asking them to comfort you. It doesn't work.

2. **Apologize.** A good apology isn't complicated, but it can be difficult to do. Ask if the other person is willing to tell

you about their pain. If they are, listen to them. Then paraphrase what you hear back to them. Describe what you did and how that hurt them. Then express your vulnerable feelings that come from knowing that you hurt them. Emphasize that you care about the other person's well-being. For example: "So, if I'm hearing you right, when I commented on how hot that movie character was, you felt I was saying you weren't as hot because I don't tell you that I find you hot anymore. You felt insulted by my comments. Is that right?" If they agree that you got your empathy right, move to the apology: "I'm sorry that I hurt you in that way. I don't want to hurt you with my comments. I'm really sad that I did hurt you with what I said. I'd like to talk about how we can prevent that from happening in the future." Apologies don't always involve accepting fault. Apologies are about recognizing the hurt and expressing sadness about having caused the hurt. You can apologize for accidents or unintended consequences, too.

3.   **Create a personal- or relationship-improvement plan.** When you are in a calm space, identify what you'll do differently next time. Identify what you did, the reasons that you did it, and a behavior that you'd prefer to do instead. Review this with your partner, and ask them if your goal behavior would have been better for them.

Be specific. For example, if your regrettable behavior was saying that the movie character was hot (because it reminded your partner you don't say that to them), then your goal might be to tell your partner more often how attracted you are to them. Next, decide what will help you move toward the goal behavior. For example, post signs around your home or set alarms on your phone reminding you of the goal behavior. Or give yourself a small piece of chocolate every time you put the goal into practice.

In some situations, such as accidental harm, the personal-improvement process is about staying aware of your partner's vulnerabilities. In this case, your goal behavior might be to review a list of your partner's needs or sensitivities so you remember them. If you don't know what you could do differently, ask the hurt person.

4. **Follow through on the personal- or relationship-improvement plan.** If nothing changes from incident to incident, your partner will stop being moved by the vulnerable feelings in your apology. You need to actually do things differently to cultivate trust in future apologies for other issues. By making changes, you maintain your partner's trust that hurts will be mended and your relationship can improve. If a couple of weeks pass and despite your efforts nothing has changed, acknowledge that: "I know that since that argument a couple of weeks ago we posted signs around the house saying 'cherish him' to remind me not to call you names when we fight. Since then, I've still done it a couple of times. I want to acknowledge that and to let you know what I'm doing differently this week to make sure I actually make this change."

One improvement process is "I can't change this. I need you to change your expectation." Only give your partner this message when your nature is the root cause of the behavior. For example, "Since I am late all the time in every aspect of my life from doctors' appointments to work to hanging out with friends, I really can't promise you that I'm going to be on time in the future. I think this is how I am. Can you accept that?" The relationship improvement you're asking for is a change in your partner's expectations. The reality is that "No, I can't accept that" is a very possible and scary answer. If you're doing this right, you'll feel vulnerable asking your partner to accept your faults. That's also why you should do this as little as possible. If every time you hurt your partner, your response is "Live with it or leave because this is how I am," then one day, your partner might leave.

■

The #MeToo movement has helped us men review past actions in a new light. You may be feeling guilty about behaviors from a relationship that you aren't in anymore, and you can learn to manage these feelings, too. If you feel guilty about not living up to the value of consent in the past, try these steps:

1. **Manage your own emotional experience.** This is the same first step as when you feel guilty for behavior in a current relationship (see page 189). Look there for ways to regulate strong feelings. Strong negative feelings—even those that tip into shame—are common, especially when being a good man is important to you.

2. **Tell someone else.** You free yourself from carrying the burden of your history and behavior alone when you tell someone else about it. Stay focused on the description of the emotional experience that you remember in the person you hurt, and the emotions you have now as you're looking back on it. This may lead to relief for finally letting out what happened.

3. **Make amends by doing something concrete in the world.** For example, donate to an organization that teaches consent, such as the nonprofit Love Is Respect; or helps people heal from sexual violence, such as the Rape, Abuse, and Incest National Network (RAINN). Helping these organizations with money or increasing their visibility on social media can help you feel like you're doing something to counteract the pain you caused. (I don't recommend volunteering for organizations like this when

you have a challenge with those behaviors; you might not make a good volunteer.) If you're concerned about finding a good match, ask your confidant from step 2 to help you decide whether the amends that you're considering could be harmful rather than helpful. You can also make amends by passing on what you learn. Teach your sons, nephews, or other men in your social circles how not to repeat your mistakes. You did what you did because you weren't taught or expected to uphold consent. Passing on what you have learned means changing that experience for the next generation. It attempts to change the underlying causes of nonconsensual sexual behavior for other men. It attempts to protect partners of the men in your life from the kind of harm that your partner experienced from you.

4. **Create a personal- or relationship-improvement plan.** This step is the same as it is when you are in a relationship (see page 190).

5. **Follow through on the personal- or relationship-improvement plan.** This step is the same as it is when you are in a relationship (see page 190).

These steps will be unsatisfying to a lot of men. Many men want to reach out to the people they've harmed with their poor consent practices. In most cases, this is a bad idea because there may be many unintended negative consequences, such as triggering negative memories, trauma, or fear in the other person. Before you reach out, think about the following:

- **Do you want to reach out so that you can feel like a good person again, or so you can offer an apology and healing?** Most men imagine that their now-enlightened confession of wrongdoing will lead to a heartfelt conversation in which the person he abused will thank him, forgive him, and praise him for how brave he is to face his demons. If this is your motivation, please don't reach out. That motivation is all about *you*—your feelings, your needs, and your ability to sleep better at night. Therefore, it doesn't provide healing to the other person. If reaching out to the other person is about acknowledging what you did, that *might* provide the other person with some healing. If you think it's the right thing to do even if the person ends up yelling at you about what an asshole you are, you might have a reason to reach out.

- **Could reaching out to the other person retraumatize them?** It's highly possible that your contact could harm them further. If you haven't had contact with the other person, you have no way of knowing for sure, so don't contact them. If you have an ongoing social relationship with the person whom you hurt, do you really know whether approaching them will or won't retraumatize them? If not, don't reach out. Somehow, that person has found a way to cope with being around a person who hurt them. Reminding them how you hurt them may shatter their coping mechanisms.

- **What if the other person doesn't want to talk?** Especially if you are in a position of power over the other person, trying to have this conversation can put them in an impossible corner. They may tell you what you want to hear just to get you to back off. They may fear telling you that they don't want to speak with you. They may fear that if they listen but don't forgive you, you will retaliate. Don't reach out to someone whom you have power over.

After considering all these important questions, some men will still want to communicate with the person they hurt. *But I still don't recommend reaching out to someone that you hurt.* If you are going to reach out despite that recommendation, at least follow these instructions. Send the person a one-sided brief communication that offers a consent-based conversation. For example, send the person an email like this:

Dear [Name],

I've been reflecting on my past behavior, and I believe I owe you an apology. If you are open to communication about that, please let me know. If you don't reply, I won't contact you about it again.

This process puts the power in the other person's hands. It doesn't open more memories than those that resurface from your reaching out in the first place. If the person doesn't reply, don't broach the topic again.

If the person does agree to meet, do so on their terms. Meet where they ask, and follow the process they request as long as it also protects your safety. Then identify your behavior, state why it was wrong, and say you're sorry for hurting them. Don't add any explanations unless asked. Even if asked for an explanation, end the explanation by repeating that you are responsible for your actions, and what you did was wrong. Allow space for the person you hurt to express their pain to you. Validate and empathize with their pain. Don't defend yourself.

This is an emotional and a relational process. It does not attempt to protect you from any criminal or civil liabilities for your behaviors. Those risks are up to you to consider.

■

Guilt is an emotion that we may not want to share. Keeping our guilt hidden feels safer, but it also creates distance between ourselves and others. Hiding our guilt prevents us from freely receiving, giving, and teaching reconciliation. To resolve guilt, we must air our faults to others and make some kind of restitution. Talking about our guilt is hard, but living in isolating silence is worse. Hiding avoids our duty to protect our communities from those harms again. By talking about our faults and learning from them, we can teach our communities how to prevent similar harm from happening to others.

SOOTHING SEXUAL SHAME

Shame makes you want to hide, curl up into a ball, and isolate. Remember, the cause of shame is believing you are bad. So when you are ashamed, you cannot imagine a path to being forgiven even if you desperately want one. This makes you dependent and desperate for other people to accept you despite how bad you think you are. Even when people do accept you, shame keeps you afraid. You fear that, if people are reminded of how bad you are, they'll stop loving you. So, you hide your "badness" from others to the best of your ability, including lying and omitting. The lies and omissions then become the source of more shame, and the cycle repeats with increased intensity.

We've discussed how when someone is shocked or disgusted by your sexual desire or identity, you might feel ashamed of your sexuality. Since you didn't choose your desire or your identity, the other person's disgust can easily lead you to fear that you have to choose between being authentic and having a relationship. Naturally, you want to be sexually authentic, but to be in a relationship with certain people, you may be tempted to compartmentalize your sexuality. The secrecy about your sexuality can lead you to believe that you're bad because of your desire. You may also fear that the truth will be discovered. That combination of secrecy and the belief that you are "bad" is often how sexual shame shows up.

Soothing sexual shame requires two things. First, you must find the right context to share the truth about your sexuality. If you are afraid that some part of you is bad and worthless, you must talk about it. Therapists, friends, lovers, and close community members can be good people to confide in about your shame. Skillful supporters won't deny your shame by saying, "But you're so great." Skillful supporters will empathize with your vulnerability and be vulnerable back. Most people have something they feel shame about. Shame thrives on the fear that if we're "discovered," we'll be ejected from our communities. When we confide in a select group of people about our shame and then experience a deepened relationship instead of rejection, shame loses much of its power.

Once we've had a couple of these experiences, our minds begin working on the second key to soothing shame: believing that we are good regardless of our sexual desire or identity. Reviewing the section from chapter 5 about healthy sexual expression (see page 137) can help you figure out how to express your desire and identity. If you express your desire in healthy ways, then what is there to be ashamed of?

Brené Brown provides an excellent and more exhaustive guide to shame and how to overcome it in her book *Daring Greatly: How the Courage to Be Vulnerable Transforms the Way We Live, Love, Parent, and Lead.* Although I hope what I've written can help you overcome shame, it can be a difficult weed to root out of our psyches. Consider reading Brown's book if you need more support.

FACING FEAR

The narrow roles and experiences allowed for men in patriarchal culture don't allow for men to experience fear, but they sure do cause a lot of fear. Because our value is equated with our manliness and sexual prowess, men are afraid of sexual rejection, the end of a relationship, failing to find someone to open our hearts to again (because our partners are often the only people we do open our hearts to), being cheated on, losing a job, being insulted, being called unmanly, not pleasing our partner, losing an erection, not being able to orgasm, orgasming too fast, masturbating, having the porn we watch exposed, and so many more things.

If you face and regulate your fears, then you can soothe them. When you don't accept and regulate your fears, you'll likely become defensive and angry when you're afraid. That can lead to trying to control other people's behavior to prevent your fears from coming true. In other words, if you don't face your fears, you may make other people afraid of you. Many men also experience anxiety. Anxiety is caused when you try to control something out of your control or when your mind loops over endless possible negative outcomes.

Here's the great news about fears generated from our fragile destructive masculinity or from anxiety—there's a relatively simple solution to these experiences: face the fear and soothe your emotional response at the same time. Here are three tools for helping you do just that.

1. **Set the process in motion.** For example, if you're afraid of having a conversation with your partner about something that is bothering you in the relationship, then start the process. You might say, "Hey, there's something that I want to talk with you about. Do you have time tonight to sit and chat?" When you sit down together, it'll be harder to avoid the conversation.

2. **Identify and scrutinize your fears.** In many cases, we are so caught up in feeling afraid that we don't really name what we're afraid of. Once we name the fear, we often realize that our fears aren't very realistic. Afraid your partner will leave you? Your committed partner of many years will not leave you for asking for a small need. We often realize that what we're trying to avoid is actually already happening. For example, "I'm afraid of talking about why I'm irritable because then my partner will know I have weaknesses." Your partner already knows you have weaknesses because you've been irritable.

3. **Plan to face your fears.** A good plan includes identifying how you'll prepare, what type of support you'll need, how you'll tolerate the fears while you face them, and how you'll recover after you've faced your fears.

When you regularly face your fears, you build resilience to face life as it is. You will still be afraid, but fear won't hold you back from being the kind of man you want to be.

EXPRESSING SADNESS

Many men have difficulty regulating sadness because they don't let it out or show it, so it rests heavy on their hearts and never leaves. Sadness isn't bad; it points to what you love. You are sad when your children grow up and move out. You are sad when your loved ones die. You are sad when your relationships end. You are sad when you depart from the people you care about. Sadness means you love something; men are allowed to love, too. To express what you're sad about, try talking to a friend about what you love about it. Here are some examples:

- "I'm going to miss my son when he's away at college. I've come to respect him so much, and I get such joy seeing him become a man of integrity and kindness."

- "My dad loved me so much. He didn't have a lot of role models for saying it or showing it, but I always knew that he cared about me by how he said, 'It's so good to see you' when I'd visit."

- "Don't get me wrong, I'm glad the relationship is over, but it was nice to be able to count on having someone in bed at night when I went to sleep. Not being alone felt so good that I was willing to put up with all the bad stuff in the relationship just to avoid it."

When you state what you love, you'll be validating the experience of your sadness because you'll bring to mind that what you love is changing or ending. Once you've identified and expressed what you love, try identifying the reason why you're sad:

- "I know that it's time for my son to move away, but I'll miss him."

- "I'm sad my dad died. I'll never hear him say how good it is to see me again, and I'll never hear him say that he loves me."

- "I'm sad about being alone in bed now."

If you're opening your heart, you'll feel the sadness rising in your body. Your throat may feel constricted, your eyes may water, your face may turn downward, and you may bend your torso inward.

The final skill for regulating sadness by expressing it is to keep breathing when this feeling of sadness arises. This is particularly good when we're feeling grief and sadness over losing something we love. When people try to stop feeling sad, they stop breathing in deeply, may stop breathing entirely, and exhale shallowly. Men tend to be masters of this technique. To allow sadness to flow, let your breath flow. Breathe in deeply. Allow your breath to shudder. Exhale fully. If your face constricts in a grimace, you're probably doing it right.

If you've held your sadness in for a long time, you may fear that it won't stop. It will. Face the fear of your sadness by letting it out.

ACCEPTING PAIN

The old cultural message is that if we are strong, manly men, we can prevent pain for ourselves, our loved ones, and our community. It says we can love but not get hurt if we're just strong and competent enough. Myths like this are objectively false and counter to reality.

Life includes pain. Your competence will never stop that. This is the first noble truth of Buddhism: life is suffering. It is a core tenet of existential philosophy and therapy: life leads to death; and includes suffering, disconnection, and meaninglessness. No matter how manly, powerful, competent, rich, or successful you are, you will experience pain in relationships, your loved ones will experience pain, and you are powerless to stop it.

Inside of this truth is the seed of liberation: if your competence cannot prevent harm and pain, then perhaps pain isn't your fault. If you will inevitably experience pain in loving relationships, then perhaps despite the pain they caused you, your lover still loves you. You can relax and set down the heavy, impossible burden of destructive masculinity. Instead of walling yourself off and isolating yourself so you don't hurt anyone, you are allowed to love despite knowing it will hurt. Instead of trying to punish others for causing you pain or controlling others to prevent pain, you can feel your pain, be sad about it, and be comforted by people who are also in pain. You can be part of your family and community instead of being a lone soldier fighting an unwinnable battle against the nature of existence.

How do you accept pain? It's so . . . painful. Accepting pain requires *paying attention* to it, *validating* its existence, *planning* what to do about it, and *acting* on the choice. Here are some examples:

- I'm feeling hurt (paying attention). I tried to do everything my partner wanted for their birthday, but they're still disappointed (validating). I'm going to comfort them, if they'll let me, and try to learn more about their needs (planning). Getting up, approaching my partner, and offering to talk about their disappointment puts the plan into action (acting).

- I can see that you're hurt because I snapped at you (paying attention). That makes sense (validating). I know you were trying to have a good day with me. How about if I eat and take a shower to emotionally reset, and when I return, we'll try to start this day over again (planning)? Assuming the other person agrees to the plan, then eating and showering puts the plan into action (acting).

- I'm hurting because my mother is dying and there's nothing I can do to stop it (paying attention). That would hurt most people (validating). I'm going to hold her hand and reduce her pain as much as I can while she's still here (planning). Going to face the hospital sights, sounds, and smells despite the pain puts the plan into action (acting).

As these examples show, there's nothing about the inevitability of pain that stops you from acting to reduce the pain. Despite the inevitability of pain, we don't stop striving for safety, meaning, or connection. In accepting the inevitability of pain, we can reduce the suffering.

Managing emotions begins with accepting that they exist—even big, painful emotions. Denying those emotions doesn't work. When we accept that those emotions exist, we can begin to regulate them. In that way, we don't pass the pain on to others, and we create a capacity for more compassion inside of us.

HEALING YOUR CORE WOUNDS

A couple of wise professors I had in grad school, Ann Gila and John Firman, said something in a lecture that stuck with me: "No one makes it through life without some joy, some love, some addiction, and some trauma."[5] Whether your issue is economic challenges, traumatic reinforcement of masculine gender norms, or something else, you have some trauma to attend to. The beauty and challenge of emotional and sexual relationships is that these relationships awaken our deepest wounds in life and make us vulnerable to them again. This is beautiful because the relationship then provides us with an opportunity to heal those wounds. This is challenging because it is easy to blame others for triggering our traumas, but the reason they do so is that we have opened our hearts to them.

Whatever hurt you, you can take responsibility for not spreading that hurt to others by attending to and regulating the emotions that come out of your wounds. I use the term *core wound*, Gila and Firman refer to the *primal wound*, and cognitive-behavioral psychiatrist and author David Burns refers to *self-defeating attitudes and fears*.[6] These terms point to a common tendency. We develop a central vulnerability that points to our worst fears and triggers our worst behaviors. Healing the core wound is more powerful than just repeatedly noticing and soothing the feelings when your core wound is triggered.

As a warning, I'm about to open a discussion about childhood wounds and traumas. I am inviting you to think about your own experiences of traumas. Take care of yourself as you read the following sections. Here are some examples of traumas, core wounds, and consequences:

Figure 6.3: Traumas, example core wounds, and common consequences of that wound

TRAUMA	EXAMPLE CORE WOUND	COMMON CONSEQUENCES OF THAT WOUND
Poverty	"I can never rest, or I'll starve."	Relentless work followed by feelings of entitlement and resentment. Inability to relax, or restlessness.
	"Nothing I ever do matters anyway."	Apathy, depression, giving up easily.
Neglect	"No one else will take care of me."	Loneliness. Difficulty naming your needs and letting others take care of you. Not being willing to take care of others, as in: "Why should I?"
	"If my needs aren't met for a moment, it means they'll never be met again."	Clinging, anxious behavior. Desperate attempts to get reassurance of commitment.
Isolation/ Exclusion	"I don't need anyone anyway."	Feeling trapped in a relationship. Not voicing your needs.
	"I need to be accepted or I'm nothing.	Fake behavior to ingratiate yourself with people. Fearing your faults will be seen, and you'll be rejected.
Violence	"I have to be tough, or I'll be a victim again."	Angry defenses. Being abusive or violent to partners.
	"If I do something wrong, I'll be hurt."	Conflict avoidance that prevents a relationship from improving.
Teased/ Picked on/ Put down	"They're just jealous. I'm actually the greatest."	Inability to accept criticism. Putting others down so you look better.
	"I'm unlovable."	Perfectionism. Pushing loved ones away. Depression, withdrawal.

This table of traumas is far from exhaustive. There are many core wounds from the same type of trauma. No one manifests their wounds in the same way.

EXERCISE: Identify Your Trauma, Your Core Wounds, and Their Consequences

Now it is your turn to see how your core wounds affect your relationships. Write down answers to the following questions:

1. What significant events in my life have changed my experience of people or the world in negative ways? This could be a childhood experience, a trauma during military service, illness, death of a loved one, your own or someone else's addiction, and many more experiences.

2. Even if I'm not proud of it, and even if I know it isn't literally true, what belief did I develop about myself, people, or the world to help me protect myself from that wound?

3. When I am in a relationship (romantic, friendship, or important business relationship), if someone does something that I fear confirms my belief from question 2, what do I do to protect myself from that fear?

Now that you have answers to these three questions, you're in a good position to begin doing something about it. Try the following steps:

1. **Begin unraveling your core wound by bringing some self-compassion to your initial trauma.** Wouldn't anyone be upset by alcoholic, neglectful parents? Wouldn't any child be hurt by being teased and picked on by peers? Write down what you would say to comfort a child who was hurt in the same way you were hurt.

2. **Counter the belief that you wrote down to answer question 2.** Can you identify a true and positive statement about yourself, people, or the world that counters the belief? If your negative belief was about other people, try to think of something that gives people the benefit of the doubt. If your negative belief was about yourself, try to think of something that acknowledges the good parts of yourself.

3. **Think about the behaviors that you want to do instead of the reactive behaviors that you described.** Look at your answers to question 3. Think about the kind of partner you want to be even when you are reacting to those core wounds. Write down the behaviors you aspire to here.

Working on your core wounds isn't as simple as this quick exercise. Even when you've identified your aspirations, you have a lifetime of work ahead of you to put those aspirations into practice. It's a difficult and challenging process. Consider therapy, community support, or talking with someone close about what you've encountered. Most people need help with figuring out what their core wounds are and how to plan for healing them.

FEELING EMPATHY

Despite what the cultural myths say, men are just as capable of empathy as people of other genders, and they learn empathy in the same ways. Empathy skills come from the ability to connect with yourself and to be kind to your own emotions. Empathy rests on the foundations you've built throughout this book. You start by acknowledging your own hurts and wounds, then noticing your own needs and emotions, then regulating your emotional experience and taking care of yourself. With your emotional experience regulated, you can pay attention to another person's emotional experience, resonate with it, and repeat it back to them.

Your capacity to do so is limited by your ability to pay attention to and take care of your own most difficult emotions. The people I know who are the most empathetic have been wounded and hurt by others and have worked to heal their wounds. Because they know what it's like to feel pain and how to tolerate their own pain, they can acknowledge, connect to, and tolerate pain in others. Without the ability to feel our own pain, we cut ourselves off from the rest of our emotions and therefore the emotions of others. Empathy doesn't mean "I know how you feel." It means "I feel our shared humanity."

Men are not trained to pay attention to our emotions, especially our vulnerable emotions. Often, our experience is that, if we pay attention to our vulnerable emotions, we'll be attacked or belittled. Because we aren't skilled with expressing the empathy we do feel, we avoid it because we don't want to get it wrong and damage our loved ones. We can face these fears. We can learn these skills. We can express our love with empathy and strengthen our relationships.

Step 1: Notice Your Emotional Experience

The first step in strengthening empathy skills is attending to your emotional experience. I'm referring to the actual physical sensations. This might be the feeling of liquid movement as the bottom drops out of your stomach in fear, the tension that quickens inside your chest in anger, the changes of breath and heartbeat that characterize anxiety, the drop of energy in the muscles of your arms and chest that characterize helplessness, or the furrowed brow of confusion or frustration. These physical processes are what we're labeling when we use an emotion word. Emotions are physical experiences. Other people have similar sensations inside of them. When you pay attention to your own emotional experience, as you learned to do in the "Get Mindful in Five Minutes" exercise (see page 128), you'll better understand what someone is telling you when they tell you about theirs.

Step 2: Regulate Your Emotional Experience

To exhibit empathy, you need to notice the emotions of another person. When you regulate your own emotional experience, you create room for your attention to focus on that person. For example, during an argument with your partner, if you're scared that they'll break up with you, you need to breathe and soothe your fear before you'll be able to listen carefully to what your partner is telling you about their pain. If you're having a hard time regulating your emotions, reread the sections in this chapter that correspond to the emotions you're feeling. Be sure to do the exercises even if you've tried them once. Some emotions require a lot of practice to soothe effectively.

Some people think that empathy means allowing your emotions to flow freely while you react to someone else's emotions. That's not the case. You need enough connection to your feelings so that they are affected by the other person and you can express that connection, but not so much that your emotional reaction becomes the focus of the conversation. Skillful empathy keeps the attention on the person who is sharing their feelings throughout the entire process, which means you need to regulate your emotional experience the entire time, too.

Step 3: Notice and Ask about Emotions

When you pay attention to other people, you don't know their emotions directly—you only get clues about their emotional experience. So even if you notice the physical and vocal cues of an emotional experience, you may not know which emotion or why. Some people cry when angry, for example. Some people raise their voice when they're sad. Some people withdraw when they are happy. Other people's emotions don't work the exact same way as yours.

So, when you see cues that someone is having an emotional experience, get curious.

Try to make explicit observations about your partner with respect to what you see. Then ask what it means. That way, you'll draw their attention to what you are noticing before asking about it. Here are some examples.

- "How are you feeling?"

- "I'm hearing the volume of your voice increase and the tension in your voice. It seems like you are angry. Is that right?"

- "I notice you collapsed around your chest and exhaled abruptly. What is that telling me about how you're feeling?"

By asking, you'll allow the other person to interpret their emotions. This avoids the trap a lot of men fall in to of telling the other person how they feel. Your empathy skills will be inaccurate, especially as you are first learning to express empathy. So, stay humble, and start by just observing what you see and asking about it out loud.

Step 4: Ask about and Listen to the Person's Emotional Experience and Story

As you get more skilled at empathy in general and as you get to know a specific person like your partner better, you may be able to form ideas about how they're feeling based on what you observe and past experience. This allows your humility to go one step further. You might ask, "Did I just say something offensive?" If they reply no, you go straight to observation: "I noticed that you turned away when I was talking. Sometimes, that means I've said something that hurt you. Did I?"

Stay humble even as you improve in this skill. The declaration "You're hurt" is much less likely to be effective (even if it is correct) than the humble question "Are you hurt?" Inquiries demonstrate to the other person that you aren't just trying to use knowledge of them to judge, control, or manipulate them. Asking if you're empathizing accurately demonstrates that your goal is understanding. I'll cover this as a communication tool in "Inquiry: Please Help Me Understand You" (see page 220).

When you're empathizing, the person you empathize with may tell you why they feel how they feel. This is important to pay close attention to for two reasons. First and foremost, the reasons they feel something can help you learn how to treat them in the future. Second, hearing another person's reasons for their feelings often creates defensiveness in the listener. For example, imagine if you forgot to pick up something for your partner at the grocery store and they say, "I feel so hurt and angry because it shows you don't care about me."

A common knee-jerk reaction to such a statement is immediately constructing two counterpoints. The first is defensive: "I do care about you." The second is argumentative or judgmental: "Just because I forgot to get a little thing one time, I don't care about you?! That's ridiculous." These reactions are not helpful when it comes to empathy. This is why regulating your emotional reactions is such an important part of the empathy process.

The person's story describes their interpretation of the experience. It says what they think the experience might mean. That story in their mind is telling you about their vulnerabilities, not an accurate story about you. In this case, the partner is telling you they feel hurt, angry, and unloved.

Empathy means focusing your attention on how the other person feels and why they feel that way (including their thought processes). Empathy doesn't focus on whether you intended to create those feelings, whether the reasons for your behavior are the ones they perceive, or even whether the concrete series of events actually happened the way they're remembering it. Empathizing is not a time to correct the other person.

Step 5: Believe the Other Person

When someone answers your questions about how they are feeling and why, believe them. Even when the person's statements about their feelings seem contradictory to your observations, remember that the only expert on a person's feelings is that person.

In the example from the last step, believing the other person would mean simply acknowledging that they're feeling hurt, angry, and unloved. So, you say, "You are angry, alone, and feeling unloved. Is that right?"

Don't be afraid. Empathizing isn't telling the other person they are right about your reasons, motivations, or feelings. Your empathy demonstrates that you care. Paying attention to their feelings demonstrates that they aren't alone. Your willingness to listen will most often reduce the need for and intensity of their anger and other negative emotions.

Step 6: Feel What They're Feeling

Your partner said they feel hurt, angry, and unloved. Resonate with those feelings. How do you feel when you're hurt, angry, and unloved? Hurt might feel like an ache in your chest. Anger might cause you to feel tension in your chest and arms. Feeling unloved might feel like you've been punched in the gut, and you may be motivated to curl up in a ball.

Keep your humility intact here. Although you are having feelings similar to the other person's feelings, the reasons something makes you feel that way may be different from theirs. Maybe the other person's feelings work differently from yours. Maybe they are more likely to fight than withdraw. Your feelings will help you know that the other person is suffering. Don't assume you know how they suffer. Just allow the recognition that they are suffering and that you have suffered create a sense of shared humanity.

Always remember emotional regulation. You do want to allow yourself to be moved, but you don't want your emotions to become the center of attention. You do want to feel the fire of the other person's anger at a perceived injustice. You don't want your anger to turn into shouts and threats that the other person then has to regulate. You do want to feel your partner's sadness. You don't want to break down in tears so intense that they end up comforting *you*.

Step 7: Have Compassion for What They're Feeling

Finally, if you have really opened your heart to the existence of the other person's pain, you'll want them to suffer less. If they're angry, you'll want justice and safety for them. If they're hurt, you'll want them to feel better. If they feel lonely, you'll want them to feel connected. If they're ashamed, you'll want them to feel confident. If they're jealous, you'll want them to feel secure. Having resonated with their pain by feeling some of their pain in yourself, you'll want for them the same relief you would want if you were going through the same feelings.

This is the equalizing experience. It doesn't matter whether your partner's reasons for their feelings seem irrational to you. Whatever the cause, you want their suffering to end. Our culture falsely teaches us that, if we argue with people's pain, we can make their suffering go away. This divides us from the other person's experience. When we have compassion for what they are feeling, we connect with them. Only when we're connected can we be effective in relieving their suffering. You might say, "I can see and hear the pain you're in. I'm feeling that pain, too, because I care about you. I want your pain to end. Is there a way I can support that?"

■

These steps focus on helping you feel empathetic. Learning how to *express* that empathy to another person is another skill we'll cover shortly. First, let's go over a common concern men have about empathy: "What if I don't have empathetic feelings?"

Quite a few men believe this process of reciprocal feelings simply doesn't happen to them. These are often men who are comfortable in a traditionally masculine identity. If this matches your experience, this section is for you. Most men—even traditionally masculine men—feel empathy.

Do you watch action movies or sports? When the hero defiantly calls out, battles, and defeats the bad guy, do you feel uplifted? When your team wins an important victory, do you cheer? These feelings of exultation, joy, and energy are empathy, too. If you feel empathy in these contexts, why do you think you have a hard time feeling empathy in your relationship? The surprising revelation for most men is that they don't experience the *absence* of emotional empathy, but rather that they are *overwhelmed* by empathy.

If you are overwhelmed by empathy, you likely have one of four responses to a partner's genuine and vulnerable expression of emotion: fix it, deny it, avoid it, or stop it. If you treat your partner in this way, it's likely how you respond to your own emotions, too.

If you recognize yourself in this description, make sure you are using the skills from chapter 6. You may also benefit from some individual therapy so that someone else can help you notice when you are using these defenses against emotion and help you learn how to open up to them. Once you can regulate your emotional response to your partner enough to be there for them, you'll be ready to try the skills in this chapter again.

EXPRESSING EMPATHY

Imagine how badly a conversation would go if someone listened to you describe your feelings and then said, "I understand how you feel, *but...*" Even if the person really does understand, you wouldn't feel understood. How different would it be if the person said, "I hear that you're angry. You didn't think I was listening to you because I interrupted you, and you found that disrespectful. Is that right?"

They haven't agreed that they disrespect you, but they expressed empathy by accurately seeing what you are going through.

In other words, your feeling of empathy by itself isn't enough. You must also express your empathy so other people can feel your connection with them. Expressing empathy is key to creating and maintaining an emotional connection.

This isn't about getting the words right. Sometimes, this isn't even about understanding at all. You could say, "I don't think I really understand, but I can see that you're in distress, and I want to ease your pain." This is skillful empathy even without accurate understanding. To express empathy, here's a simple formula.

State the event that affected the person

+

recognize how they felt

+

explain how you feel, knowing their feelings

=

expressing empathy

Here are some examples, all of which presume that you've already checked your ideas about how the other person is feeling or heard from them directly how they are feeling.

- "When I didn't follow through on our conversation last week (event), you felt sad, confused, and angry (their feeling). I feel disappointed in myself, too (your feeling)."

- "When I hear how your boss treated you (event), it makes sense to me that you're feeling depressed, demotivated, and disempowered at work (their feeling). I feel sad hearing it, too (your feeling), because I don't want (your feeling) anyone to treat you that way."

- "When we were having sex, you were experiencing pain, and I kept thrusting (event). You felt scared and mistrusting (their feeling) because you thought I knew you were in pain, but I didn't care to stop (their feeling). I'm shocked (your feeling). I didn't know you were in pain, and I have a lot of regret (your feeling) and disappointment in myself (your feeling) that I didn't notice."

Empathy can also demonstrate a shared emotional life because it shows your partner that your emotional life is connected to their emotional life.

- Your feeling is connected to their feeling: "I don't want to make you angry."

- You know your behavior affects them: "I recognize that when I forget to follow through on what we discussed, it makes you angry."

- I feel this way when I hear you feel that way: "I'm feeling turned on hearing how aroused you are."

- All three at once: "It is hard for me to hear you say how I hurt you. It wasn't my intention to hurt you with those actions. Hearing that I did makes me sad."

If you have spent time listening to and inquiring about feelings and expressing and checking your empathy, then you can use empathy and the connection you've formed together to reduce the other person's suffering. Many people jump to this solution-oriented step far too quickly. Men are especially prone to that leap. I recommend getting consent before moving into solutions like this. Here are some examples:

- "Now that we've talked about how this made you feel, would this be a good time for me to offer some ideas I had about how to fix this?"

- "I'm glad that you told me how I hurt you. Now that I know, I wonder if we could talk about how to work together to help prevent this from happening again."

- "Now that I know we're both turned on by the same things, how would you feel about discussing which of those things to do with each other right now?"

Expressing empathy skillfully can create a connection with the other person and let them know that you are together in the process. Empathy alone doesn't solve any problems, but togetherness can ease suffering, especially for situations that have no solution, like the death of a loved one.

Chapter 7

HOW DO I COMMUNICATE EFFECTIVELY?

EMPATHY FOR YOUR PARTNER is a good start to the communication process, but real communication requires a back-and-forth flow. The skills in this chapter help you engage your partner in communication at the right time (conversational consent), in a way that makes your intentions clear (metacommunication), focuses you on connecting instead of being right (inquiry), and keeps you engaged with your partner (active listening). These communication skills will help you enter a genuine relationship with another person. That genuine relationship will help you practice consent, as described in chapter 8.

CONVERSATIONAL CONSENT: CAN WE TALK?

Imagine that you're watching your favorite show and your romantic partner walks into the room and begins talking to you: "You'll never guess what happened to me today. Well, I was at work, and

I went into a conversation with my boss and . . ." At best, your thought process and emotional process have been interrupted. At worst, your partner will not have your attention at all, and they'll share everything they want to say while you continue watching. There are many opportunities for conflict, hurt feelings, and misunderstandings in a situation like this.

Just like you don't walk up to someone and start having sex with them without some conversation to facilitate that process, it is skillful to ask for the other person's attention, time, and readiness before engaging them in conversation. Here are some examples.

- "Remember how you spoke to me earlier about the dinner tomorrow? I'm having some reactions; can I share them with you?"

- "I want to talk with you about some serious topics. I know you have a lot of work stress this week, and I don't want to add to your stress. Can we schedule a time to talk on Saturday morning?" and then when Saturday morning arrives, "Is now still a good time for us to have a talk about some serious topics?"

- "I'd like to have a no-pressure, collaborative discussion about our sex life. Are you open to that?"

When you get the other person's consent for a conversation, you allow them to bring their best self to the table. You've prepared them to participate with you in the conversation as a team member. If you use conversational consent, the other person can trust you to not ambush them. The consent base of the conversation establishes your goodwill from the beginning.

METACOMMUNICATION: I'M SAYING THIS BECAUSE...

The traditional definition of the word *metacommunication* is all elements of communication beyond the words, like body language, pacing, and tone. When I use this term, I'm referring to communicating about the conversation. When you engage in metacommunication, you tell your partner about your reactions, interpretations, and intentions.

- **Reaction:** "When you told me that you're angry about this dinner because I'm not making it special enough, I felt sad and hurt. I'm trying to make it special for you, but I don't know how to convey that. Then when you said you're angry, I started getting defensive."

- **Interpretation:** "We said last week we need a conversation about our intimacy. I know you've been busy with work, so we haven't had this conversation yet. I interpret that to mean that you don't have the bandwidth for that conversation until after your promotion goes through, and I'm willing to wait."

- **Intention:** "Thank you for setting aside some time to talk about our sex life. Now that we're here, my intention is to spend a little time checking in about your satisfaction with our sex life. I also want to bring up some ideas for new experiments to try in our sex life, but I don't want you to feel pressured or criticized by those suggestions."

You also ask your partner about their reactions, interpretations, and intentions: "Would you be willing to share with me what was going on for you when you raised your voice with me in the kitchen this morning?" Metacommunication in a relationship can help both partners defuse the reactive negative stories we some-times end up telling ourselves about our partner. In this way, when you sit with your partner who thinks you don't listen, they directly hear you say, "I want to hear you more clearly." This may not be a perfect antidote to those negative stories, but it can help.

INQUIRY: PLEASE HELP ME UNDERSTAND YOU

You don't know what's really going on inside of other people. If you have humility about this, you'll be inclined to ask a lot of ques-tions to fill in what you don't know. Here are a few examples.

- "Now that I've shared my reactions, would you like to tell me anything about what's going on for you or how I can help you feel better about this dinner?"

- "Is my interpretation accurate that you're too busy with work right now, or do you still want to have that conversa-tion sometime soon?"

- "Are you open to having a conversation about your sexual satisfaction and some new ideas? Is there anything I can do during this conversation to make sure you don't feel criticized or pressured?"

Inquiry demonstrates that your primary goal is to connect. After empathizing with your partner's feelings, instead of telling your partner, "I get it," you ask, "Do you feel like I understand you?" Instead of offering something to soothe your partner and declaring, "Here, this will make you feel better," you can use meta-communication and inquiry: "I brought you a piece of chocolate because it seems like sometimes that helps you transition from a rough day. Would you like it?" After summarizing what your

partner said, you ask, "Did I miss anything?" Inquiry as a communication tool smooths over many inevitable errors in listening or
empathy because it shows that you want the truth, not just empathizing as a way to silence the other person.

When we put consent, metacommunication, and inquiry
together, they are a powerful hat trick for any type of relationship.
You might ask, "Would you be open to talking about your mom's
illness?" If they say yes, then you continue: "I'd like to be here for
you during this tough time. What's going on for you as she's in the
hospital?" These three simple communication tools together can
significantly improve the quality of your friendships, family relationships, romantic relationships, and sexual relationships.

LISTEN ACTIVELY: UH-UH, MM-HMM, OH!

If you can attend to and manage your big emotions, then by opening your heart to feeling empathy, you are ready for the first step in
forging and maintaining a relationship: learning about your partner by listening skillfully and feeling deeply.

Active listening is a way of responding to the other person—with
your facial expressions, body language, and words—that expresses
engagement. You don't have to agree with the other person to do
active listening. You just have to believe the other person when they
express their own feelings and respond to those feelings tenderly.

If you are listening to a hurt partner, your brow might furrow,
you might lean in but allow your head to drop a little with the
weight of what you are hearing, and you might say simple sounds
or words that express the feeling—like "Ooooh"—that drops in
tone at the end to reflect the dejected mood you are hearing and
feeling as you listen.

When the person comes to a natural pause, pair an empathetic
statement about their feeling with inquiry:

- "When you turned away and sighed like that, what were you feeling?"

- "Are you feeling sad?"

- "If I went through what you went through, I'd feel angry. Is that how you feel?"

Most people want to be understood, so even when a person trying to empathize gets it wrong, the inquiry allows the other person to correct you without skipping a beat. They'll say, "Oh no, I'm not angry, I'm hurt," and then they can explain why they're hurt. Don't worry about getting it right. You *will* get it wrong, at least sometimes. Humility and inquiry can keep the relational bond strong so that a "wrong" attempt at empathy won't be a problem in most cases. Usually, only inaccurate empathy asserted confidently leads to problems. If you have ended with inquiry, the other person is likely to just correct you and keep expressing themselves: "No, it is more like this . . ."

If your active listening is skillful enough, the other person may say something like "Yeah," "Exactly," or some other affirmative declaration. When people feel heard, they also add more information and repeat something. Usually, they repeat details but add emotional or meaningful elements. This may exhaust you if you're already struggling to manage your emotional reactions and maintain attention. Remember that the other person is adding or repeating information because you're doing a good job. That'll help give you stamina to keep listening.

The more skilled you get at active listening, the more tuned in you will be to these nuances. Then you'll be able to empathize with this new nuance: "Ah, so earlier you said you were sad, but you're not just sad, you're despairing and tempted to give up. Is that it?" Identifying the person's new emphasis will help form bonds with the person you're listening to.

The purpose of active listening is to make the *other person feel understood*. When you say, "I understand," it won't create the feeling of being understood in the other person. To convey understanding, you must demonstrate that what they said is inside of you now. You repeat back to them what you've heard by telling them a coherent story about their emotions. This expresses comprehension. You might say something like "So, you're feeling sad because you don't think that I understand you. Is that right?" or "When I didn't take out the garbage even though we talked about it twice last week, you didn't know what to do anymore, and so you felt angry. Is that right?" Ending with questions maintains an inquiry process. The questioning language demonstrates that, even if you aren't right, you're trying to connect to the person, and you want to get it right.

All these skills for connection are at the core of the consent process. A consent conversation is not just about sharing the play-by-play for who is going to do what to whom. It is about developing an empathetic understanding of emotional goals and how sexual activity creates those emotions.

Chapter 8

HOW DO I PRACTICE CONSENT?

ALL THE FOUNDATIONAL SKILLS of this book have led up to this topic. In the early chapters, you learned how destructive masculinity hurts people of all genders, including men. You also learned about the unique configuration of your sexuality and how your desire shapes your emotions and what you notice. Chapters 5 and 6 showed you how to take care of your whole self, including your sexual desire and your emotional needs. With that self-care in process, you learned some foundational communication tools in chapter 7. Now, you're ready to bring all of that knowledge and all of those skills to bear in putting consent into practice.

HOW TO NEGOTIATE CONSENT

This is a simple, easy-to-remember way to negotiate consent. When you're working toward consent *before* sexual acts, talk and think about three things:

1. How do each of us want to *feel* and *not feel* during the process?

2. What are we each going to *do* so we both experience the feelings we want?

3. What are we each *not* going to do so that we don't experience the feelings we don't want?

Feelings tell the real story and are the primary focus of this process. It's fine if your goal is to feel pleasure. It's fine if your goal is to feel emotional connection. It's fine if you and your partner have similar or different goals. The goal of a consent conversation is to make sure that, after the behaviors and acts are done, you *and* your partner had the feelings you wanted and are both leaving with good feelings about the acts and behaviors.

If you only have *acts* as the focus of your behavior, at best you seem selfish. At worst, you create feelings of violation or trauma for your partner. Focusing on what to do and what not to do doesn't consider the other person's feelings.

Remember the lesson from chapter 4: our feelings are created out of our goals and the priority of those goals. If your first goal is consent and your second goal is to try a threesome, then your whole approach changes. You'll only try a threesome with other people who want to try a threesome. You'll talk with those people about which feelings they hope to get out of the experience and which behaviors they think will create those feelings. If someone says, "I thought this would be sexy, but actually it feels awkward," it'll be easy for you to set the behavior aside because the behavior wasn't the goal. Now, let's break down each part of negotiating consent.

How Do Each of Us Want to Feel and Not Feel During the Process?

Start by asking your partner how they want to feel. Make this a simple, direct question: "Before we go any further, how do you want to feel while we're having sex?" You already begin to get different ideas of what's being asked of you if your partner says, "I want to feel respected," "I just want to have fun," or "I want to feel loved." But notice that nothing about those feelings describes which physical actions take place. Three different partners could give three different answers, but all might want the same sexual acts to create their desired feeling. (In the next section, you'll find out more about connecting the feelings your partner wants with the behaviors they want.)

You'll also need to say what you want to feel. If you just want a hot onetime sexual experience, pleasure, and hopefully an orgasm, then say that clearly: "I just want to have a fun, casual, and playful experience. I'm not wanting to develop an emotional connection tonight." Most men feel wary about admitting something like this. To change our culture of sexual shame and sexual assault, we can claim our desire shamelessly.

If your potential partner wants something different from you, give them the chance to say, "No, thank you." Someone will want the gift of our desire just as it is. If we describe our desire clearly, only the people who want it will say yes, and their satisfaction will be higher. It is what they wanted. It is what they expected. It is what we gave them.

If you are looking to express your developing emotional connection with someone, say something like, "My feelings for you are growing, and I want to feel closer to you." Most men feel scared to share their feelings directly because it makes them vulnerable. By saying clearly what we want, we give our partners a chance to fulfill our wildest dreams and take the risk of having our hopes disappointed.

Your potential partner may say no. You may say no to them. No is a gift; respecting it gives you the chance to show your character. No can simply indicate a lack of compatibility and nothing else. Sometimes it can teach you where you need to grow for someone to say yes. No can tell you that you aren't looking for partners in the right community. For example, if you have some kinky desires, you'll find more yes if you date people with matching kinks. In other cases, no can teach you how to weigh your values and desires. For example, do the things this person offers you in a relationship outweigh the things they say no to—so that you want to say yes to the complete relationship package?

It is possible that you won't find a sexual partner. Remember, no one is guaranteed partnered sexual experiences. If you've been clear and have looked for partners in the right kinds of communities, then because you asked clearly for your desires to be met, you'll find it easier to express your grief at not finding anyone. Expressing that grief will set you up to better live in acceptance of, or to adapt to, what other people are interested in.

What Are We Each Going to Do So We Both Experience the Feelings We Want?

This question helps you identify the specific behaviors that you both anticipate will create your desired feelings. Only do the things to or with your partner that you've both agreed to. This is what's meant by the terms *affirmative consent* and *explicit consent*.

The ways people interpret a sexual behavior can be so different that it's like speaking different languages. One partner might say, "I just want to feel loved and have intercourse." But what is it about intercourse that makes this partner feel loved? Maybe, for you, pulling your partner's hair helps you feel sexually powerful. Your partner might want to feel desired by a sexually powerful partner, but having their hair pulled makes them feel controlled and violated. The same behaviors aren't likely to be interpreted the same way by different people. So, before you can really understand what sexual behavior your partner is asking for, you need to understand why that behavior makes them feel the way they want to feel.

Ask follow-up questions: "Can you help me understand what parts of intercourse make you feel loved? Like eye contact or close embraces in the dark? Like saying 'I love you' during the process? Or hungry moans?" These kinds of questions can help you clarify the connections between the desired feelings and the acts being requested. The answers will help you understand not just *what* to do, mechanically, but *how* to do those things to create for your partner the feelings they are looking for. When *you* answer this question, you can also be clear about your desired behaviors and how they create your desired feelings.

When you discuss the behaviors that create different feelings for you and listen to the behaviors that create different feelings for your partner, eventually you start to get a picture of what making love, fucking, having sex, or doing kink with this person would look like. Share your ideas about what they'd like back to them. Make sure you both agree to and understand what you would do to create the desired feelings.

Since communication and feedback loops are a big part of sexual behavior, you'll also want to discuss how you'll know what to do more of and when to stop doing something. Planning how to communicate during sex is an important part of the consent process.

One trap to avoid in this process is telling other people how *they'll* feel if they do something you want. If your potential partner tells you that they find giving oral sex demeaning, believe them. Don't try to wheedle them into doing it anyway. Being pressured will almost certainly reinforce the negative feeling. Maybe for you, receiving oral sex feels like a great gift and you feel deeply grateful and adoring. But your feelings and the other person's feelings are different. Don't assume otherwise.

Conversely, if something turns your partner on but doesn't turn you on, that doesn't mean they are wrong. You are the expert in your turn-ons and turnoffs, and your partner is the expert in theirs. Say no when you don't like the feelings a certain behavior creates for you, but don't discount your partner's expressions of desire.

If what your partner asks for doesn't turn you off but also doesn't turn you on, you may consider trying it. You might say, "I've never done that before. It doesn't sound like something that would turn me on, but I'd be willing to try it with you if that's something that turns you on." This kind of generosity can go a long way toward building goodwill with a sexual partner, whether this is a onetime encounter or a life partnership.

You might also reserve the option to say no after trying something. Say, "I'd be willing to try that with you because I trust you. If it isn't working for me, I'd like to stop and move on to something more mutually pleasurable. Would that work?" Giving your partner the same option can help reduce a sense of pressure.

It can be enjoyable and engaging to try new sexual behaviors. It can also be a lot of fun to introduce someone to a new sexual behavior. But you need to keep in mind that learning goes at the learner's pace, not the pace of the teacher's arousal. So, if you're interested in having anal sex because you have enjoyed that in the past with other partners, and your new partner is willing to try, that's great. Just remember that trying something new means going slowly. Learn how it feels for them. Be open to learning that they don't enjoy it. Because sexual consent conversations are for you, too. You get to ask for that same patience and freedom to stop when you try receiving anal pleasure (or any other new sexual experience).

What Are We Each Not Going to Do So That We Don't Experience the Feelings We Don't Want?

This question invites a description of the specific behaviors that each person doesn't want. The things you and the other person state here are behaviors known to trigger trauma, major turnoffs, or things that one person asked for that the other person isn't interested in. Repeat what you hear back to your partner. Do not do those things.

If your potential partner brings up something they don't want you to do and you aren't sure that you can comply, it may be best for you to be the better man and opt out of the sexual experience altogether. Let's look at two examples of when it could be difficult to avoid what your partner doesn't want unless you say no to the encounter.

> **An essential behavior for you is a no for them:** Imagine there's a behavior you think of as essential for expression, like tongue kissing, but your partner is turned off by it. In this scenario, it might be better for you to say no to the sex being offered. Perhaps you'll want to acknowledge your doubts: "I hear you say that tongue kissing is off-limits for you. I want to respect that. I also know it is a common sexual behavior for me. I'm not certain that I won't do it unconsciously if I get really turned on. How would that affect you?" Perhaps you'll want to create a plan: "So, you won't feel violated if I unconsciously push out my tongue to kiss you, but you'll tap me gently to remind me, and I need to stop right away. Is that right? And you're sure that you feel okay with helping me learn how to be with you this way?"

> **You can't guarantee an outcome they want:** Imagine that your partner has made it clear that they don't want any emotional attachments from this hookup. You want to hook up, but you're well aware that you can't control whom you fall in love with. You may be tempted to just say to yourself or the other person, "I won't fall in love this time." But the thing your partner has said they don't want you to do is literally not in your control. In this situation, you're giving a false promise. Instead, state frankly that what they're asking isn't in your control. You may add that it isn't your desire to fall in love, if that's the case. Don't make promises outside of your control

just to have sex with someone. A similar situation might arise if your partner says they don't want you to ejaculate but you know you ejaculate easily.

■

Between what you and your partner agree *to do* (question 2) and what you agree *not to do* (question 3), there's a large gulf. For example, your partner says they like "a little tongue" with kissing but not a tongue "rammed deep into my mouth." So how much is too much? If you notice these gaps during the consent conversation, ask about them. But inevitably, some undefined territory remains between what has been asked for and what has been asked to be off-limits. The best practice is to stay on the safe side of these ambiguities. But even if you think that you are staying on the safe side, checking verbally and explicitly is even better. You might pause briefly after a kiss and ask, "I know you said 'a little tongue.' Have these kisses worked, or would you like something different?"

An ongoing consent conversation is taking place in any sexual encounter. Making that conversation verbal and explicit—"That hurts," "More," "Yes, like that"—can really facilitate the process. One side of that conversation includes the resilience to receive that guidance and stay engaged or, at minimum, to acknowledge when you've run out of that resilience—"I think I need to stop. I'm glad you're giving all this feedback, but I think I've hit the limit of my capacity for learning today." Let's turn now toward a few tools that can help you have that ongoing conversation.

Figure 8.1: Three-step consent process

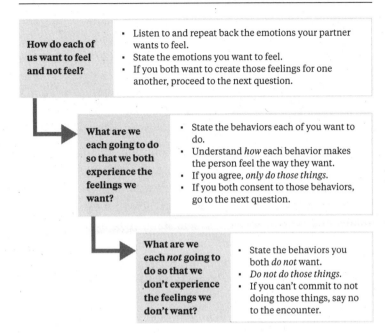

How do each of us want to feel and not feel?	• Listen to and repeat back the emotions your partner wants to feel. • State the emotions you want to feel. • If you both want to create those feelings for one another, proceed to the next question.
What are we each going to do so that we both experience the feelings we want?	• State the behaviors each of you want to do. • Understand *how* each behavior makes the person feel the way they want. • If you agree, *only do those things.* • If you both consent to those behaviors, go to the next question.
What are we each *not* going to do so that we don't experience the feelings we don't want?	• State the behaviors you both *do not* want. • *Do not do those things.* • If you can't commit to not doing those things, say no to the encounter.

HOW TO MONITOR CONSENT

If you are with someone who's willing to have sex with you and you've negotiated consent skillfully enough to make it happen, your work is not done. Consent is an ongoing process, not a once-and-done activity. Because body language and vocal tone aren't clear signals, you need skills for monitoring and maintaining consent *during* sexual activity.

A few concrete skills can help you monitor and maintain consent with minimal impact on either person's pleasure. Maintaining consent creates the potential for more hot sex in the future.

Receive, Follow, and Give Feedback

Although you've negotiated what to do and what not to do, plans can't anticipate real life. Little deviations from the plan in the form of feedback are common during sex. Your partner might say "A little to the left," "Faster," or "Not so hard." This process is an example of the metacommunication (see page 219) at work in a sexual context.

Listen to what your partner is saying and try to follow it. Especially when you are having sex with someone who isn't used to being listened to (like a lot of women, for example), you might want to say thank you when you get feedback. This will reinforce the communication process. When you try to adjust your behavior to match (like to move left, as requested), you might say, "Is this better?" or "How's that?" By listening to and inviting more feedback, you're being an attentive lover. You're much more likely to give your partners pleasure if you listen when they tell you about how to give them pleasure.

You may also need to give feedback. You have just as much right to give feedback and to guide your partner to pleasure. Sometimes you can make the process sound sexy—"Yeah, baby, just like that." But make sure that you already negotiated the kind of language that you're using. Some partners won't like to be called "baby," "slut," "lover," "beloved," or whatever other word you might think is sexy and well intentioned.

Feedback doesn't necessarily change who is doing what to whom. Feedback is about saying how something already negotiated and agreed upon is going. Renegotiation is a different kind of process that requires a different set of responses.

Renegotiation: Stop, Think, Talk, and Resume

Let's say that your partner offered more sexual activities than you were ready to accept while you were negotiating consent. Because of that, you turned your partner down regarding some of the offers. Now, the situation is feeling comfortable, and you've actually become interested in some of the behaviors that you made off-limits before. That's fine, but since you initially put them off-limits, and you now want to change that, do so with a clear head, and go back to the negotiation process.

Stop. Because people can make bad decisions when aroused, you need a way to clear your head. Do something to stop the process; here are some examples:

- Get up and get some water for yourself; offer some to your partner, too.

- Go to the bathroom and splash some water on your face.

- Stop kissing or caressing, move to a more sexually neutral position, and ask to catch your breath for a minute.

Think. Once you've stopped the encounter, review the process, your sexual values, and how you are feeling. In the middle of making out, you were fantasizing about taking this next step. Think carefully before renegotiating.

- *What do you really want?* You may want to move to a new sexual activity when you're really aroused, but once you step back from the pleasure and really think about it, there may be lines you're not ready to cross. Don't renegotiate if the existing boundaries are what you want to maintain.

- *Is renegotiating a good idea?* Maybe this is a good time to call it a night because you will get goal oriented if you get more aroused. Renegotiating to increase activity when you know you get irritable when you stay aroused for too long is not a good idea. Maybe you want to renegotiate because your partner is getting pushy, and you want to clarify or add new limitations to protect yourself. Renegotiating is important in that case.

- *What are the potential consequences of renegotiating?* If what you negotiated at the beginning was something like, "Let's make out and see where things go," then there was already an openness between the two of you for renegotiating. Although you always have a right to say no, and should do so regardless of how your partner may feel, there can be negative consequences (like your partner feeling pressured) to trying to increase sexual behavior after you negotiated the first time. When and how you renegotiate makes a difference to your partners; pay attention to that process.

Talk. Ask how your partner is feeling about the encounter so far. Ask if they feel like doing some new things, keeping the activity at the same level, or de-escalating. The options demonstrate your openness to any answer. If they say they're interested in doing some new things, ask what they're interested in. Ask if they'd like to hear what you were thinking of, and if they say yes, tell them. In other words, renegotiating is the same as negotiating consent in the first place.

A quick check-in during a steamy episode can establish deeper trust, lay positive groundwork for more open sexual receptivity in your partner, and reaffirm your freedom to pursue pleasure together.

Resume. Once the consent process has been completed again and you're both in agreement, feel free to resume, introducing the new mutually agreed-upon activities.

"Stop, think, talk, resume" works equally well when your partner wants to advance sexual activity past their prior limits, too. If you're with a partner and they suddenly begin undressing but they'd told you they didn't want to undress that night, then stop. Back away from the situation, and cool your own head. Your partner consented to one thing but then did another. Even if you wanted that behavior prior to negotiating consent, think now about what you want and how you feel about the fact that your partner has done something you both agreed they wouldn't do. Approach this process with extreme caution. Now talk with your partner. Why did they do that? Was it because they felt sexy? Or did they feel pressured or coerced? If they did it because they were feeling sexy, ask what the new feeling goals are, what the new yes behaviors are, and if there are any changes to the no behaviors. Only resume the activity when you feel that the new agreements are clear and keeping you both safe.

"Stop, think, talk, and resume" is a way to monitor consent. You may be tempted to believe that you can have these renegotiations while trying to continue sexual behavior, but in many cases, that is a bad idea.

Let's say that you are about to have anal sex with your partner when they tell you they have an upset stomach. Many men have a lot of assumptions about what might happen next like, "Well, if they were up for anal, that's freaky, so even though that's off the table, they should still be open to giving me a blow job," and they will just start moving toward that or telling their partner to do that without renegotiating. Wrong. The information changed. Maybe their mood changed entirely, and they're no longer interested in having sex at all.

Since the information changed, you need to check in about the rest of the plan. Stop, think, talk, and resume. Try it using the empathy formula you learned in chapter 6.

It might come out as, "I know that your stomach is upset [event]. I assume you aren't feeling up for anal sex anymore [how they feel]. I'm really glad [how you feel knowing how they feel] you told me what's going on. Does that mean you're still up for other types of sex, or does that mean sex is off the table for you tonight?"

Here are some other examples of reasons to stop, think, talk, and resume:

If you negotiated a kinky scene where you were going to tie your partner up, but you forgot the rope, don't assume that this now means that it's okay to hold their hands down with yours or replace the rope with your belt. Stop the process—"Oh, hold on. Pause scene. I forgot the rope." Think—*Okay, I feel I can be flexible about this, but I can't assume my partner will be.* Talk (and you can make this sexy)—"I'm sorry I forgot the rope, but that doesn't need to stop me from holding you down with my hands. Are you open to that?" Resume only if you find a mutually agreeable path forward.

If you negotiated receiving oral sex from your partner, but they developed a head cold, don't assume they'll still be interested in giving oral sex. Stop the process—"Hey, I know you're not feeling well. Can we pause and check in about what that means for the night?" Think—given your partner's head cold, how do you feel? And what do you really want? A blow job around sniffles may not sound that sexy once you think about it. Maybe you're more interested in giving your partner pleasure, now that you think about it. Talk—"I know we negotiated for you to give me oral pleasure. With your head cold, I was thinking about reversing that, and I'll give you oral pleasure. How does that sound to you?"—followed by a flirting facial expression and waiting for an actual response.

If you negotiated sexual contact that night while out for dinner, don't assume as you enter the front door that the consent is still in place. The *stop* has already happened during the after-dinner walk, the drive home, and the paying and excusing the babysitter. Think—*What am I still interested in, and what do I have the energy for?* Talk—"Hey, are you still up for everything we talked about?" Resume only when you're clear that you have a mutually agreed plan for right now.

Checking in and renegotiating might sound difficult at first, but these examples show that you can make it sexy. Like most activities, consent is a skill; once you get better at it, you'll be able to do it without having to think about it ponderously or letting it interrupt your energy.

HOW TO FOLLOW UP ON CONSENT

People can have very different perceptions of the same event. One person can experience a consent violation even though the other person was trying to preserve consent and may not know they violated consent. The discrepancy between the two perspectives doesn't necessarily make one person right and the other person wrong. It means that two different experiences took place. If you want to repair the situation with that person, you need to understand that, in their experience, you did violate them even if that wasn't your intention.

Negotiating and monitoring consent helps prevent those differences in experience, but no consent process is foolproof. Sometimes you need to attend to and learn from experience. The following process describes how to follow up on consent, and it's especially helpful when you have a new sexual partner or after trying a new sexual behavior with any partner.

Step 1: Prepare for Follow-Up

In a negotiated one-night stand, it can be helpful to offer the other person a way to contact you.[1] Giving the other person your number puts them in control of contacting you if they want to give you feedback about the process. When you are leaving the sexual encounter, you might say, "Hey, I know we set this up as a onetime thing, but if there's anything that didn't work for you and you need to process that, call me. Here's my number." Leaving the contact in the other person's hands while expressing an openness to hearing about their feelings and to processing them establishes respect.

When you negotiate for a one-night stand, ask for the other person's contact information or a way to follow-up on social media. For some partners, asking for their contact information may feel like a violation of the terms of the hookup. On the other hand, if you're feeling violated by something your partner did, it might be helpful to ask to process that with them. In that case, you might say, "Some of what happened here isn't sitting well with me. I might want to talk with you about it, if you're open to that. May I have a way to contact you in case I do?"

In a long-term relationship, preparing to follow up means identifying ahead of time when you will talk about the sexual encounter after it has happened. Although pillow talk immediately following sexual activity can feel bonding, it's better to have follow-up consent conversations the next day or later, with your clothes on and in a nonsexual context. Allowing for time to pass before talking can let you both sort out your thoughts and prepare for the conversation.

Step 2: Ask about the Other Person's Experience

If you connect with the sexual partner again, ask them how things went: "How are you feeling about our night together?" In a long-term relationship, when you sit down as agreed upon, you might say, "Hey, how are you feeling now about those new things we tried in bed the other night?"

Asking the person about their experience demonstrates that you value them. In a best-case scenario, you're so respectful of one another that you're both offering to let the other person go first. In that case, don't be afraid to go first, but keep your comments short and to the point; then ask again about the other person's experience.

To be very explicit, do not at this stage ask the person out again. Do not use a sexual tone or attitude. This is a listening-and-gathering-information process, not the beginning of a new hookup.

Step 3: Listen, Reflect, and Be Open

If the partner tells you something positive, express your appreciation for it and the encounter, state your commitment to learning, and move on. If this was a onetime hookup, there's no need for additional discussion.

If this was the beginning of a potential relationship that you want to pursue, feel free to ask the person out again. If this is part of a long-term relationship and you're getting positive feedback, you can ask about whether, how, and when the person might be interested in trying those new behaviors again. In these two cases, make a mental note of, and retain the elements, that created the positive experience for your partner.

If your partner tells you something neutral or noncommittal, express a willingness to hear negative feedback and put the ball in their court. You might say, "If you had a negative experience and you're uncomfortable sharing, you don't have to. If you're willing to share, though, I'd like to hear about it so I can learn and avoid creating that experience for you again (or "for others" if it was a one-time thing). Thank you for your feedback so far. Is there more?" Doing this might require that you engage in the emotion-regulation techniques from chapter 6. If the person doesn't offer a more conclusively positive or negative reflection on the experience, don't pressure them for it. See step 5 (page 211) for ideas on how to cope with ambiguous feedback.

If your partner tells you something negative, first and most important, regulate your emotional experience using the tools from chapter 6. Don't fall into anger, dismissiveness, denial, or gaslighting (manipulating the other person by trying to make them question their own experience). If you can't regulate these reactions, at least have the humility to admit it: "I know that I asked about your experience. I'm sorry, but I'm finding that my reactions to what you've said are too big for me now. If I continue this conversation, I'll probably make it worse. I'm going to try to take this in. Do you want me to contact you again when I've figured out how to regulate my reactions, or would you prefer that I just leave you alone?" Use this exit strategy anytime you need to during the feedback process. If you can regulate your reactions to the negative feedback, keep going.

Use feeling empathy (see page 206) and expressing empathy (see page 213) to let the person know you hear them. This includes all the tools for listening, which reflects to the other person what you've heard. For example, you might say, "So, if I'm hearing you right, when I asked to have sex with you later in the night after you told me at the beginning of the date that you didn't want to have sex yet, that felt like pressure to you." Be sure to ask them if you are understanding accurately—"Is that right?" Then you believe what they're telling you about their experience, and cultivate your vulnerable feelings responses in empathy.

Next, ask if they are open to hearing your reaction to what they've shared: "Would you be open to hearing how I feel after hearing what you've shared, or did you just want me to know about your experience?" If they're not open to hearing your reaction, thank them for the disclosure and go to step 4 (see page 209).

If they are open to hearing your reaction, state how you feel having heard their experience. You might say, "I was pretty shocked at first when you said you felt pressured. I didn't realize my actions would have that effect on you. It's really painful for me to hear because I don't want to be the kind of person who makes other people feel that way." Ask if there is a way that you can help them heal from the experience. For example, "Is there a way I can help you recover from that experience of pressure?"

Finally, listen to and do what they say as long as it doesn't violate your integrity. If they ask you not to contact them again, don't. If they ask you to just learn from it, express a commitment to doing so. If they express an interest in maintaining a connection with you, having sex with you again, or doing the same sexual things again—and you are interested in the same—make sure that you know in concrete detail how you created the negative experience and how you can prevent it from happening again (see step 5, page 241, before agreeing). If they say they don't know how you could participate in their healing, express a willingness to hear ideas if something comes to mind at a later time: "Well, I can understand that. Since my actions hurt you in this way, you may not know how I can help you heal from the experience. But if something comes to mind later, I'm open to hearing it. Until I hear that from you, though, I'll respect your process and not contact you again. Does that work?"

Step 4: Learn from the Feedback

It isn't enough to be a "nice guy" who receives feedback and makes people feel good when they have difficult feelings about you. You need to make concrete changes. A lot of people will say things like, "Well, I just won't pressure anyone again." This underestimates the power of behavior patterns. In the absence of planning how to change your behavior and practicing change, you'll probably keep doing the same things.

Just like an athlete who practices to unlearn bad behaviors on the field, if you want to change your sexual repertoire to include more consent and pleasure for your partners, you may need to take things slowly, get feedback during the process, and try again. This is one reason why you need friends and a community, as discussed in chapter 5.

Talk with friends, a therapist, or your community about the feedback you've gotten, and use that information to plan changes. Create follow-up conversations with your support system to create accountability for the next time. As scary as it may be for you to talk about negative feedback you received, when you share, learn, and make changes, you create a culture of consent in your community. Other men will expect themselves to live up to the same standard you've followed.

Ask your support system questions like "How might I have known beforehand, or even in the moment, that my partner was having this experience?" and "What clues might I have missed or ignored that showed that my partner was having a bad experience?" By the end of this learning step, you want a detailed list of things that you will do differently in the future. That list won't do you any good if you never review it. Read and reread that list before you go into similar situations.

Step 5: Protect Yourself

You need a sexual environment and communication that ensures your sexual safety. That sexual safety includes all the usual high school health-class elements, like STI prevention and pregnancy prevention (if applicable)—but it also extends to your emotional safety. You don't want to hurt anyone. You don't want your sexual partners to regret sharing their sexuality with you. You want your heart to be protected. These desires are not just about covering your ass legally or socially. This is about you being the kind of person that you want to be—admired, desired, respected, and cared for. The best way to protect those needs is to talk about the sex you are *going* to have and to learn from the sex that you *have* had.

If one of your partners had a bad sexual experience with you, you might not want to have sex with that person again. If you aren't confident that your intent will be read accurately by that partner, that means you don't feel safe with them. This is another way in which the consent process is for you. If you feel, despite your best attempts and willingness to learn from your behavior, that you didn't get detailed enough feedback about how to prevent a negative experience for your partner, listen to that information and protect yourself with it. You don't have to have sex with that person again.

Step 6: Make Changes with This Partner

The purpose of a consent follow-up conversation is to inform you how to give your partner pleasure, comfort, and safety. Even if all you learn is to do more of what you did, that's a valuable conversation. Put that information into practice as rigorously as you would changes from a negative experience.

For every positive piece of input, there's something important to learn and apply to maintain a positive experience with that partner the next time you have sex with them. If you engage in this kind of process over a lifetime, you can become a very attentive lover.

Even if you received neutral or unclear feedback, you should at least have enough information to know where to add more explicit consent conversations and to check in more during the sexual activity to improve the communication process.

Whether a partner offers feedback that is positive, neutral, or negative, if you decide it is safe for you to have sex with them again, then there's something about that feedback to bring back to your next sexual experience with them.

As you enter the next experience, review the prior feedback. You might say, "Okay, I remember you said you don't like anything that restricts your ability to move your head. Is there anything I'm forgetting?" or "You said circles with my hand, not an up-and-down motion, right?" or "I remember that I need to keep checking in verbally and looking for eye contact this time. Should we find a way for you to help me remember if I'm forgetting?"

Learning and making changes after the conversation demonstrate that you've given your partner's personhood and your own integrity a higher value than sexual gratification. That will help your partners be more sexually open, free, and generous. In the long run, this process will generate more sexual gratification for everyone involved.

Step 7: Make Changes for All Partners

Look at all the experiences you've had, and learn from the collective feedback you've received. If necessary, start by admitting your weaknesses and blind spots.

For example, some men get fixated on their relationship hopes. They interpret feedback from their partner as confirming their hopes and unconsciously minimize any hesitation. If that's you, compensate for this blind spot by focusing on what your partner is telling you. When you engage in active listening, repeat back to your partner what you hear them tell you about their reluctance or barriers to a relationship with you. If you get emotionally attached to sexual partners—even in a hookup—then maybe casual sex isn't for you. If you've gotten feedback that you create pressure for your partners, focus on figuring out how to follow a partner's lead.

If there are consistent themes in the feedback you receive from your sexual partners, it may reflect something about your sexual nature. Review your notes from the "Know Your Turn-Ons" exercise in chapter 3. Notice if there's any connection between the feedback you're getting and what turns you on. For example, do you get negative feedback when you keep trying that one sexual behavior that feels like the sexiest thing in the world to you? Make an effort to protect yourself and your partners from hurt by knowing your nature and learning how to address the blind spots that are part of it.

Figure 8.2: The cyclical process of following up on consent

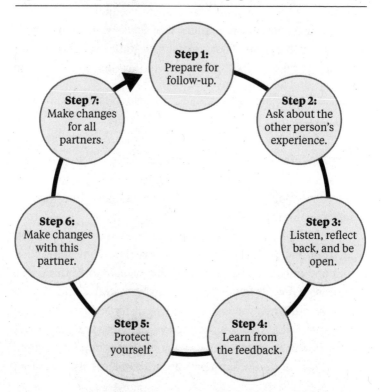

EXERCISE: Plan to Be the Better Man

Now it's your turn to take these lessons, see how they apply to your sexual history, and identify the changes you might need to make. This is a big exercise, but the more effort you put into it, the more value it will have for you and your future partners.

Step 1: Take stock of the feedback you've gotten. Think back to all your prior sexual partners. For each that you're able to, write down the kind of feedback you got. Be sure to include the positive, neutral, and negative feedback. Do your best to write down what the partner said, with minimal interpretation or editorializing of your own. After writing it all down, you might try cutting and pasting the feedback into positive, neutral, and negative categories. What summaries can you make for yourself about the things you are good or so-so at doing? Where could you improve your sexual technique? When do you need to be more careful so you can improve your consent practice?

Step 2: Learn from the feedback. Synthesize what you've written down into declarative statements about yourself. For example, you might write, "I can get tunnel vision when I'm close to orgasm," or "When I'm hooking up, I avoid eye contact, and that means I can miss important cues." Take special note here of contradictory information. One partner might have said you gave the best oral sex of their life; another might have said that they didn't like how you gave oral sex at all. The learning statement might be "I'm not the perfect oral-sex partner for everyone. When what I'm doing isn't working, I need to be more open to guidance."

Step 3: Plan for change. Create a plan of action, and write it down. For example, you might say, "I'm going to tell partners that I get tunnel vision when I'm close to orgasm and ask them how we can make sure that doesn't hurt them," or "I will try to maintain eye contact more when I'm hooking up the next few times. I'll reevaluate how that's working for me after each time," or "The next time I give a new partner oral sex, I'm going to ask for in-process feedback before I start." Identify someone you can talk with about this feedback. Share what you've written, and make a plan for reviewing your change plan with them again in the future.

WHEN SOMETHING GOES WRONG

Sometimes, you're going to be in a situation where your partner gives some negative feedback. We must be ready to stop and listen. Stories from #MeToo reveal that men, riding on a mix of narrowed attention and patriarchal entitlement, often exhibit a lack of empathy when they receive feedback about how a partner feels. They often become:

- **Defensive:** "Well, I wasn't trying to make you feel uncomfortable."

- **Dismissive:** "That's absurd. I'm a feminist. Just relax. Everything is fine."

- **Angry and combative:** "Everything was fine, and now you're ruining it."

- **Prone to gaslighting:** "What's wrong with you? That's ridiculous. I'm not doing anything to make you uncomfortable."

Some men exhibit a degree of apparent empathy—"How about we just chill, but this time with our clothes on?"[2]—but it isn't really empathy if the narrowed attention and the goal-oriented mindset remain their primary foci. Empathy is not a feeling inside of you; it is ethics in action—something that you do. Empathy when a partner expresses discomfort requires stopping your emotional experience of arousal, shifting your attention to their emotional experience, and then having and expressing reciprocal and tender emotional responses to their feelings. In a sexual situation, empathy might sound like the following statements:

- **Validate and repeat what was communicated:** "I'm really glad you told me that you feel uncomfortable. I'd much rather hear it than keep going without your enjoyment."

- **Actively identify reciprocal feelings:** "Oh! I feel uncomfortable, too, now that I know how you feel."

- **Use metacommunication and inquiry:** "I'm interested in finding out what I did that caused that feeling in you, so I don't do it again. Are you willing to help me learn from this experience?"

- **Express the desire for the partner to feel positive things:** "I'd like you to feel comfortable and safe. Is there something I can do to help you have that feeling?"

- **Seek direction:** "What would you like me to do right now?"

- **Most important:** Back away and assume the sexual encounter is over!

It might be difficult for you to attend empathetically in this way when you are turned on, but you are the only person who can manage your arousal—so it is your responsibility to manage it. If necessary, just be honest about how difficult it is for you: "I'm sensing that you're uncomfortable or not feeling safe. I'm having a hard time attending to those feelings the way that I want to because I am really aroused. I'm going to go to the bathroom, splash some water on my face, and try to clear my head. When I come back, I'd like to hear more about what you are feeling."

Once they become more attentive and empathetic, a lot of men assume they know what a partner would want. You might try to take your partner's mind off the discomfort by resuming the sexual activity. But that might create pressure for your partner because resuming the activity worsens the issue. Or you might try putting an arm around your partner and offering physical comfort, but your partner might prefer to talk.

You need to *find out* what your partner needs instead of *thinking you know* what your partner needs. Simple questions can really help:

- "Would you feel more comfortable if I got closer or moved farther away?"

- "Would you like me to leave?"

- "Would you prefer to talk to me about how you feel or be silent?"

Wait in silence for an answer. If no answer comes after a couple of minutes, calm any anxiety you have about that using the emotional regulation tools in chapter 6. Then withdraw, saying what you're doing and why: "Since you haven't answered, I'm going to go into the other room for a while because I want you to feel safe. If you don't come out after a while, I may come back and check on you and see if you want me to leave." Get dressed if necessary, and then do what you said you were going to do.

When your partner is ready to talk about their feelings, listen to them and repeat the feelings back. You might find yourself saying, "So, when I moved, you thought I was going to touch you there. You felt pressured because we hadn't talked about me touching you there, and you became afraid because you thought I had expectations about what was going to happen next. Is that right?"

Remember, there isn't always an identifiable reason for an emotion. The absence of a reason doesn't invalidate an emotion. Sometimes emotions just arise. Those emotions still exist, and they are still shaping that person's experience of you in the encounter. You can empathize with emotions even if you don't know the reasons behind them: "So, it wasn't anything in particular that I did. You were enjoying everything, but something just made you feel uncomfortable and you wanted to stop. Am I getting it?"

Try using consent-based conversations about how to proceed, like, "Are you open to a conversation about what you need to feel safer right now?" or "I'm interested in learning how to help you feel safer. Are you open to helping me?"

If your partner felt uncomfortable, don't assume that the sexual activity will resume if they feel safer again. If your partner attempts to resume sexual activity, ask questions about what has shifted and what has made it safe to proceed. Make sure that you have negotiated the expectations for physical intimacy better this time than last time. Most important, don't agree to have sex after an uncomfortable moment unless you are completely comfortable and feeling safe, too.

■

Consent isn't just another impossible demand being put on your shoulders or another impossibly small box that you're being asked to fit into to be a "good man." The invitation to consent is one element in your liberation from the oppression you've experienced under the patriarchy. I believe that the developmental process you've followed in reading this book can liberate what is good about men's sexuality—your sexuality—from shame, into a healthy expression. To prepare for consent, you learned about the real nature of your desire, how to regulate that desire, and how and when to set it free. Whole-person wellness supports consent, so you learned to take care of your health in multiple dimensions of your life, including your emotions. To further your capacity for consent, you learned communication skills that strengthen your ability to form and maintain relationships with friends, family, your community, lovers, and life partners. You're now more prepared to use consent to protect you and your partners from harm and to create hotter sex. But this process is ongoing. Keep listening to your community. Keep growing. Keep on striving to become the better man.

AFTERWORD: I'M FLAWED, TOO

I HAVE HESITATED to write about consent. I've also been unsure how to write about it to teach others from my professional role without including me as a person. If I'm going to write to men about consent, power, and sex, it doesn't feel right to me to stay safe behind a veil of professionalism without acknowledging my own experiences. I have learned a lot since becoming a sex-positive psychologist before #MeToo took social media by storm, but the cut-to-the-bone growth that caused me to rewrite my image of myself came because I hurt women even though I didn't intend to. When I read Katie Way's piece on babe.net about a woman's experience with Aziz Ansari, I recognized myself and my clients enough that I felt I had something to contribute to the ongoing consent conversation in our culture.[1]

The women I hurt have a right to their anonymity, so there aren't any real names here. Because I'm using the experiences I had and what I learned from those women, I want to dedicate this writing to them. These women suffered before I learned what I didn't know about the power of my own sexuality, about sexual consent, and how to be a better person. It is possible there are more people whom I've hurt that I don't know about. I might have been so blind that I wasn't even aware of the pain I caused. There may be times when a partner was hurt by me but was too afraid to tell me they were hurt. Those potential situations are reasons to restrain my sexual enthusiasm, and reasons for me to be scared, too, when I try to bring the gifts of my sexuality to my partners. My partners might also be scared because of their experiences with past partners. I hope that what follows will honor the people I have hurt. In addition to dedicating this writing to those people, I want to dedicate this chapter to "Grace," whose description of a date catalyzed my impulse to join the conversation in this way.

CONSENT FOR THESE STORIES

I debated a lot about these stories and vetted my process for including them in this book through many other people. By sharing these accounts, even using pseudonyms of the women in them, I risked that these women would be hurt by my writing about them. My story about them could remind them of the pain they experienced. Also, it could miss a crucial element of the harm I caused and leave them feeling voiceless about their own experience. Some reader or other writer might speak negatively about these women. Or someone else might have outed their real identities. I tried my best to prevent those possibilities. I certainly considered leaving out the stories to do so.

However, if I left my accounts of inadequate consent out of the picture, I'd be hypocritical. The women in these stories would have every right to feel hurt. I considered taking on that risk by naming my faults in abstract terms instead of specifics. But the message of this book—and what I'm trying to teach other men—seemed important enough to at least consider including my personal experiences. If I'm going to teach *you* how to reconcile yourself with your past behavior, I'd better model the same courage myself. I wanted to be transparent, so that you, the reader, can question me.

I decided that I didn't want to include these stories without asking for permission from the women described in them—in other words, I asked for consent. I'm sharing one story here, and the woman gave consent to share the story. Some women did not give approval, and those stories have been omitted. The consent lessons I learned from those experiences are summarized at the end of this afterword in abstract form.

"SUSAN"

As an adolescent in junior high school, I was nerdy. I hung out with a group of like-minded kids, and we called ourselves the Nerd Herd (yes, for real). There were more girls than boys in the Nerd Herd, which was heaven for seventh-grade me. I flirted with many of them. We engaged in precocious innuendo, I tickled them relentlessly, and the question of which girl I would "go out with" became a focus of my attention.

When one of the members, Susan, and I started focusing on each other, the rest of the group ostracized us. My new girlfriend and I clung to each other. We had no social life other than each other, and no pastime other than our sexual fumbling. This probably sounds like an awkward but not uncommon path to sexual discovery. But in hindsight, I can see that I pressured Susan to kiss, to be touched, and to go further. I see now that our social isolation may have made it difficult for her to say no—she may not have wanted to risk her only relationship. When she did say no, I listened in the moment, but a day or two later, I would verbally or physically push to cross the boundary she established. I would not be surprised if she told me that I waited mere minutes—not the days that I remember—before pushing the boundary. Yes, she had sexual desire of her own, but I know now that pressure can exist even in the presence of your partner's desire.

Somehow, we weathered eighth grade together. One summer day before high school, I invited Susan over to my house because my family was away. We had sex for the first time. We anticipated that it would be painful, and it was. But what I didn't anticipate was the distance between us. She was not present. In my memory, she never said no. But I recognize now that her body language did not say yes. I vividly remember the absence of eye contact, her downturned chin, and the disengaged movements of her limbs. I stopped what I was doing, but I should have stopped sooner. We found a way to have penetrative sex another time. It was not a substantively different experience. Despite my sexual pressure and coercion, we stayed together until high school, when we made new friends and our relationship fell apart.

By the standard of the times, I had a good sexual education. I knew about reproduction because I had accurate sex education in fifth and sixth grades. At fourteen years old, I had the courage to buy condoms at the drugstore. I practiced with them and used them during our sexual experiences. My sex safety was a "success." Losing my virginity that young was a "success" by the metrics of hypermasculinity. But I fell short of the standards I have now when it came to respect and consent. I sincerely, if naively, loved Susan, but I pushed her beyond her boundaries, and we were both too young. I am not proud of this story, and I regret it.

OTHER LESSONS ABOUT CONSENT

I've had other experiences with partners that helped me see that my self-regulation and consent processes were inadequate and not living up to my values. This section is my best attempt to identify the elements of consent that I learned the hard way, illustrated in the stories that I did not receive permission to tell.

I Need to Be Authentic and Meet My Own Needs

My wife gave permission for me to share the affairs I describe here, but I'm putting these stories in this section because, though the affairs were consensual relative to the partners, those affair partners did not consent for the stories of those relationships to be told. I'm describing the affairs relative to my relationship with my wife. On three occasions, I cheated. Each affair followed a pattern. After a period of dissatisfaction with the emotional and sexual connection in my marriage and after an extended period trying to resolve those differences, I stopped trying. I stopped monitoring my relationship satisfaction or life satisfaction, and my unmet sexual desires and emotional needs continued to exist inside of me. When an opportunity to have an affair arose, I took it.

During the affairs, I felt relieved and happy to have a person expressing sexual desire for me and sharing an emotional connection with me. I sought out and savored every escalation in sexual contact. I also felt guilty or angry. My wife tells me that I was quite irritable during the affairs. I am usually a very ethically minded person, so the inauthenticity and hiding behaviors created an intense dissonance with those values, even when I didn't always understand the connection.

When my wife learned about the affairs, it hurt her. Each time, my affair partner was also deeply hurt. These women that I cared about felt sad and maybe even betrayed by me. During some affairs, I also engaged in other negative behaviors.

After my first two affairs, which happened around the same time, I did my best to figure out how to better manage my sexuality. I was so shocked by my behavior that I went through a six-month period of abstinence, including forgoing masturbation. I read books about sex and relationships and tried to figure out how to manage my desires. During the healing period with my wife, I finally understood that she loves me deeply but that how she shows her love is different from how I feel loved. I decided that being loved was more important than feeling loved, and that her willingness to accept me as I am and her forgiveness were things I wanted to honor. I knew that I had to work to honor her love for me.

I lacked male friends, which I saw as a problem, so I worked to develop new friendships. I used a new method to monitor my sexual feelings and to keep them in check. Some parts of the method worked: I developed mindfulness practices, opened lines of communication with my wife, and employed the unpleasant focus on crushes, all of which you've read about in this book. But I was also repressing my sexuality and denying my relationship needs, which was not sustainable. It worked for twelve years; then everything fell apart.

I loved the woman that I had my third affair with, but it didn't stop me from hurting her. I developed an emotional connection with her that I wasn't going to follow through on, and that hurt her deeply. My wife found out about this affair and dealt with it with characteristic grace. We repaired our relationship and began to take a closer look at the nature of my sexuality and relationship capacities, and we eventually opened our relationship to allow me to express my polyamorous nature. That is why I stress in this book that it's important for all people to be honest about their sexuality in order to bring it into alignment with their nature and values.

Only Yes Means Yes

Aside from "Susan" described earlier, I took the absence of no for yes one other time. I hadn't negotiated physical contact with my partner ahead of time. I pushed the boundary of my touch without checking in with my partner. However, her absence of a verbal no was not the presence of a yes. She set the boundary, and I immediately acknowledged and reset my behavior. I felt so much guilt and shame because I truly believe that I knew better, but I hadn't put my knowledge or values into practice.

Be Honest about the Nature of My Sexuality

One time my partner learned about some of my kinky sexual interests while I was sleeping. When I was confronted about the evidence of my fantasies, I engaged in gaslighting and lied. I made up a plausible story about the nature and meaning of the evidence to deflect responsibility for its impact on my partner— and to keep my desire safe from scrutiny and judgment. Now, I've integrated those kinky desires into my sexual life in ways that my partners know about, that do no harm, and that create no shame for me. But the harm to the past partner is done. My lying about it probably intensified the hurt she experienced when discovering my fantasies, which is why I advocate for open communication in this book.

Don't Get Stuck in My Head

I have a rich internal imagination. I used to write fiction and was in a creative writing program in high school for several years. My primary hobby as an adult is role-playing games like *Dungeons and Dragons*, which includes creating and enacting epic improvised stories and playing out characters. I have learned over the years that my creativity can exacerbate the daydreaming characteristic of early relationships. When I "fall in love," I can get caught up in my internal narrative about the developing relationship.

This has caused me to miss cues from my partner that my relationship goals were different from their relationship goals. I've dismissed or minimized my partner's concerns about differences between us. I've also ignored when my partner has told me that I want things that are fundamentally incompatible with their goals. A similar thing can happen after the newness of a relationship wears off. My wife says that I have "a big personality." She means that I can enthusiastically articulate a vision and get people to join me without noticing or asking for dissenting perspectives. I've had to work very hard to temper this tendency in me, and I still have not perfected it at all.

Because of this, I have left partners feeling pressured to engage in a deeper relationship with me than they desired, which caused them to end the relationship. I've lost out on what could have been fun, sexual, or kinky explorations with an eager partner because I got stuck in my own head and couldn't see and accept my partner's sexual generosity.

I Need to Manage My Grief in Respectful Ways

My mother was physically abused and stalked by men repeatedly throughout my childhood. Our car windows and apartment windows were smashed several times by one man in particular. The behavior of those men terrorized and traumatized me, too. I wanted to be different from men like that and consciously tried to observe and follow the model of men who didn't act like that. Even so, I have made women afraid through my behavior.

There have been times, especially during breakups, when I lost sight of the potential impact of my actions. I continued activities from the relationship, such as walking through an ex-partner's neighborhood or sending casual messages after the relationship was over. I learned that, due to the history of men's violence, these behaviors look and feel like stalking behaviors. I wasn't trying to stalk anyone. I wanted to express and resolve my grief. However, in not thinking about the potential impact of my actions on the partner, I created fear. I was not trying to perpetuate violence against women, but my unskillful behavior did not heal it, either. As soon as I learned about the impact of this behavior, I immediately apologized and stopped the behavior.

Are These the Only Ways I've Hurt Partners?

I don't know if these are the only ways I've hurt partners. There is always a gap between any two people's experience of the same event. I don't know how other partners remember me. There is a possibility that my former partners remember our time together more positively or negatively than I did. It is also possible that I've made women feel uncomfortable without knowing it. I've never heard feedback that I project a "creepy" vibe, but due to the power dynamics in our culture, it's possible that women may have been too afraid to give me that feedback. Just because I don't know about those experiences doesn't mean they don't exist.

I wrote this afterword to say this clearly: I'm not perfect. I know I've hurt people. I have examined that history and tried to learn from it. These life lessons have directly informed this book: it is important to me that I try to teach men emotional regulation and sexual consent skills and the importance of honesty. If I had omitted my own flaws and mistakes, I could have damaged your trust in me. Question everything here. Take what is of value, and march toward your principles and values. They are your best guide.

IS MY HISTORY DISQUALIFYING?

Sometimes I wonder whether I have any right to speak about consent issues and destructive masculinity. I suspect some people will say I don't. Ultimately, I decided to write this book because these issues appear in my office. When I teach men who are consciously or unconsciously pressuring their partners for sex, I am able to help heal those experiences. When I provide therapy to men who are dating and need help with these skills, they seem to hurt fewer people, feel more confident, and be more loving. I felt called to amplify the potential of those tools by publicly joining the conversation. I hope that is the right choice.

I also believe in a person's capacity for healing and improvement—I wouldn't be a good therapist if I didn't. Many of my clients who are depressed will grant other people kindness and acceptance that they will not grant to themselves. I try to teach them that holding oneself to a higher standard than everyone else is arrogant. That is, I can only hold myself to a higher standard if I believe that, somehow, I am better than others. I don't believe that

I am better than others. If I believe that other people are worthy of redemption and that they can be better, I must be, too. If I am a better man now than I was, then perhaps other men will benefit from what I have learned. Hopefully, by sharing this book and these stories, you—the reader—won't hurt people in the way I did to learn these lessons. My experience in my office bears this out.

I have considered leaving this discussion out of the book. Maybe it will open me to the accusation that I am "white knighting," or holding myself up as a self-proclaimed redeemed paragon who swoops in to save women from men by teaching men how to be. That's not what I feel in my heart. What I've written here is my best effort to help, and I've included the stories in this section because they are part of how I learned. If there is a critique of my process, I'd rather expose the whole process to you so that you can critique it skillfully.

IS IT RIGHT TO MAKE MONEY OFF OF WHAT I LEARNED HURTING PEOPLE?

I would not publish this book without agreeing to give a portion of my earning to the charity Love Is Respect, which teaches sexual consent skills to youth across the United States; and RAINN (the Rape, Abuse, & Incest National Network), which works to protect and support victims of sexual violence. To the degree that I am capable of it, I've written this book by enacting the processes of consent that I teach. But I'm also looking outside of myself for indicators of whether I've attended to restorative justice, like the call of Roxane Gay regarding Louis C. K.'s return to comedy:

> He should pay until he demonstrates some measure of understanding of what he has done wrong and the extent of the harm he has caused. He should attempt to financially compensate his victims for all the work they did not get to

do because of his efforts to silence them. He should facilitate their getting the professional opportunities they should have been able to take advantage of all these years. He should finance their mental health care as long as they may need it. He should donate to nonprofit organizations that work with sexual harassment and assault victims. He should publicly admit what he did and why it was wrong without excuses and legalese and deflection. Every perpetrator of sexual harassment and violence should follow suit.[2]

I hope that my writing here demonstrates a "measure of understanding" of what I have done wrong and how it hurt others. I did not harm the careers of women by silencing them, but I am compensating an organization that teaches consent. I'm not sure what I could do now to help the condition of the women whom I have harmed, but if I discover it, I will seek to take that action. I have admitted my wrongs. I hope I haven't used excuses, legalese, or deflection. I have attempted to understand the origin of my behavior. I acted to stop myself from doing the behaviors that caused harm. I'm trying my best to understand the experience of the people whom I hurt. Finally, this whole effort is designed to prevent behaviors like mine.

Does that earn me the right to make money from this book? I don't know. I know that I have worked hard to write it. My labor to create a book can't be stacked up and measured against the pain I've caused. Does it matter that this labor intends to prevent harm from coming to others? Does that cleanse the labor enough to merit compensation? Would it be better if this book went unwritten if I need compensation to promote it? I can't answer these questions. But I will dialogue with you, my community, to keep facing these questions because they are good ones. My intention is to engage in restorative justice with this book. I invite your help to make sure that I succeed in fulfilling my intention.

ACKNOWLEDGMENTS

I'VE WANTED TO BE A WRITER since I sat down to my uncle's giant humming electric typewriter the summer before fourth grade to peck out a four-line story that seemed epic in my imagination and appeared minuscule when typed on the page. Since then, I've written creatively and professionally, but I wouldn't consider myself a "real writer" until I had a book published. I just wish that, when the muse struck, she could have demanded an easier topic. I was conscious throughout the writing process of how many people's traumas, shame, and delicate capacities for pleasure I was writing about. I hope that I have addressed yours sensitively here. If I have, it is due in no small part to the support I have had in bringing this work to the world. It is a cliché but true: I could not have done it alone.

Doug Braun-Harvey, Stephanie Buehler, Joe Kort, and David Ley
James and Marisa
Pamela, Martha, Kathryn, and JD
Men of Soul Fire
Dave, Ryan, Tucker, Kevin, Luke, and Marc
Hope
Anabel and Michelle, always.

ENDNOTES

Introduction

1 The #MeToo hashtag has encouraged victims of sexual abuse to speak about their experiences by using the power of social media to demonstrate how common the experience of sexual abuse is.

2 *Consent* is the act of agreeing to what you are doing with someone or their body. The word can also be used to refer to the ongoing process of making sure each person has given consent and is still consenting to a shared experience.

3 *Polyamorous* means I have more than one loving relationship at a time, with the knowledge and consent of all involved.

4 Being *kinky* means that I engage in some BDSM (bondage, discipline/domination, sadism/submission, and masochism) sexual behavior.

5 b. hooks, *The Will to Change: Men, Masculinity, and Love* (New York: Washington Square Press, 2004), 66.

Chapter 1

1 See metoomvmt.org.

2 For example, see pewresearch.org/social-trends/2022/09/29/more-than-twice-as-many-americans-support-than-oppose-the-metoo-movement.

3 For example, see vox.com/culture/2018/1/17/16897440/aziz-ansari-allegations-babe-me-too.

4 For example, see theatlantic.com/entertainment/archive/2018/01/aziz-ansari-and-the-paradox-of-no/550556.

5 Institute for Strategic Dialogue and McCain Institute, "The Threat Landscape: Incel and Misogynist Violent Extremism," US Prevention Practitioners Network, 2021, mccaininstitute.org/wp-content/uploads/2021/10/incel-and-misogynist-violent-extremism-read-ahead-materials-august-2.pdf.

6 For example, see theatlantic.com/international/archive/2019/08/anti-feminism-gateway-far-right/595642.

7 R. E. Morgan and J. L. Truman, "Criminal Victimization, 2019," US Department of Justice, Office of Justice Programs, Bureau of Justice Statistics, September 2020, bjs.ojp.gov/library/publications/criminal-victimization-2019.

8 Morgan and Truman, "Criminal Victimization, 2019."

9　"About," Good Men Project, accessed February 22, 2023, goodmenproject.com
/about.

10　E. C. Levine, D. Herbenick, O. Martinez, T.-C. Fu, and B. Dodge, "Open Relationships, Nonconsensual Nonmonogamy, and Monogamy among US Adults: Find-
ings from the 2012 National Survey of Sexual Health and Behavior," *Archives of
Sexual Behavior* 47, no. 5 (2018): 1439–1450, doi.org/10.1007/s10508-018-1178-7.
This report found that 32 percent of gay men reported being in "open relationships," an umbrella term for consensually nonmonogamous relationships.

11　L. F. Brathwaite, "Why Dating Apps Are Racist AF—With or Without Ethnicity
Filters," *Rolling Stone*, August 21, 2020, rollingstone.com/culture/culture-features
/dating-apps-grindr-ethnicity-filters-1047047. Grindr, the most popular gay
hookup app, only removed its race filters in 2020.

12　"National Census of Fatal Occupational Injuries in 2021," Bureau of Labor
Statistics, US Department of Labor, December 16, 2022, bls.gov/news.release
/pdf/cfoi.pdf.

13　"Employed Persons by Detailed Occupation, Sex, Race, and Hispanic or Latino
Ethnicity." Bureau of Labor Statistics, US Department of Labor, 2002, bls.gov
/cps/cpsaat11.pdf.

14　"2019 Crime in the United States," Federal Bureau of Investigation, US Department of Justice, 2019, ucr.fbi.gov/crime-in-the-u.s/2019/crime-in-the-u.s.-2019
/topic-pages/tables/table-42.

15　A. L. Roberts, K. A. McLaughlin, K. J. Conron, and K. C Koenen, "Adulthood
Stressors, History of Childhood Adversity, and Risk of Perpetration of Intimate
Partner Violence," *American Journal of Preventive Medicine* 40, no. 2 (2010):
128–138, doi.org/10.1016/j.amepre.2010.10.016.

16　M. J. Breiding, K. C. Basile, J. Klevens, and S. G. Smith, "Economic Insecurity
and Intimate Partner Violence Victimization," *American Journal of Preventive
Medicine* 53, no. 4 (2017): 457–464, doi.org/10.1016/j.amepre.2017.03.021.

17　M. J. Brown, R. A. Perera, S. W. Masho, B. Mezuk, and S. A. Cohen, "Adverse
Childhood Experiences and Intimate Partner Aggression in the US: Sex Differences and Similarities in Psychosocial Mediation," *Social Science Medicine* 131
(2015): 48–57, doi.org/10.1016/j.socscimed.2015.02.044.

Chapter 2

1　*Sexual pressure* is the process of not respecting a person's boundaries, such as
continuing to ask for what has already been declined. *Sexual coercion* is using
nonphysical threats or deception to elicit sexual behavior. *Sexual assault* is
sexual contact or behavior without consent. *Rape* is penetration without consent. The exact line between each of these may be open to interpretation, and
the legal lines between each of them may vary by state. For more information,
see rainn.org/articles/sexual-assault and justice.gov/archives/opa/blog/updated
-definition-rape.

2   "This Metaphor for Consent Might Be Just the Thing You Need to Make It Click," *Everyday Feminism*, July 18, 2016, everydayfeminism.com/2016/07/metaphor -for-consent.

Chapter 3

1   F. Toates, *Biological Psychology*, 3rd edition (London: Pearson Education Unlimited, 2011); and D. B O'Connor, J. Archer, and F. C. W. Wu, "Effects of Testosterone on Mood, Aggression, and Sexual Behavior in Young Men: A Double-Blind, Placebo-Controlled, Cross-Over Study," *Journal of Clinical Endocrinology & Metabolism* 89, no. 6 (2004): 2837–2845, doi.org/10.1210/jc.2003-031354.

2   C. F. Donatucci, "The Institute of Medicine White Paper on Testosterone: Current Perspective," in *Androgen Deficiency and Testosterone Replacement: Current Controversies and Strategies*, ed. W. J. G Hellstrom (New York: Humana Press, 2013): 21–14.

3   S. Basaria, et al., "Effect of Testosterone Administration for 3 Years on Subclinical Atherosclerosis Progression in Older Men with Low or Low-Normal Testosterone Levels: A Randomized Clinical Trial," *Journal of the American Medical Association* 314, no. 6 (2015): 570–581.

4   T. G. Travison, J. E. Morley, A. B. Arajuo, A. B. O'Donnell, and J. B. McKinlay, "The Relationship between Libido and Testosterone Levels in Aging Men," *Journal of Endocrinology & Metabolism* 91, no. 7 (2006): 2509–2513, doi.org /10.1210/jc.2005-2508.

5   Donatucci, "White Paper on Testosterone," 2.

6   C. Fine, *Testosterone Rex: Myths of Sex, Science, and Society* (New York: W. W. Norton, 2017).

7   *Competition motivation* is the term used by biologists and medical professionals to describe the effect of testosterone on an organism. The term suggests that testosterone causes us to strive, compete, venture, test our capacities, and be active. Notice that there's nothing about this term that suggests that testosterone inevitably creates violence.

8   For more details about this kind of sex difference not necessarily leading to different capacity, I recommend Cordelia Fine's book *Testosterone Rex: Myths of Sex, Science, and Society*.

9   A. S. Book, K. B. Starzyk, and V. L. Quinsey, "The Relationship between Testosterone and Aggression: A Meta-Analysis," *Aggression and Violent Behavior* 6, no. 6 (2001): 579–599, doi.org/10.1016/S1359-1789(00)00032-X.

10   Toates, *Biological Psychology*, 71.

11   E. R. Montoya, D. Terburg, P. A. Bos, and J. van Honk, "Testosterone, Cortisol, and Serotonin as Key Regulators of Social Aggression: A Review and Theoretical Perspective," *Motivation and Emotion* 36, no. 1 (2011): 65–73, doi.org/10.1007 /s11031-011-9264-3.

12 M. L. Batrinos, "Testosterone and Aggressive Behavior in Men," *International Journal of Endocrinology & Metabolism* 10, no. 3 (2012): 563–568, doi.org/10.5812/ijem.3661.

13 A. Wittmeyer, "Eight Stories of Men's Regret," *New York Times*, October 18, 2018, nytimes.com/interactive/2018/10/18/opinion/men-metoo-high-school.html; emphasis mine.

14 S. Marche, "The Unexamined Brutality of the Male Libido," *New York Times*, November 25, 2017, nytimes.com/2017/11/25/opinion/sunday/harassment-men-libido-masculinity.html.

15 b. hooks, *The Will to Change: Men, Masculinity, and Love* (New York: Washington Square, 2004): 80–81.

16 hooks, *The Will to Change*, 87.

17 See drericfitz.com/wp-content/uploads/2021/06/Figure-Erotic-Riverbed-2-1.pdf.

18 See, for example, the reporting on masturbation data from the National Survey of Sexual Health and Behavior at Indiana University Bloomington: fivethirtyeight.com/features/dear-mona-i-masturbate-more-than-once-a-day-am-i-normal.

19 G. Ogden, *Expanding the Practice of Sex Therapy: The Neuro Update Edition—An Integrative Approach to Exploring Desire and Intimacy*, 2nd edition (New York: Routledge, 2018).

20 Ogden, *Expanding the Practice of Sex Therapy*, 80.

21 G. Corona et al., "Autoeroticism, Mental Health, and Organic Disturbances in Patients with Erectile Dysfunction," *Journal of Sex Medicine* 7, no. 1 (2010): 182–191, doi.org/10.1111/j.1743-6109.2009.01497.x. High masturbation is actually correlated with higher testosterone.

22 For example, see aasect.org/position-reparative-therapy.

23 J. J. Lehmiller, *Tell Me What You Want: The Science of Sexual Desire and How It Can Help You Improve Your Sex Life* (New York: Hachette, 2018).

24 For example, see ncbi.nlm.nih.gov/pmc/articles/PMC3194801.

25 J. Roughgarden, *Evolution's Rainbow: Diversity, Gender, and Sexuality in Nature and People* (Berkeley: University of California Press, 2004). See especially "Section III: Cultural Rainbows."

26 "Answers to Your Questions for a Better Understanding of Sexual Orientation & Homosexuality," American Psychological Association, 2008, apa.org/topics/lgbtq/orientation.

27 R. Levin, "Sexual Activity, Health, and Well-Being—The Beneficial Roles of Coitus and Masturbation," *Sexual and Relationship Therapy* 22, no. 1 (2007): 135–148, doi.org/10.1080/14681990601149197.

28 E. H. Mereish and V. P. Poteat, "A Relational Model of Sexual Minority Mental and Physical Health: The Negative Effects of Shame on Relationship, Loneliness, and Health," *Journal of Counseling Psychology* 62, no. 2 (2015): 425–437, doi.org/10.1037/cou0000088.

29 W. Pollack, *Real Boys: Rescuing Our Boys from the Myths of Boyhood* (New York: Henry Holt, 1998).

30 This line of reasoning comes from *The Will to Change* by bell hooks.

31 If you have any doubt that women can and do want sexual intensity, consider reading *The New Topping Book* by Dossie Easton and Janet Hardy, which describes, among other kinky scenes and identities, some pretty intense lesbian kinky scenes.

32 This process is described in more detail in Sue Johnson's *Hold Me Tight: Seven Conversations for a Lifetime of Love*, "Conversation 5: Forgiving Injuries."

33 For example, ADHD, OCD, bipolar disorder, substance abuse, sexual shame, trauma, or a sexual or relationship identity that hasn't been integrated into the relationship.

Chapter 4

1 Much of what follows from this chapter is described in more scientific detail in Frederick Toates's *How Sexual Desire Works: The Enigmatic Urge* (Cambridge, UK: Cambridge University Press, 2014) and C. S. Carver and M. F. Scheier's *Self-Regulation of Action and Affect* in *Handbook of Self-Regulation: Research, Theory, and Applications*, third edition, K. D. Vohs and R. F. Baumeister eds. (New York: Guilford, 2018).

2 The most common use of this term describes the set of people without autism but can also refer to people with neurological typical patterns of thought and behavior. I identify here that these insights only apply to neurotypical people as a way of continuing to recognize the diversity in our human community.

3 E. Janssen and J. Bancroft, "The Dual Control Model: The Role of Sexual Inhibition & Excitation in Sexual Arousal and Behavior," in *The Psychophysiology of Sex*, ed. E. Janssen (Bloomington: Indiana University Press, 2007).

4 F. Toates, *How Sexual Desire Works* (Cambridge: Cambridge University Press, 2015), 97.

5 E. Nagoski, *Come as You Are: The Surprising New Science That Will Change Your Sex Life* (New York: Simon & Schuster, 2021).

6 The evaluation takes place unconsciously through a "fast" processing route in our amygdala (threat response system) and our hippocampus (spatial awareness, memory, and emotion system) and creates an emotion.

7 C. S. Carver and M. F. Scheier, "Self-Regulation of Action and Affect," in *Handbook of Self-Regulation: Research, Theory, and Applications*, 3rd edition, eds. Vohs and Baumeister (New York: The Guildford Press, 2016).

8 Nagoski, *Come as You Are*, 265.

9 This next skill comes from David Deida's book, *The Way of the Superior Man*. Although I now find his work problematic, especially his gender binary assumptions, there are a few elements with value.

Chapter 5

1 For example, see ncbi.nlm.nih.gov/pmc/articles/PMC3150158.

2 For example, see ncbi.nlm.nih.gov/pmc/articles/PMC1323317.

3 For example, see journals.plos.org/plosmedicine/article?id=10.1371/journal.pmed .1000316.

4 For example, see forbes.com/sites/forbescoachescouncil/2018/07/12/why-soft -skills-are-harder-than-they-look.

5 For example, see pewsocialtrends.org/2016/10/06/1-changes-in-the-american -workplace.

6 J. Kabat-Zinn, "Mindfulness-Based Interventions in Context: Past, Present, and Future," *Clinical Psychology: Science and Practice* 10, no. 2 (2003): 145, doi.org/10.1093/clipsy.bpg016.

7 For example, see cdc.gov/nchs/data/vsrr/VSRR10-508.pdf.

8 W. Dement, *The Promise of Sleep: A Pioneer in Sleep Medicine Explores the Vital Connections Between Health, Happiness, and a Good Night's Sleep* (New York: Penguin Random House, 2000).

9 D. Braun-Harvey and M. Vigorito, *Treating Out-of-Control Sexual Behavior: Rethinking Sex Addiction* (New York: Springer Publishing Company, 2016).

10 Braun-Harvey and Vigorito, *Treating Out-of-Control Sexual Behavior*, 47.

11 For more information, see the Sex Workers Outreach Project at swopuse.org.

12 M. Reece et al., "Sexual Behaviors, Relationships, and Perceived Health among Adult Men in the United States: Results from a National Probability Sample," *Journal of Sexual Medicine* 7, no. 5 (2010): 291–304, doi.org/10.1111/j.1743-6109.2010.02009.x. Statistics range from 96.6 percent of men twenty-five to twenty-nine years old who are single and dating, reporting having masturbated alone within the past ninety days, to 26.9 percent of men seventy and older who are married, reporting having masturbated alone in the past ninety days.

13 E. Coleman, "Masturbation as a Means of Achieving Sexual Health," *Journal of Psychology and Human Sexuality* 14, no. 2-3 (2002): 5–16; doi.org/10.1300 /J056v14n02_02.

14 For example, see M. P. Kafka, "Hypersexual Disorder: A Proposed Diagnosis for the DSM-V," *Archives of Sexual Behavior* 39 (2010): 377–400, doi.org/10.1007 /s10508-009-9574-7.

15 M. Reece et al., "Sexual Behaviors."

16 M. Reece et al., "Sexual Behaviors."

17 Ogden, *Expanding the Practice of Sex Therapy*.

18 PrEP is a medication recommended for anyone with sexual behaviors that put them at a higher risk for contracting HIV. See prepfacts.org/prep/the-basics.

19 F. Fejes, "Bent Passions: Heterosexual Masculinity, Pornography, and Gay Male Identity," *Sexuality and Culture* 6, no. 3 (2002): 95–113, doi.org/10.1007 /BF02912230. Arguments that gay male porn suffers under patriarchal oppressive norms, that an active gay performer mirrors the heterosexual man, and that the passive or receptive gay performer mirrors the heterosexual woman belie a heteronormative belief akin to asking a gay couple, "Who is the woman in your relationship?"

20 N. Prause, "Viewing Sexual Stimuli Associated with Greater Sexual Responsiveness, Not Erectile Dysfunction." *Sexual Medicine* 3, no. 2 (2015), 90–98, doi.org /10.1002/sm2.58.

Chapter 6

1 W. Pollack, *Real Boys: Rescuing Our Sons from the Myths of Boyhood* (New York: Henry Holt: 1998).

2 b. hooks, *All About Love* (New York: William Morrow, 2001).

3 If you're being physically abusive or abused, get help immediately. Don't wait until the next time you hurt someone. Do it now. Call the National Domestic Violence Hotline, 1-800-799-SAFE (7233). They are used to fielding calls from abusive people and can help connect you with a battery of intervention and prevention programs. You may also find more information at thehotline.org/help /for-abusive-partners.

4 D. Anapol, *Polyamory in the 21st Century: Love and Intimacy with Multiple Partners* (New York: Rowman & Littlefield, 2010).

5 For more information, see their book *Psychosynthesis: A Psychology of the Spirit* (Albany: State University of New York Press).

6 D. Burns, *The Feeling Good Handbook* (New York: Penguin, 1999).

Chapter 8

1 If you are worried about your own safety, privacy, or security, go through the process of getting a separate number for hookups that directs to your phone. If you happen to connect with someone who is harassing you, change numbers.

2 K. Way, "I Went on a Date with Aziz Ansari. It Turned into the Worst Night of My Life," Babe.net, January 13, 2018, babe.net/2018/01/13/aziz-ansari-28355.

Afterword

1 K. Way, "I Went on a Date with Aziz Ansari. It Turned into the Worst Night of My Life," Babe.net, January 13, 2018, babe.net/2018/01/13/aziz-ansari-28355.

2 Roxane Gay, "Louis C.K. and Men Who Think Justice Takes as Long as They Want It To," *New York Times*, August 29, 2018, www.nytimes.com/2018/08/29 /opinion/louis-ck-comeback-justice.html.

ABOUT THE AUTHOR

ERIC FITZMEDRUD is a therapist specializing in relationship and sexual issues in the San Francisco Bay Area. His specialty is helping men improve their sex lives by learning to regulate their emotions, removing sexual entitlement, and honing their sexual consent and negotiation skills. FitzMedrud is a member of the American Association of Sexuality Educators, Counselors, and Therapists (AASECT). He has been published in an academic book and academic journal and has spoken at multiple conferences. He has also trained therapists and taught many graduate courses in psychology. FitzMedrud has a PhD in clinical psychology from the Institute of Transpersonal Psychology. He is polyamorous and bisexual and lives with his wife of twenty-three years and his life partner of six years in San Francisco's East Bay area.